One Law for All?

Eigene und fremde Welten

The series "Eigene und fremde Welten" is edited by Jörg Baberowski, Vincent Houben, Stefan Beck, Thomas Mergel, and Gabriele Metzler in connection with the Collaborative Research Center no. 640 "Representations of Changing Social Orders: Cross-Cultural and Cross-Temporal Comparisons" based at Humboldt-Universität, Berlin (Germany).

Volume 25

Stefan B. Kirmse, Ph.D., is a Research Fellow at the Collaborative Research Unit 640 »Representations of Changing Social Orders. Intertemporal and Intercultural Comparisons« at Humboldt University Berlin.

Stefan B. Kirmse (ed.)

One Law for All?

Western Models and Local Practices in (Post-)Imperial Contexts

Campus Verlag
Frankfurt/New York

Bibliographic Information published by the Deutsche Nationalbibliothek.
The Deutsche Nationalbibliothek lists this publication in the Deutsche Nationalbibliografie; detailed bibliographic data are available in the Internet at http://dnb.d-nb.de
ISBN 978-3-593-39493-0

Cover illustration: © Stefan B. Kirmse, photo by the author: Autopsy report from 1908, National Archive of the Republic of Tatarstan
Cover design: Campus Verlag, Frankfurt-on-Main
Printing office and bookbinder: CPI buchbuecher.de, Birkach
Printed on acid free paper.
Printed in Germany

This book is also available as an E-Book.
www.campus.de
www.press.uchicago.edu

Contents

Acknowledgements

I am greatly indebted to the study group "law" at Humboldt University's Collaborative Research Center 640 (better known as SFB 640) for their ongoing intellectual input and encouragement, without which the conference "One Law for All?" and this edited volume would not have seen the light of day. Some of the group's members have contributed articles to this volume, others have helped to make the conference a stimulating and successful event. I am also grateful to all those conference participants who offered their insights, energy and wit, yet did not take part in this book project, which chose a focus slightly different from the conference.

The SFB provided the academic environment and, crucially, the funding necessary for this project. Special thanks go to Jane Burbank for her guidance on how to proceed from the conference to the book, and to Jörg Baberowski for his continuing support. As far as the practical realization of this book project is concerned, I would also like to thank Anika Kreft and, in particular, Sascha Stingl for their layouting skills and their patience with a never-ending flow of draft chapters. Finally, as proof-reader of this volume, Andrew Tarrant never ceased to alert my attention to mistakes and inconsistencies, thus improving the final text in many more respects than just grammar and orthography. Needless to say that I bear full responsibility for any remaining flaws.

Stefan B. Kirmse
Berlin, May 2012

Introduction

Stefan B. Kirmse

To avoid potential misunderstandings: "one law for all?" is not used as a political slogan in this book. Admittedly, along with related concepts in other languages, such as *idem ius omnibus* or *gleiches Recht für alle*, the phrase has been used to further a wide range of political agendas. Feminist, civil liberties and gay rights groups have utilized the slogan to call for greater equality; racist groups in North America have exploited it as a means to denounce the allegedly preferential treatment of minorities; and most recently, a secularist movement in the United Kingdom has adopted it as the title for its campaign against *shari'a* law, which it views as gaining influence among British Muslims.

In this book, the phrase is neither employed to advocate a political cause nor used to refer solely to legal equality (or the lack of it). Offering a point of entry into the study of legal debate and practice in imperial and post-imperial contexts, it served as a guiding research question for a conference hosted by the Department of East European History (which explains the strong representation of historians of Russia in this volume) at Humboldt University in the fall of 2010. It struck the organizers of the conference, on which this volume is based, as a useful tool to capture different aspects of legal reform in the nineteenth and early twentieth centuries: the drive for "modernization" and the importance of legal borrowing in various parts of the globe; claims to legal integration and greater equality; and the continuing specificity of legal practice and interpretation.

That said, to a degree "one law for all?" is a rhetorical question. Neither has legal homogenization ever materialized on a global scale, nor have most polities ever put "equal justice for all" into practice. Some forms of inequality persist even in today's liberal democracies. What is more, if the question is used to investigate the worldwide diffusion of "Western" law, as in the sociological "world polity" approach (see, in particular, Boyle and Meyer 2002), it faces a twofold problem: analyses of diffusion tend to claim either the obvious or the impossible. If diffusion is taken to refer "only" to the imitation of Western law in different parts of the world, it is a commonplace. Mimesis is part of most legal reform processes. On the other hand, the spread and use of European legal norms and institutions is best not discussed in terms of a transfer of laws from one country to another. As critics of Watson's concept of "legal transplants" (1974) have argued, such transfer is impossible since the law consists not only of words but also of the culturally specific meanings attached to these words (Legrand 2001). As a result, any analysis of legal borrowing must not only take local adaptations and reinterpretations into account but also acknowledge the complete novelty of the resulting laws.

Regardless of these caveats, "one law for all" remains valid not only as an ideal for lawmakers. Thanks to its multi-dimensionality, it can also be a useful guide for inquiry. It directs our attention to the dynamic relationship between two competing, but often overlapping, trends that characterize most imperial and post-imperial spaces: legal integration, on the one hand, and the recognition and promotion of difference, on the other. The latter, at times, even included forms of legal segregation. Framing the inquiry in such terms allows an analysis of different steps towards, or away from, legal equality while revealing an array of local interactions with Western law(s).

The role of "Western" law must indeed be given careful consideration. A focus on East-West or North-South interaction admittedly runs the danger of being charged with "Eurocentrism"; and past inquiries into the role of Western legal blueprints and institutions in the South, such as the Yale Law and Modernization project in the early 1970s, have been rightly criticized for their developmental assumptions, that is, the idea that the adoption of "one type of law—that found in the West—[was] essential for economic, political and social development in the Third World" (Trubek 1972, 2; see also Trubek and Galanter 1974). This volume, by contrast, has no interest in extolling or denouncing any particular normative order. Yet, it suggests that a close consideration of interactions with Western laws is helpful—in fact, it is necessary—for a cross-cultural discussion of legal debate and practice in the nineteenth and early twentieth centuries.

In many parts of the globe, European legal reforms and institutions were among the most common points of reference at this time, as efforts to rationalize local judicial systems and make them more efficient gained momentum. Policies of centralization and the standardization of legal practice were meant to create both stability and a minimum of legal certainty. This frequently involved an overhaul of laws and legal institutions in accordance with European models, or at least a partial appropriation of such models. Legal reforms were usually designed and presented as part of the wider project of "modernization" and linked to related efforts in the political, economic and cultural spheres. Subscribing to the idea of universal, mono-linear progress and Europe's advanced position on this developmental path, many elites were convinced that non-European regions could learn from the experience of European nations—usually by following their lead, but sometimes also by avoiding previous mistakes.

To be fair, there was no such thing as a singular "Western model". The legal reality in Europe was a multitude of different and differently interpreted models. Thus, it is worth exploring which of these (and why!) Russian, Latin American, Afghan and other reformers decided to draw upon. What is more: how did local actors re-interpret and adapt these models to local circumstances? For reform movements throughout the South and East, "modernization" often consisted of a selective re-combination of European and local ideas and practices (in which the former were discussed less in terms of their "superiority" than in terms of their compatibility with the latter). The resulting, new legal systems could then be promoted as regional models. The new Turkish legal system of the mid-1920s, for example, though based on a mixture of Swiss, Italian, German and French influences (Örücü 1992), soon became a reference point in neighboring Muslim majority states. The question of borrowings and references in legal debate and practice, then, forms one key set of questions addressed in the chapters that follow.

This volume is also designed to examine the discrepancy between the claims of reformers, on the one hand, and the implementation and reception of legal change, on the other. It highlights the simultaneous development of growing uniformity in some areas of law, both within and between countries, and diversity in others. The promotion of universal legal norms in reform debates and the resulting legal institutions often bore striking similarities whereas legal practice often remained idiosyncratic, not least because local actors behaved pragmatically. All cases discussed in this volume were legally "plural" in one way or another. Local administrators, judges and litigants could pursue their own agendas by drawing on different legal traditions at different times.

In short, this volume examines law as both debate and practice in the imperial and post-imperial world. Case studies from Latin America, Russia, Africa and East Asia explore the ways in which rulers, parliamentarians, jurists, mid-level bureaucrats and ordinary people talk about and actively use the law. Before introducing the individual chapters by identifying a number of common themes, I briefly discuss the role and meaning of law in (post-)imperial contexts and offer a short summary of the disciplinary background and premises on which this volume is based.

Exploring Law during and after Empire

For the regions and time period under scrutiny in this book, law was of utmost importance. Rulers and policy-makers took pains to refine their legal systems and individual laws in order to make their rule more secure and efficient. At times, they employed laws and law-enforcement agencies to keep opponents at bay and neutralize troublemakers. On a day-to-day basis, however, they put enormous resources, financial and social, into the administration of their polities and the maintenance of law and order. While many empires—and some post-imperial spaces—are portrayed as realms in which the law mattered very little or could be bent by rulers and bureaucrats at any time, many of them were, in fact, full of legal forums. Ordinary people interacted with the law in numerous ways. Instead of being confined to legislative chambers and courts, law was an everyday experience.

In order to capture this experience in its specific cultural and historical contexts, this volume views the law both from "above", as a set of individual laws or legal systems designed and debated by lawmakers, and from "below", as an array of manners in which the system was implemented, used, and experienced. The former perspective concentrates on legal reforms and, in particular, on the ways in which they were negotiated, justified, and communicated to the people. Processes of prolonged debate could take place either in parliament, as in the Russian Duma, or between the ruler and regional or tribal leaders, as in the case of Afghanistan.

The view from "below" then introduces the perspectives of local officials and legal practitioners as well as litigants, witnesses, and defendants, alerting us to the everyday operation of law. The focus on legal intermediaries and on local judicial, administrative and police institutions helps us explore the connections between governors and governed. It also highlights the importance of choice in the legal sphere. Lower and mid-level officials reveal a spectrum of approaches in dealing with cases—a spectrum particularly wide in colonial contexts where vague instructions and the usually military background of judges gave much discretion to local officials. Choice is also fundamental to the analysis of court use. This analysis documents the ways in which ordinary people dealt with legal change, and appropriated institutions for their own ends. The combination of these perspectives offers a vantage point from which multiple meanings of law can be examined, in both discourse and practice.

While written by historians, this volume is indebted to the field of "law and society" research, a form of interdisciplinary socio-legal inquiry that became institutionalized in the United States in the 1960s and is concerned with the study of law in its social and cultural context (Levine 1990; Munger 1998). In Germany, this field is only beginning to emerge (Wrase 2006).[1] Law and society research tends to focus on the social and cultural embeddedness of legal institutions—trials, lawyers, juries and courts; at the same time, scholars in this tradition have also turned to interpretive theory, which links the notions of culture, meaning and agency. As Geertz famously argued, "the 'law' side of things is not a bounded set of norms, rules, principles, values, or whatever from which jural responses to distilled events can be drawn, but part of a distinctive manner of imagining the real" (1983, 173). What is more, at any point in time and space there is more than one distinctive manner of "imagining the real" (Aguirre and Salvatore 2001, 14). From the perspective of interpretive theory, then, the law is best understood as a series of interactions and the meanings that ac-

1 The Berlin-based study group "legal reality" (*Rechtswirklichkeit*) was created in 2005, with the associated research program "legal cultures" launched in 2010.

tors attach to these. Litigants, lawyers and lawmakers continually produce the law as they give meaning to it as part of their everyday interaction. Law and everyday life thus "interpenetrate" (Yngvesson 1988).

One of the key insights of this interpretive perspective—the fact that legal action produces culture—proved influential among legal anthropologists, who then examined the process under conditions of colonial rule (Merry 1991; Mann and Roberts 1991). By the early 2000s, the "cultural turn" was in full swing in law and society research (Sarat and Kearns 1998; Sarat and Simon 2003). Historians have been slower at exploring the culturally productive role of legal systems. Early anthropological studies on law and culture across Asia, Africa and the Americas (especially Nader 1969) were neglected by many historians working on these regions. In recent years, studies of colonial history have become more interested in the different facets and effects of legal culture—a development that has been accompanied by a turn among scholars of imperial history away from the discussion of administration and towards cultural analysis (Benton 2006, 177). This volume seeks to contribute to this growing body of the cross-cultural and interdisciplinary study of law in the nineteenth and twentieth centuries.

Why was law so important to imperial and post-imperial governments? The law was not only a means to an end but also an end in itself (Fisch 1992). Imperial expansion was often justified in terms of spreading the "rule of law" (even if access to it was skewed in practice). Local legal traditions could also be promoted as the embodiment of "authenticity" and thus a form of defiance to the project of Westernization. Clearly, legal traditions were potent political weapons.

But most importantly, the legal sphere served imperial and post-imperial governments as an instrument of governance. They used it to establish and strengthen their control and authority, thereby encouraging new forms of state-centered "legal pluralism"—a plurality of differently legitimated legal systems and authorities in which categories of people were assigned specific rights and opportunities for legal action. This pluralism was highly unequal, with some of its constituent legal orders greatly depending on others.[2] It was reinforced, and constantly modified,

2 Some scholars, in fact, reject "legal pluralism" as a concept because it does not neatly capture this inequality and dependence (for example, Starr and Collier, 1989, 9).

by ongoing imperial expansion. Thus it was common in colonial empires, where it was particularly shaped by the encounter of European laws and local legal ideas and practices (Hooker 1975; Merry 1988, 871). Forms of legal segregation and discrimination, rooted in racial, religious, social or other distinctions, were often used as safeguards for the "superiority" and privileges of colonial rulers and thus helped to create and perpetuate social hierarchies. Many colonial officials had little interest in undermining the asymmetrical power relationship between colonizers and colonized (even if this boundary became blurred in practice as the subalterns used legal mechanisms to make claims, defend their autonomy and contest colonial abuse).

The commitment to control and regulation spurred many empires, and some post-imperial nation-states, to codify religious and various local legal traditions. As it was usually state-sponsored commissions that "froze" sets of highly flexible and diverse local practices into formal rules, "customary law" is a prime example of "invented traditions" (see Colson 1976; Ranger 1983; Chanock 1985; Gordon and Meggitt 1985; Jersild 2002, 89–109). Such codification efforts enhanced the role of the state in the legal sphere, and enabled officials to draw on local customs under certain conditions. In the German colony Cameroon, colonial officials could rule in accordance with local customs in both civil and criminal lawsuits between Africans (though they were obliged to take German law in criminal cases into account). With few exceptions, in the Russian Empire the consideration of religious legal traditions and custom was limited to village courts and certain types of civil law (especially family and inheritance law). At the same time, and in contrast to other imperial powers such as the British in India, the Russian authorities insisted on a strict adherence to religious orthodoxy in family law (Crews 2006, 143–191). In post-imperial China, customs could only be taken into consideration in civil cases not covered by the Civil Code. Thus, the integration of local legal traditions with state law differed considerably across time and space. However, state law(s)—which was not a unitary system but a mosaic of different laws, codes and practices—tended to play a privileged role in this constellation of orders. The state, for example, usually retained the right to dismiss customs that it saw as either a threat to public order or an insult to (state-defined!) social mores.

In many empires the legal sphere developed in a disjointed and contradictory fashion. Frequently, there was no such thing as a "legal policy"—rather, a set of incoherent views, reform proposals and decisions that differed over time and between individuals and institutions. Yet, overall a basic tension emerged, for the reliance on legal diversity as a mechanism of rule was increasingly met with strides towards legal unification. Both policies could be justified in terms of the developmental logic widespread among nineteenth and early twentieth century thinkers and policy-makers: the maintenance of legal differences could be advocated where groups were seen as not sufficiently "developed" to merit legal equality; and unification could be pursued as a reward and encouragement for "progress" towards a higher degree of "civilization". Thus, as my own article in this volume argues, some ethnic and religious minorities were more fully integrated in the state legal system than others.

Yet, legal pluralism was increasingly perceived as a problem in that it caused complications in matters of jurisdiction and authority, the training of legal practitioners, and the resolution of cases that affected several orders at the same time. Against this background, legal integration was used as a strategy to increase the efficiency of rule and strengthen central power.

Post-imperial nation-states tended to take steps towards legal unification as part of their state and nation-building efforts. Some sought to model all legal relations on state law and administer them through state institutions. Yet, even those states that strove towards homogeneity rarely achieved it. Multiple legal cultures coexisted and were deeply entangled with each other. Minorities did not just disappear. Ethnic, religious and social prejudice inherited from the imperial period often continued to inform new legal orders, as the Latin American cases in this volume illustrate. Around the globe, in fact, some groups remained outside the jurisdiction of regular courts, sometimes at their own insistence, especially in civil law. As the case of republican China shows, such diversity could even be entrenched in new civil codes and be accompanied by further efforts at codifying non-state law. States with long-standing religious and "customary" legal practices, such as Indonesia, chose to integrate these with the state legal order while giving particular weight to religious norms (Benda-Beckmann 2008). Legal pluralism, in short, remained the rule in many states even after empire.

There are differences in what this pluralism looked like. Since a coexistence of different forms of normative ordering (court-based or other) can be found in virtually every society (Merry 1988), the challenge is to find the specificity of each individual case of legal pluralism. Is it parallel, inclusive, or does it take the form of aggressive competition (Benda-Beckmann 2010)? How does it evolve over time, and how does it differ between and within states? More importantly, how much freedom do litigants have to step outside the legal category to which they have been assigned and to engage in so-called "forum shopping" (Benda-Beckman 1981), that is, to move and choose between legal forums? Some constructions of legal pluralism are not state-centric at all and therefore best analyzed in different ways (Benton 2002, 30; Benda-Beckmann 2008; Randeria 2006). That said, for the cases presented in this volume the state is a key player.

The case studies also underline that institutional and normative designs were usually rather different from the legal reality, which could not be fully scripted. Formal segregation of different groups in society, often along racial lines, did little to stop these groups from developing legal relations with each other. The legal institutions created for different parts of the population were deeply entangled and developed multiple forms of cooperation. In addition, by relying on the help of informal legal practitioners to go to court or other legal forums, the disenfranchised masses utilized the very instruments that were originally put in place to ensure the domination of elites. The plurality of legal forums and the selective use of such forums by litigants, moreover, helped to determine the authority of different legal institutions, and thus had an impact on legal practice. The design and use of new laws and legal institutions were closely linked; different legal forums were affected by each other's existence. As a result, the making, use and internal differentiation of law during and after empire must be studied together.

For all their commonalities, the debates and practices discussed in this volume were part or the result of specific reform programs. In imperial Russia, the Judicial Reform of 1864 established an independent judiciary and court system. Trials began to be held in public, and a new generation of trained jurists put emphasis on the lawfulness and accountability of police and court actions. The new courts turned into interactive spaces in which jurists, policemen and ordinary subjects of the Empire shaped and experienced state policy. As some (albeit not all) minorities were granted access to the new legal system, a hesitatingly unified legal space emerged. Along with the emancipation of the serfs, the Judicial Reform was perhaps the most radical and successful element of the so-called Great Reforms of the 1860s. These were a watershed in imperial history, even if debates over new legal codes and individual laws continued, and certain amendments were passed over the years that followed. Western Europe supplied key reference points in the process of legal change while in some legal initiatives, such as legislation on the death penalty, Russian reformers saw themselves as being at the forefront of European progress.

In China, legal reforms were more gradual, spanning across the imperial and republican periods. They were part of a much wider reform process underpinned by the universalization of Western norms, the establishment of a new political order and the transformation of the social and economic spheres. In the course of the first four decades of the twentieth century, a series of legal codes kept defining and re-defining "criminal" acts as well as opportunities for lawsuits. Legal behavior changed only gradually: by the mid-1930s, the choices of litigants and judges were still influenced by imperial codes. The universalistic model of legal modernization, moreover, did little against *de facto* legal pluralism; on the contrary, the state continued to integrate different local practices with this model.

The reform program in Afghanistan was gradual yet ambitious. As long as the country was under British influence (albeit not part of the British Empire), rulers were busy trying to strengthen the central state. Yet, before full independence in 1919, efforts were already made at codifying existing (Islamic) laws and restructuring the judicial system. The 1920s then witnessed a period of dramatic reform. Like their fellow reformers in the Ottoman and Russian Empires, the "Young Afghans" sought to implement their vision of a "modern" Afghan state and society. Beginning with a new constitution, the post-independence ruler soon announced far-reaching changes that would enhance state control in both private and public law, over taxes, army service and religious institutions. This strengthening of the state legal system entailed the disempowerment of those in charge of coexisting legal orders, which ultimately led to the ruler's downfall. Yet, many elements of his "one law for all Afghans" policy remained and were continued by his successors.

Like other post-colonial states, Peru faced a number of legal challenges in the mid-nineteenth century. It had to develop a new set of codes and norms to replace colonial legislation (which took several decades and led to a multiplicity of state legal norms); it had to create new institutions and agents—tribunals, courts, local magistrates, schools for lawyers, and others—that would meet the needs of the new legal system. And crucially, it had to address the existing legal discrimination against its large indigenous population which had been considered inferior and unworthy of citizenship rights by colonial elites. The emerging state-centered legal system was thus forced to reconcile ideas of race, status and power inherited from colonial rule with new liberal concepts about the rule of law and citizenship rights. Given these challenges, Benton characterized legal systems in post-independence Spanish America as "fractured" (2002, 211). Peru offers a good example of such a fractured system. While independence brought equality before the law to all Peruvians, the reality was ridden by exceptions and continuing inequalities that kept women, rural and indigenous people marginalized.

The legal challenges faced by early to mid-nineteenth-century Mexico were broadly similar. The replacement of the colonial system with a new legal order that would suit the needs of the newly independent state was an arduous and violent process. Monarchists and republicans, conservatives and liberals, elites and peasant rebels were locked in battle for decades, giving rise to a rapid succession of wars, political leaders and forms of government (for one, two short-lived "Mexican Empires" were interspersed in the post-independence, republican period). As the reformers emerged victorious from these power struggles, the new Constitution (1857) and Penal Code (1871), inspired in large part by Western European models, reflected the liberal ideal of universal equality before the law for all citizens of the Mexican Republic. Jury trials were introduced, at least in the capital city, in order to increase popular participation in state institutions—another liberal ideal—and educate the masses as "citizens". Like in Peru, however, "one law for all" remained an ideal that large parts of the population did not experience in practice. Regardless of all efforts at legal unification, a multiplicity of legal cultures continued to coexist and interact. Older, imperial notions, especially racial prejudice, persisted. At the same time, as liberal thinking became enmeshed in popular ideas of crime and punishment, ordinary people began to express support for the work of state legal institutions.

As the only case of an existing colonial state and society in this book, the German colony Cameroon unsurprisingly showed the least interest in introducing greater equality, or even in "modernizing" its legal system. It offers a prime example of a territory in which the law was used as a tool for maintaining colonial domination and repression. Legal segregation along racial lines, justified in terms of different stages of "development", helped to keep the "natives" in a subordinate position. While there was some support for the idea that African law should be slowly transformed towards idealized European legal principles and practices, no serious attempts were made to further legal equality. Greater equality, in fact, would have eroded the racist foundation on which the entire colonial system was built. After 1905, the Colonial Office in Berlin attempted to bring the legal decisions of colonial officials more closely in line with German criminal law. At the same time, the colonial government tried to increase the autonomy of "native" courts and subjected court cases that involved both Europeans and Africans to greater regulation (mainly to increase the predictability of legal decisions for the European party). "One law for all", however, was not considered an option. At the same time, Schaper's article suggests that litigants tended to perceive the highly differentiated legal sphere as a single space, also because strict segregation was more of a utopian vision than a description of legal reality. In practice, there much was interaction and "forum shopping" across legal spheres.

In the remainder of this opening chapter I highlight a number of themes that form the core of this volume: legal borrowing, agency, legitimacy, performativity, and inequality. The first of these themes is most prominent in debates over and the implementation of legal reform at the "top"—be it in parliament or between the ruler and regional interest groups. It is particularly pronounced in the first sections of the volume, which focuses on the role of Western models in the context of the Russian and Afghan reform processes. This is not to suggest that non-Western models were insignificant. Benjamin Buchholz points to the influence of Turkish and Iranian experience and advisors on debates in Afghanistan, while research on Russia highlights the role played by the Ottoman Empire as a model for some spheres of law—especially, the integration of the *shari'a* with the state legal system (Crews 2006, 143–191). Directly or indirectly, however, European antecedents were decisive for the cases covered in this volume, which reveal an array of engagements with European models ranging from mimesis and adaptation to their use as templates against which alternative, "local" ideas were formulated.

By the late nineteenth century, Russian jurists, scientists and leading politicians were referring to "Europe" predominantly as a positive example. Lena Gautam, for one, shows that Western European scientific claims concerning criminal responsibility were discussed among the educated public and selectively appropriated by legal scholars and policy-makers (who then communicated their contributions back to the "West", thus creating a degree of reciprocity). As some of these debates popularized new ideas about human behavior, stressing social or physiological constraints on the free will, they helped to change the ways in which criminals were viewed and treated in court. The keepers of new expert knowledge had vested interests in disseminating such knowledge in Russia: since the courts became dependent on expert testimony, they also offered livelihoods to medical-legal specialists (who often had few other sources of income). The growth and increasing professionalization of this new social group, in turn, and their integration into courtroom practice, turned some imported scientific claims into locally accepted "facts". Nevertheless, the legal reality in the courtroom remained distinctive, as Western ideas about criminal responsibility were integrated with the Russian codes and court design.

Benjamin Beuerle's analysis of the debate over the death penalty in the Russian Duma exposes a more ambivalent engagement with Western models. The discussion shows that in the minds of Russian lawmakers Western experience was to be given close attention but not necessarily to be followed. Opposed to the death penalty as a symbol of the hated autocratic regime, most Duma deputies insisted that Russia had to pursue a different path (rather than join most of her European neighbors in maintaining the death penalty). The idea of "Europe" thus dissolved into a multitude of states and individual thinkers, some of which—the "true West"—deserved emulation while others were suddenly presented as being more "backward" than Russia herself. In fact, some parliamentarians proudly asserted that for once, Russia stood at the forefront of European "development". Yet crucially, the arguments on all sides indicate the importance of European states, policies and thinkers as points of reference in Russian debates on new legislation.

The reception and selective use of Western references in the legal system is also illustrated by the Mexican case. A diverse set of imported scientific ideas and legal models interacted not only with local understandings but also with each other, as Manuel de los Reyes García Márkina shows in his article. The Mexican Penal Code of 1871, which drew on over twenty European and North American codes (with an emphasis on French models), reflected liberal ideas of freedom, equality before the law, and the importance of individual agency. In the decades that followed, however, a new generation of legal scholars emerged who—like their contemporaries in Russia—cast doubt on the free will of the individual and focused on the social and biological reasons for crime. This new generation thus challenged the new legal order, inspired by European models, by using legal arguments put forward by French, Italian and British theoreticians.

Such multi-layered and explicit engagement with European models was unthinkable in Kabul. While Afghanistan's post-independence ruler Amânullâh Khân sought to strengthen the fledgling Afghan state by supplying it with a more "modern" political, legal and social system, he had to couch this project in local terms. The ruler's legitimacy depended on his public respect and support for Islamic and "traditional" norms. As long as he presented himself as the chief defender of Islam, framed innovation in terms of adaptations of earlier Afghan institutions, and assured both tribal leaders and higher Islamic scholars of their moral and political authority, he managed to implement reforms (including a new constitution). Iran and the Ottoman Empire served as surrogate reference points for legal borrowings from the West, granting these borrowings an air of Islamic legitimacy. The ruler took pains not only to construct his reforms around religious terms and institutions but also to leave the power of established elites untouched. Thus, it was not until Amânullâh Khân changed course and called for an all-out revolution in accordance with European models (inspired by the ruler's own tour of European countries) that the ruler's authority began to crumble and open confrontation ensued. While on the surface this conflict was about competing values (which mattered on a symbolic level), first and foremost it was a conflict over resources based on legal authority.

The second and third sections of this volume move the discussion from debates over legal reform and competing reference models to legal practice. The chapters tease out the role played by different local legal actors and forums during and after empire. They show that state efforts at universalizing legal norms across the judicial landscape were accompanied by a continuing diversity of legal practice.

The key concept for this discussion is agency. In analogy with the three parts of the book, we may distinguish between the agency of central authorities, the agency of lower-level officials and legal practitioners, and the agency of ordinary people in legal institutions. The behavior of actors in key state institutions, both legislature and executive (which were often hard to separate in imperial contexts), was critical to the success or failure of legal reform and administration, especially where central power was tenuous and contested, either because of the vastness of territory—a feature of many empires—or because of a short history of statehood, as in Afghanistan. Central authorities could not rely on force alone in governing such territories, but had to try and insert themselves into existing networks of power at the local and regional levels. In Afghanistan, for example, the *loya jirga* was first and foremost a site for negotiation and alliance-building without which legal reform would have been unthinkable. While the contested operation of state law has been widely discussed in "law and society" research on the contemporary period, it has received only occasional attention among historians and cultural anthropologists working outside Western contexts (for example, Moore 1986; Mann and Roberts 1991; Collier 1994; Lazarus-Black and Hirsch 1994; French 1995).

The Afghan case also points to a crucial constraint on the agency of central authorities: legitimacy. While the power of Russian rulers, by contrast, rested in their perceived ability to "modernize" the Empire, the Afghan amir's legal authority and right to introduce reforms was rooted, in some measure, in his defense of Islamic norms. More importantly, and given the weakness of his law-enforcement authorities, his legitimacy was dependent on his readiness to satisfy the demands and interests of elites and to consult with them in all major policy areas. Reform proposals that undermined the authority and resource base of elites were unlikely to succeed. By taking the concerns of elites into consideration, however, the ruler could use legal reform as an opportunity to enhance his own legitimacy.

A number of chapters address the agency of legal intermediaries and local officials. The second section of the volume addresses the operation of law by such individuals in greater detail, offering case studies from early twentieth century Russia and nineteenth century Peru. Jane Burbank's in-depth study of two cases from one of Russia's most multiethnic provinces looks at law from the perspective of intermediary officials. She argues that these officials—usually above the village but below the central authorities—served crucial functions in the Russian Empire, a territory characterized by long distances and the devolution of administrative and judicial power to local authorities. Crucially, the everyday legal interaction between subjects and officials expressed and reinforced the authority of the state in the countryside. While interpreting and enforcing the law on a day-to-day basis, officials communicated the state's authority to peasants of various ethnic groups who, in turn, reported crimes, incriminated community members and lodged appeals, thereby accepting and utilizing this authority for their own ends. It was this interaction that ultimately imbued the "state" with life in rural areas.

Carlos Aguirre also addresses the role of intermediary actors in linking the population with the state, but shifts the attention from administrative and judicial institutions to informal legal practitioners. He explores the activities and functions of the so-called *tinterillos* in post-independence Peru in order to scrutinize the relationship between the disenfranchised masses and the state legal system. Legal practitioners helped to disseminate and re-appropriate notions of justice, rights, and legality among the lower classes. Aguirre's analysis illuminates ordinary people's understanding and use of state law while highlighting the ways in which language, location, and social and economic status hindered their access to it. Pointing out that after independence *tinterillos* were allowed to represent litigants in towns and villages where no or few certified lawyers existed, Aguirre contends that these practitioners provided a link between indigenous peoples, the state, and local elites; between the oral and the written world; and between urban and rural spaces. Despite their predominantly negative image in contemporary debates and literature, they gave shape to a culture of contestation and helped to promote the rights of indigenous peasants and communities. While recent scholarship on lawyers and legal practitioners in the colonial world has focused on their contribution to the formation of colonial identities (for an overview, see Sharafi 2007), Aguirre presents the *tinterillo* as a social and political actor in local, regional, and national networks of power (but without vilifying or glorifying this figure, as some scholars of the new field of "colonial lawyering" are wont to do).

Various articles in this volume show that the actions of local agents and institutions allowed ordinary people to experience the "state" at the village level. The discretion of these officials was admittedly at the root of much legal uncertainty and usually least beneficial for disadvantaged groups. Yet, this discretion was so intrinsic to the maintenance of colonial rule that legal constraints on the officials' legal powers were often kept to a minimum. Informal legal practitioners, by contrast, tended to be viewed with skepticism, if not outright hostility, by the legal establishment and ruling elites. They became influential where state expansion was limited (see also Macauley 1998). Finally, Buchholz's discussion of *loya jirga* delegates introduces another type of intermediary whose actions illustrate the ways in which the meaning of state institutions was re-appropriated by those who interacted in them. The delegates had little interest in debating the proposed constitution but used the opportunity to confront the ruler with their pressing concerns. Delegate agency was more critical in the *loya jirga* than institutional structure.

The operation of law is also greatly dependent on the behavior of the litigant. The practice of going to court has been a research focus of legal anthropology since at least the 1960s (Gibbs 1963; Nader 1969; Collier 1973; Starr 1978; Lazarus-Black and Hirsch 1994) and more sociologically-oriented scholars of the "law and society" tradition since the 1970s (*Law and Society Review* 1974, 1975; Munger 1998, 30). Along with these studies, the work of historians such as E.P. Thompson (1975) helped to expose and undermine the assumption that the law is mainly a tool wielded by elites to defend their hegemonic power. Yet, in works on imperial history, the agency of the masses, especially outside the cities, was long neglected. For historians of Russia, among others, what mattered was not what peasants did, but what was done to them. It is only in the last twenty-five years that scholars have begun to explore how the Empire ruled with the masses, rather than over them (Gaudin 2007, 7;

Burbank 2004). Among scholars of empire there is increasing agreement that the dominant mode of interaction between imperial powers and local populations was accommodation (Aguirre and Salvatore 2001; Benton 2002, 27; Burbank and Cooper 2010, 14). Law is only gradually being incorporated into these discussions. Yet, as Carlos Aguirre puts it in this volume, "the peasants' approach to law and legal intermediation was much less naive than what the standard literature want[s] us to believe."

Examining litigation in China, sub-Saharan Africa, Latin America and Russia, various authors in this book discuss ordinary people's use of the state court system and other legal forums to deal with crime, settle family and community disputes, or to improve their life chances. State courts were attractive for people who sought protection from officials (and many of the legal reforms in the nineteenth and early twentieth centuries were aimed at making officials more accountable for their actions). They also offered possibilities for those who preferred external mediation, for example because their communal support networks were weak or unreachable (in cases of travelling). These courts also appealed to those who feared that alternative—communal, religious or other—legal forums were likely to rule against them.

Yet, the degree to which people could engage in "forum shopping" differed from context to context: we shall see, for example, that litigants happily jumped between forums in the German colony Cameroon (despite formal legal segregation) whereas they were more limited in their options in imperial Russia. That said, extra-legal arrangements were an alternative in both (and most other) cases; and where people reached out-of-court solutions, they were quick to drop their cases. Litigants knew the rules of the game. As Xiaoqun Xu's discussion of marriage and divorce in republican China shows, they manipulated cases and fabricated grounds for litigation when it was in their interests to do so. The chapters by Burbank, Kirmse and Gautam on court use in the Russian Empire reveal the same pattern: aware of the forms of activity that constituted "crimes" or the mental states that would allow for mitigating circumstances in cases of criminal indictment, litigants skillfully utilized this knowledge to gain advantages. However, as officials were also aware of such forms of legal behavior and did not just accept denunciations at face value, court use was about ongoing negotiation. Peasant masses, women and ethnic minorities turned to the courts in significant numbers to argue their cases (despite continuing discrimination). By choosing one legal authority rather than another, moreover, they also enhanced or diminished the legitimacy of individual legal forums.

In several chapters of this volume the notions of interactive spaces and performance play a central role. The performative dimension of trials—even their "theatrical" qualities—has been noted many times (Merry 1994; Aguirre and Salvatore 2001, 13, 21; Benton 2002, 16). The courtroom is discussed in such terms in Gautam's and, to a degree, in my own article (though I offer a more detailed discussion of ethnic minority representation in imperial courtrooms elsewhere [2012]). Gautam views the court as a space for the public enactment and dissemination of new psychological and medical ideas and discourses whereas my own analysis shows Russian courts as arenas of encounter for ethnic and religious minorities and the wider society around them. How many of the ideas, images and power constellations the participants and audiences in the courtroom actually internalized is difficult to gauge; yet, there is little doubt that the post-1864 courts presented a new public forum—a major change from the closed courts before the Judicial Reform—that offered constant exposure to new ideas of equality, citizenship, and criminal responsibility.

Beuerle and Buchholz discuss legislative assemblies rather than courts as performative spaces. Short of being parliaments in a democratic sense, both the Duma and the *loya jirga* had limited political influence; yet, they were spaces in which the tsar's and amir's power could be either staged and thus reinforced, or challenged and symbolically diminished. The Duma's unanimous vote for abolishing the death penalty may have had no legal consequences in 1906; yet it sent a symbolic message, a widely noted public signal, that the government was not speaking on behalf of the people, forming a legal precedent later used by the Provisional Government and the Bolsheviks both of whom abolished capital punishment as one of their first measures in 1917. The *loya jirga*, by contrast, was a symbol of the ruler's "new order" and his willingness to negotiate on controversial issues; it was also a tool to achieve this new order and build alliances against opponents. Keen to increase his own legitimacy, he used it as an instrument for staging, negotiating and revising reforms. Yet, it remained a temporary consultative space, as the amir had no intention of sharing his power indefinitely. When his last summoning of the *jirga* marked a turn away from consultation and toward the use of this space for Afghanistan's visual embrace of European "modernity"—in clothes and appearance, women delegates and Western entertainment—his strategy broke down.

Finally, the partially rhetorical nature of the question "one law for all?" already hints at the importance of inequality to this volume. While several articles choose the perspective of the underprivileged masses, granting agency to the disenfranchised at the same time, they suggest neither an equality of power nor an equality of opportunities. The law has always been a double-edged sword in that it creates and sustains the hegemony of the powerful while it can also facilitate the resistance of the poor (Hirsch and Lazarus-Black 1994, 8). Hegemony and resistance are inherently contested and come in multiple shapes. More often than not, the key form of interaction between the haves and have-nots was accommodation.

To be sure, inequality must be part of any discussion of law, for the law is never neutral and impartial, but always constructed by human agency in a way that is advantageous to some at the expense of others (Starr and Collier 1989, 3, 7). Beuerle's discussion of the death penalty offers one of many examples: in the eyes of many contemporaries, capital punishment mainly targeted the politically active poor and thus served as a tool for the ruling elites to maintain their hold on power.

Due to the influence of structuralist and functionalist theory, until at least the early 1970s, the law was widely perceived as an integrative instrument that helped to create and sustain social order. Since then it has come to be seen as a contingent cultural and political force experienced differently by differently situated people. While the British social history of crime acknowledged that legal institutions defended the interests of the ruling classes, it also showed that they offered voice and opportunities to the oppressed (Thompson 1975; Hay et al. 1976). In both "law and society" research and legal anthropology, access to justice and the experiences of underprivileged groups are key fields of enquiry (Galanter 1974; *Law and Society Review* 1976; Starr and Collier 1989; Lazarus-Black and Hirsch 1994); and the work of "poverty lawyers", who give voice to the poor, is now an important subfield of socio-legal research (for example, *Cornell Law Review* 1992; Montoya 1994).

Studies from imperial and post-imperial contexts contribute rich material to these discussions as they offer a wide range and stark forms of inequality, from formal legal segregation rooted in social and racial prejudice, to an indirectly skewed access to the legal system and more subtle forms of discrimination against women, the poor, and ethnic minorities.

Numerous barriers including social and legal status, economic resources, rural-urban discrepancies, language, literacy and gender put parts of the population at a disadvantage regarding the use of these courts. Economic constraints were particularly acute in civil lawsuits, which involved substantial litigation fees, so that it was mainly those with the necessary resources who launched them. Where writing and literacy became the key criteria for full citizenship rights, as in Peru, indigenous communities were *de facto* denied access to these rights. At the same time, indifference and even the boycott of state legal institutions on the part of disenfranchised people were hardly uncommon. While the legal reforms in most of the cases discussed in this book were underpinned by liberal ideals about universal equality before the law, in reality they were particularly beneficial for the urban, male population who commanded significant economic and social capital. Xu's discussion of women's marriage and divorce lawsuits in China, for example, shows that regardless of a *de jure* transformation towards equality between the sexes from the imperial to the republican periods, lower legal institutions and functionaries continued to discriminate against women in practice.

The legal status and experiences of groups that did not share the religion or ethnicity of the ruling elites were highly context-specific. These indigenous groups formed the majority of the population in imperial possessions overseas, such as the German colony Cameroon, and in newly independent states that emerged from overseas empires, such as Mexico; yet, they suffered a range of racial, religious and other discriminations. In some contiguous empires, such as Russia and China, by contrast, these groups remained a smaller part of the population, which perhaps spurred efforts at integration in the late nineteenth and early twentieth centuries. Burbank's research on Russia's multiethnic Middle Volga region suggests that ethnicity or religion did not figure as a decisive or even relevant legal category for the authorities; my own research comes to the same conclusion for Muslim subjects in this region, but also emphasizes that the integration of Muslims differed significantly across the Empire. While some minorities profited from legal unification, others experienced stricter forms of legal segregation (see also Kirmse 2012). Even those minorities who did receive the same legal opportunities as the rest of the Empire's (Russian) subjects after the Judicial Reform of 1864 continued to be judged on the basis of Civil and Criminal Codes that dated back to the pre-Reform period and contained various forms of religious discrimination. Integration was always selective and partial.

In sum, then, the articles in this volume present law as a site of struggle. They are mostly works in progress. The authors raise questions and try to offer some tentative conclusions. The volume thus neither intends to be exhaustive, nor to answer all the questions. Yet what emerges from the discussion is a story of contested European hegemony, local assertions, and multiple legal borrowings.

Works Cited

Aguirre, Carlos and Salvatore, Ricardo D. (2001). Introduction: Writing the History of Law, Crime, and Punishment in Latin America. In Ricardo D. Salvatore, Carlos Aguirre and Gilbert M. Joseph (eds.) *Crime and Punishment in Latin America. Law and Society since Late Colonial Times*, 1–32. Durham, NC: Duke University Press.

Benda-Beckmann, Franz von (2008). Pluralismus von Recht und Ordnung. *Behemoth. A Journal on Civilisation*, 1, 58–67.

Benda-Beckmann, Franz von (2010). *Gleiches Recht für Alle?* Talk presented at the GTZ Eschborner Fachtage.

Benda-Beckmann, Keebet von (1981). Forum Shopping and Shopping Forums. Dispute Settlement in a Minangkabau Village in West Sumatra. *Journal of Legal Pluralism*, 19, 117–159.

Benton, Lauren (2002). *Law and Colonial Cultures. Legal Regimes in World History, 1400–1900.* Cambridge, UK, and New York: Cambridge University Press.

Benton, Lauren (2006). Constitutions and Empires. *Law & Social Inquiry*, 31, 1, 177–198.

Boyle, Elizabeth H. and Meyer, John W. (2002). Modern Law as a Secularized and Global Model: Implications for the Sociology of Law. In Y. Dezalay and B. Garth (eds.) *Global Prescriptions: The Production, Exportation, and Importation of a New Legal Orthodoxy*, 65–95. Ann Arbor: University of Michigan Press.

Burbank, Jane (2004). *Russian Peasants Go to Court: Legal Culture in the Countryside, 1905–1917*. Indianapolis: Indiana University Press.

Burbank, Jane and Cooper, Frederick (2010). *Empires in World History. Power and the Politics of Difference*. Princeton: Princeton University Press.

Chanock, Martin (1985). *Law, Custom, and Social Order: The Colonial Experience in Malawi and Zambia*. Cambridge: Cambridge University Press.

Collier, Jane (1973). *Law and Social Change in Zinacantan*. Stanford, CA: Stanford University Press.

Collier, Jane (1994). Intertwined Histories: Islamic Law and Western Imperialism. *Law and Society Review*, 28, 2, 395–408.

Colson, Elizabeth (1976). From Chief's Court to Local Court: The Evolution of Local Courts in Southern Zambia. In M.J. Aronoff (ed.) *Freedom and Constraint*, 15–29. Amsterdam: Van Gorcum.

Cornell Law Review (1992). Symposium: The Emperor's Old Prose. Reexamining the Language of the Law, Vol. 77.

Crews, Robert D. (2006). *For Prophet and Tsar. Islam and Empire in Russia and Central Asia*. Cambridge, MA, and London: Harvard University Press.

Fisch, Jörg (1992). Law as a Means and as an End. Some Remarks on the Function of European and Non-European Law in the Process of European Expansion. In Wolfgang J. Mommsen and J.A. de Moor (eds.) *European Expansion and Law. The Encounter of European and Indigenous Law in 19th- and 20th-Century Africa and Asia*, 15–38. Oxford and New York: Berg.

French, Rebecca R. (1995). *The Golden Yoke. The Legal Cosmology of Buddhist Tibet*. Ithaca, NY: Cornell University Press.

Galanter, Marc (1974). Why the "Haves" Come Out Ahead: Speculation on the Limits of Legal Change. *Law and Society Review*, 9, 95–160.

Gaudin, Corinne (2007). *Ruling Peasants: Village and State in Late Imperial Russia*. DeKalb: Northern Illinois University Press.

Geertz, Clifford (1983). *Local Knowledge. Further Essays in Interpretive Anthropology*. New York: Basic Books.

Gibbs, James L. (1963). The Kpelle Moot: A Therapeutic Model for the Informal Settlement of Disputes. *Africa*, 33, 1–11.

Gordon, Robert J. and Meggitt, Mervyn J. (1985). *Law and Order in the New Guinea Highlands: Encounters with Enga*. Hanover, NH: Vermont.

Hay, Douglas et al. (1976). *Albion's Fatal Tree: Crime and Society in Eighteenth-Century England.* New York: Pantheon.

Hirsch, Susan F. and Lazarus-Black, Mindie (1994). Introduction/Performance and Paradox: Exploring Law's Role in Hegemony and Resistance. In Mindie Lazarus-Black and Susan F. Hirsch (eds.) *Contested States: Law, Hegemony, and Resistance*, 1–31. New York and London: Routledge.

Hooker, M.B. (1975). *Legal Pluralism. An Introduction to Colonial and Neo-Colonial Laws.* Oxford: Clarendon Press.

Jersild, Austin (2002). *Orientalism and Empire. North Caucasus Mountain Peoples and the Georgian Frontier, 1845–1917*. Montreal: McGill-Queen's University Press.

Kirmse, Stefan B. (2012). New Courts in Late Tsarist Russia: Of Imperial Representation and Muslim Participation. *Journal of Modern European History* (forthcoming).

Law and Society Review (1974). Litigation and Dispute Processing: Part One, 9, 1, 1–160.

Law and Society Review (1975). Litigation and Dispute Processing: Part Two, 9, 2, 163–391.

Law and Society Review (1976). Special Issue on Delivery of Services. 11, 2, 167–415.

Lazarus-Black, Mindie and Hirsch, Susan F. (eds.) (1994). *Contested States: Law, Hegemony, and Resistance.* New York and London: Routledge.

Legrand, Pierre (2001). What "Legal Transplants"? In David Nelken and Johannes Feest (eds.) *Adapting Legal Cultures*, 55–70. Oxford: Hart.

Levine, Felice (1990). Goose Bumps and the Search for Signs of Intelligent Life in Sociological Studies: After Twenty-Five Years. *Law and Society Review*, 24, 1, 7–33.

Macauley, Melissa Ann (1998). *Social Power and Legal Culture. Litigation Masters in Late Imperial China.* Stanford, CA: Stanford University Press.

Mann, Kristin and Roberts, Richard L. (eds.) (1991). *Law in Colonial Africa.* Portsmouth, NH: Heinemann.

Merry, Sally E. (1988). Legal Pluralism. *Law and Society Review*, 22, 5, 869–896.

Merry, Sally E. (1991). Law and Colonialism. *Law and Society Review*, 25, 4, 889–922.

Merry, Sally E. (1994). Courts as Performances. Domestic Violence Hearings in a Hawai'i Family Court. In Mindie Lazarus-Black and Susan F. Hirsch (eds.) *Contested States: Law, Hegemony, and Resistance*, 35–58. New York and London: Routledge.

Montoya, Margaret E. (1994). Mascaras, Trenzas, y Greñas: Un/Masking the Self While Un/Braiding Latina Stories and Legal Discourse. *Harvard Women's Law Journal*, 17, 185–220.

Moore, Sally Falk (1986). *Social Facts and Fabrications: Customary Law on Kilimanjaro, 1880–1980.* Cambridge: Cambridge University Press.

Munger, Frank (1998). Mapping Law and Society. In Austin Sarat et al. (eds.) *Crossing Boundaries: Traditions and Transformations in Law and Society Research.* Evanston: Northwestern University Press.

Nader, Laura (1969). *Law in Culture and Society.* Berkeley, CA, and London: University of California Press.

Örücü, Esin (1992). The Impact of European Law on the Ottoman Empire and Turkey. In Wolfgang J. Mommsen and J.A. de Moor (eds.) *European Ex-*

pansion and Law. The Encounter of European and Indigenous Law in 19th- and 20th-Century Africa and Asia, 39–58. Oxford and New York: Berg.

Randeria, Shalini (2006). Entangled Histories: Civil Society, Caste Solidarities and Legal Pluralism in Post-Colonial India. In John Keane (ed.) *Civil Society: Berlin Perspectives*, 213–242. New York and Oxford: Berghahn.

Ranger, Terence (1983). The Invention of Tradition in Colonial Africa. In Eric Hobsbawm and Terence Ranger (eds.) *The Invention of Tradition*. Cambridge: Cambridge University Press.

Sarat, Austin and Kearns, Thomas R. (eds.) (1998). *Law in the Domains of Culture*. Ann Arbor: University of Michigan Press.

Sarat, Austin and Simon, Jonathan (eds.) (2003). *Cultural Analysis, Cultural Studies, and the Law. Moving beyond Legal Realism*. Durham and London: Duke University Press.

Sharafi, Mitra (2007). A New History of Colonial Lawyering. Likhovski and Legal Identities in the British Empire. *Law & Social Inquiry*, 32, 4, 1059–1094.

Starr, June (1978). *Dispute and Settlement in Rural Turkey: An Ethnography of Law*. Leiden: E.J. Brill.

Starr, June and Collier, Jane F. (eds.) (1989). *History and Power in the Study of Law. New Directions in Legal Anthropology*. Ithaca, NY, and London: Cornell University Press.

Thompson, E.P. (1975). *Whigs and Hunters: The Origins of the Black Act*. New York: Pantheon.

Trubek, David M. (1972). Toward a Social Theory of Law: An Essay on the Study of Law and Development. *The Yale Law Journal*, 82, 1, 1–50.

Trubek, David M. and Galanter, Marc (1974). Scholars in Self-Estrangement: Some Reflections on the Crisis in Law and Development Studies in the United States. *Wisconsin Law Review*, 4, 1062–1102.

Watson, Alan (1974). *Legal Transplants: An Approach to Comparative Law*. Edinburgh: Scottish Academic Press.

Wrase, Michael (2006). Rechtssoziologie und Law and Society. Die deutsche Rechtssoziologie zwischen Krise und Neuaufbruch. *Zeitschrift für Rechtssoziologie*, 27, 2, 289–312.

Yngvesson, Barbara (1988). Making Law at the Doorway: The Clerk, the Court, and the Construction of Community in a New England Town. *Law and Society Review*, 22, 3, 409–448.

Discussing Legal Reform

A Step for the "Whole Civilized World"? The Debate over the Death Penalty in Russia, 1905–1917

Benjamin Beuerle

Introduction

Despite the substantial polarization of politics in Russia between the revolutions of 1905 and of 1917, there existed a common denominator in most of the (otherwise highly contentious) reform discussions.[1] Debaters from diverse political and ideological backgrounds frequently referred to Western Europe and "the West" in general, when they wanted to prove the value of and rationale underlying their own proposals, as well as the disadvantages and senselessness of their opponents' positions. This did not always mean that a Western European model would be regarded as one worth following in Russia. It did usually mean, however, that Western Europe was seen to have experience that Russia was lacking, and that the overall result of this experience was rather positive. The days when Russian Slavophiles—who denied the analogy between Western and Russian history and believed Russia should follow its own path—held considerable sway within influential political circles were over.[2] Notwithstanding some exceptions, to be found mainly in the ranks of the social revolutionaries (SR) and some extreme rightist parties (most importantly, the *Soiuz Russkago Naroda* [Union of the Russian People]) (Hildermeier 1978, 21–28, 74–75, 78–83; Ascher 1988, 239–242), the vast majority of those

1 The following arguments are based on my current research about the role and content of representations of the West and Western Europe in reform debates of the late tsarist Empire (1905–1917). As far as I can see, the terms "the West", "Western Europe" and "civilized countries" were used as synonyms in these debates; I use them here as terms from the Russian sources rather than as analytical tools or my own definitions.

2 Most notably the Great Reforms of the 1860s (especially the liberation of the serfs) were influenced by prominent Slavophiles. See, for example, Riasanovsky (1954, 128–131).

who participated in the Russian reform debates of this period agreed at least on a number of common presuppositions: the West and Russia were advancing on the same path of development; the West was further ahead on that path; and Russia could learn from Western experience, adopt the measures which had proven a success there and avoid those that had failed or had negative effects. These common presuppositions reflected an ideology of universal, mono-linear progress, which was prevalent in many parts of Europe and beyond during the nineteenth century (Rapp 1992, 77–83, 153–163; Koselleck 1980, 222–225). However, they constituted the only case in which the political elites of a great power believed (Russia having been part of the concert of European powers throughout the nineteenth century) that other powers had reached a higher stage of development and that their own country lagged behind. The aforementioned beliefs greatly influenced both legislative debates and their outcomes. The West thus supplied important "reference societies" for Russian debates on new legislation.[3]

The debate over the death penalty is a touchstone for these hypotheses. This debate was but one of a series of reform controversies in Russia between 1905 and 1917. Following the Empire's defeat in the Russo-Japanese War and the outbreak of the Revolution in 1905, the necessity of far-reaching reforms became widely acknowledged. At the same time, the Revolution created the conditions for discussing reform projects in public and without restraint, including Russia's first ever elected parliament with legislative competencies and a partial breakdown of censorship.[4] The range of the debated reforms included agrarian and workers' legislation, local self-government, the rights of different national groups, and numerous other subjects. In view of this list of often undisputedly urgent reform topics, it is remarkable that the abolition of the death penalty could rise to the top of the agenda.

The death penalty reform debate is of further special interest due to the fact that public opinion in Russia took a different stance than most of Western Europe and the United States at the time. For the liberal and,

3 On the concept of "reference societies", see Luhmann and Schorr (1988, 340–341); Bendix (1980, 12–13, 292).

4 For details, see von Hagen (2002, 104–110); Waldron (1998, 35–36); Ascher (1992, 58–63); Hosking (1973, 8–12); Morison (1999, 141–145).

to some extent, socialist opposition championing the cause, it was thus at first glance inadvisable to use "Western" reference points in this debate. The death penalty was widely practiced in Western Europe and the United States, and far less debated than in the Russian Empire at the time. The prominent role of Western reference models in the Russian death penalty debates, and the way these models were used, can therefore tell us a lot about the place of the Western world in the Russian political mindset and political culture in the early twentieth century.

Death penalty abolitionists had three modes of argumentation available to them. They could simply omit any reference to the West, which might have been the most convenient and natural way to deal with an issue over which they wanted Russia to part ways with the West. Second, they could point to Western countries as negative models, to show explicitly that it made sense for Russia to take a distinctive path. Or, they could try to find positive Western reference models in order to boost their point, which would have been the usual approach, though would have been more difficult in this instance. That many of these reformers did not choose the first option, but rather a mixture of the second and the third ones, illustrates the popularity of the idea of mono-linear "progress" in Russia at this time. This mindset made it virtually impossible for any debater who wanted to be taken seriously to claim that Russia was simply different and should follow its own path.

To investigate this point, this chapter first explores the reasons for the importance of the death penalty debate for large parts of Russian imperial society. It then follows the legislative initiatives concerning the death penalty in the Duma and the State Council. It also touches upon the discussion in the press and a number of other publications. At each stage, it explores the main arguments exchanged during these debates. In doing so, it explores the place and importance of Western reference models within the political culture of early twentieth-century Russia while highlighting Russian society's attitude towards the death penalty.

The Significance of the Death Penalty in Late Imperial Russia (1905–1917)

While there were many reform projects on the agendas of opposition liberals and government bureaucrats in the wake of the Revolution of 1905, only one legislative draft made it through all the regular stages of the first Russian parliaments' legislative work. It then reached the State Council for its, and the tsar's, approval. This draft provided for the total abolition of the death penalty in Russia (Emmons 1983, 503).

There were several reasons for this: The Duma was dissolved by the tsar after just 72 days of work, which did not give it much time to discuss and pass other legislative drafts. Even earlier, after the deputies' first clearly oppositional (if not revolutionary) statements, the government had simply refused to cooperate with the Duma. As the first right of initiative belonged to the specific ministries, the legislative work of the Duma was largely blocked in most matters of regular legislation (Emmons 1983, 361–362). That the first Duma did manage to forward the draft bill to the State Council under such constraints is testimony to the importance that the people's representatives attached to the death penalty issue.[5] Why is it that this issue occupied such an important place on the political agenda of early twentieth-century Russia?

There are several answers to this question. First, long before the turn of the century, Russia's state and society had developed an attitude much more critical towards the death penalty than most of its western neighbor states. In the 1750s, Empress Elizabeth had abolished the death penalty, which was confirmed later on by Empress Catherine II, except in cases of attacks on the tsar and his family and for the violation of some rules of quarantine (Fel'dshtein 1909, 5–6; see also Nethercott 2007, 111–112). As a consequence, the overall number of executions in Russia was far below those reached in Western European states and the United States in most of the nineteenth century. Furthermore, the total abolition of the

5 The State Duma was elected four times during the late tsarist Empire: The first convened in April 1906 and was dissolved by the tsar at the end of June 1906; the second came together in February 1907 and was dissolved in May 1907; the third Duma was the only one to serve its full term and lasted from autumn 1907 until 1912; the fourth was elected in 1912; between the outbreak of World War I and 1917 it was in session only irregularly.

death penalty was vigorously demanded in the late nineteenth century by prominent writers such as Vladimir Solov'ev and Lev Tolstoy as well as by several eminent Russian criminologists (Nethercott 2007, 110–119). It was therefore all the more shocking to large parts of Russian society that, after the outbreak of the Revolution in 1905, executions soared to numbers not seen since the time before Elizabeth's decree 150 years earlier. In regions under a state of emergency, from 1881 governors-general or (where these did not exist) special administrative officials could order all civilians accused of a certain category of crime to be tried by military courts and according to military law (Rawson 1984, 41–42; Daly 1995, 613). When almost all regions of the Empire were placed under a state of emergency in the wake of the 1905 Revolution, governors made extensive use of this provision as a means to suppress revolutionary unrest (Rawson 1984, 43, 46–47; Daly 1995, 621–625). Unlike regular courts, military courts could sentence people to death for a wide range of crimes (Rawson 1984, 34). As a result, in contrast to less than 20 death sentences per year on average during the three decades preceding the Revolution, more than 770 people were sentenced to death in the first six months of the year 1906 alone, of whom some 240 were executed (Liessem 1989, 496, 502, 508).

Those convicted and executed had often indeed participated in violent (terrorist) acts against state officials. The liberal and revolutionary press however, extensively covered cases where either innocents or minors had been sentenced to death (for example, Eliashev 1905; Slonimskii 1905, 736; Tagantsev 1906, 33–34). Indeed, the very format of military justice, harsh orders by the superiors of the military judges, and the general climate of violence all favored the occurrence of such cases. Most notably, military law left judges in most cases only the choice between acquitting the defendant (which was rarely the case) or sentencing him or her to death. This meant that, by provision of the extraordinary laws, governors and other officials could *de facto* decide the fate of civilians simply by ordering to have them judged by military instead of civilian courts. As Vladimir Maklakov, a prominent liberal lawyer at the time, wrote in his memoirs, executive officials thus took over legal functions, which opened the door to arbitrary judgments (Maklakov 1964, 145–146). To Russian society, whose majority was in an oppositional if not revolutionary mood, the sentencing of vast numbers of civilians by military courts and the huge numbers of death sentences and executions (which contradicted Russian legal tradition and the Empire's regular penal laws) came to be seen as a striking symptom of the arbitrary nature of Russian governance and the weakness of the rule-of-law. It is this symbolic role of the death penalty, representing repression and arbitrariness, which helps to explain the extraordinary importance accorded to this issue in the first State Duma, which convened late in April 1906.

The First Duma's Assault on the Death Penalty: Lessons from Western History and the Idea of the "True" West

In their defiant response to the tsar's address to the Duma during its fourth session, the majority of the deputies demanded a general amnesty for all political prisoners and the (total) abolition of the death penalty.[6] As the tsar did not show any reaction to this demand, in the Duma's eleventh session on May 18, 1906, the prominent Kadet Nabokov[7] and a number of other Deputies introduced a draft bill, which contained two provisions: "§1: The death penalty is abolished. §2: Until the [according] revision of the penal legislation, in all cases where the penal laws stipulate the death penalty, it is to be replaced by the next severe penalty."[8] It was one of the first draft bills introduced into the Duma, and it was the only one regularly passed and transmitted to the State Council for deliberation. There was some debate about it in the plenum, though it was hardly contentious.[9] On June 19, 1906, the draft bill was (with some clarifications) *unanimously* approved by the Duma (Nabokov 1960b, 4027; Tagantsev 1906, 5).[10]

6 *Gosudarstvennaia Duma. Sozyv I. Sessiia I. Stenograficheskie Otchety.* St. Petersburg (1906, 99–101); Nabokov (1906b, 4015–4017).

7 The Constitutional Democrats ("Kadets") were a leftist liberal party and constituted the strongest faction in the first and in the second Duma. For further information on Nabokov, see below.

8 *Gosudarstvennaia Duma, Otchety* (1906, 421).

9 Only Minister of Justice Shcheglovitov argued unequivocally against the draft: *Gosudarstvennaia Duma, Otchety* (1906, 1478–1480).

10 *Gosudarstvennaia Duma, Otchety* (1906, 1503–1504).

This clearly demonstrates the enormous importance that large parts of Russian society and its representatives attributed to this issue.

It is interesting to examine the justifications for this decision by its proponents. It was common among Duma representatives to point to Western reference models in order to substantiate their positions and projects. But would it be the same in the case of the abolition of the death penalty, the proponents of which would be hard pressed to find positive examples in Western states? Indeed, the majority of deputies who spoke on this question did not refer to Western Europe or the West in their speeches. Most of these were short and condemned the application of the death penalty by military courts in Russia as unjust, repressive measure used by a government that ignored the will of the people and its representatives.[11] That said, the three *main* speakers on this question each made use of European references, despite the difficulties with this rhetorical strategy. What were their main lines of argument?

Vladimir Kuz'min-Karavaev, a prominent military judge and participant of the "zemstvo" movement who had first been a member of the Constitutional Democrats before joining the (slightly more moderate/rightist) Party of Democratic Reform, was one of the main proponents of the total abolition of the death penalty in Russia (Terebov and Khailova 1996; Khailova 2008; Liessem 1989, 501; Emmons 1983, 359). In the debate about the Duma's response to the tsar's address and as rapporteur of the Duma commission that dealt with the draft bill for the total abolition of the death penalty, he delivered two fervent abolitionist speeches. He referred to the experience of the French Revolution and of the French king who had been killed "not by the hands of a murderer, but based on a formal law, […] killed by the hands of an executioner, killed by decision of this legal power, such as it was at that moment." To him, the lesson this demonstrates was clear. Now was the moment to abolish the death penalty, unless more "murders based on law" should occur: "If one side acts like this, the other one will act in the same way."[12] Thus, Western history bore lessons for Russian politics. This was particularly true of the French Revolution, which in the eyes of many Russians served as a precedent and historic model to follow for the next revolutions in other

11 *Gosudarstvennaia Duma, Otchety* (1906, 421–435, 438–444, 639–658).

12 *Gosudarstvennaia Duma, Otchety* (1906, 101, 1469, 1478); Nabokov (1906b, 4023).

countries, including Russia. History had shown that it was possible or even likely in an ongoing revolution—such as the one the Russian Empire was experiencing at the time—that the side holding power at one moment could be subject to the power of the other side at the next moment. If this was so, it was clearly in everyone's interest to abolish the death penalty, which otherwise could be used against oneself at the next shift in fortune. Kuz'min-Karavaev, in short, drew pragmatic advice from Western European experience.

Maxim Kovalevskii was another prominent speaker in the death penalty debates. He was a well-known lawyer, journalist and historian who could look back on a brilliant academic career. He had written works on the British parliamentary system and French constitutionalism, had received part of his academic education in Germany and France, and had been invited to hold lectures on various subjects at universities in the United States, Great Britain and France (among others). After being suspended in the late 1880s from his post at Moscow University because of his oppositional views, he lived in France for years. He was a co-founder of the Party of Democratic Reform, which he represented, like Kuz'min-Karavaev, in the First State Duma (Khailova 1996; Khailova 2008b).

In his speech on May 18, 1906, he stated that if the Russian Duma deputies abolished the death penalty, they expressed "the consciousness not only of the Russian people, but of the whole civilized world as well". According to him, "the societal opinion of the whole world pronounces itself against the death penalty".[13] In order to demonstrate this, he had asked "the most outstanding foreigners, scientists, literary figures, jurists, to tell [him] their opinion about the death penalty." All of them had given statements for the abolition of the death penalty. Among them were such famous and honorable personalities as the French politician and jurist Frédéric Passy (winner of the Nobel Peace Prize in 1901), the historian and member of the Académie Française Ernest Lavisse and the historian Anatole Leroy-Beaulieu (Wild 1987; Dictionnaire Encyclopédique 1999, 543–544; Grand Larousse Universel 1984, 6236). Lavisse had stated that the death penalty "undoubtedly contradicts the moral conscience of the civilized world", and Leroy-Beaulieu expressed his hope that by abolishing

13 *Gosudarstvennaia Duma, Otchety* (1906, 435–436).

the death penalty the Russian parliament would "accelerate the progressive development of humanity by decades".[14] Thus, Kovalevskii's line of argument was clear: while parts of the Western world stuck with the death penalty, their most civilized representatives (the "true West", so to speak) were against it. Moreover, he believed that "the whole civilized world" looked to the Russian parliament and hoped it would take this important step, placing Russia at the forefront of worldwide progress in this matter. This put enormous responsibility on the Duma deputies, which effectively left them with little choice.

The third prominent speaker on the death penalty was Vladimir Nabokov, who introduced the bill stipulating the abolition of the death penalty on behalf of the Kadet faction. He belonged to a family of noblemen and famous jurists (his father had been Minister of Justice under Alexander III), was himself a criminal law expert and journalist, one of the founders of the Kadet Party, the deputy chairman of its central committee and the editor of the party organ Vestnik Partii Narodnoi Svobody (Kanishcheva 2008; Fedorenko 1993). In connection with the introduction of the draft bill into the Duma, he published an article in *Pravo*[15] in which he explained in detail his motives and the significance of this bill. Again, references to the West played an important role in his argumentation. The death penalty, he stated, was part of the "old justice" in contrast to the "new justice", which did not know any "bloody sacrifices". It was a tool of the "old barbarism" that was "generated by despotism and violence". He continued: "The new, free state must not know it, must not require it." It was indeed well known that "the majority of the Western European states" had not yet abolished it, which could be explained by the fact that the "lowermost instincts unfortunately crop up even under the dominion of totally developed and cultured forms of society". However, the "more subtle and truly humane representatives of western European thought" had recognized the cruelty and dangers of the death penalty "already long ago" and had led a campaign for its abolition "for a hundred years". The lasting existence of the death penalty, whose

14 *Ibid.*, 436–437.

15 *Pravo* (Law) was a liberal legal journal whose editors were closely related to the Kadet Party.

defenders grew "steadily fewer", was thus "a deplorable anachronism" (Nabokov 1906a, 1901–1902).

In addition to this argument, which paralleled the one of Kovalevskii, Nabokov introduced another point to the discussion: Only in Russia was the death penalty reserved for "political crimes" (for example, the mere preparation of acts against the authorities), whereas it had been abolished for "the bloodiest crimes". Civilians could be put on trial before military courts in areas under a state of emergency even in times of peace, which in practice gave the authorities room to apply the death penalty whenever it suited them. Nabokov subscribed to a statement by Kuz'min-Karavaev, who wrote in 1905 that "no civilized state knows such a wide field of application for the death penalty" (Nabokov 1906a, 1902–1905). Thus, Russia, while *de jure* ahead of Europe concerning the death penalty, *de facto* lagged far behind. Consequently, its total abolition was even more necessary and urgent for Russia than for the western European states.

Conflicting Representations of the West in the State Council and Further Legislative Initiatives (1906–1908)

Eight days after the unanimous passing of the bill by the Duma, it was discussed by the State Council's plenum. In contrast to the Duma, a vivid debate between opponents and defenders of the bill and a number of undecided members ensued. The opponents of the bill, although outnumbering its supporters, were put on the defensive by the unanimous decision of the elected Duma and, even more, by the fact that virtually all contemporary Russian criminal experts denied any positive effects of the death penalty.[16] The bill's opponents based their case above all on the argument that the death penalty was applied in most western European, "civilized" countries. Moreover, they argued, several western countries including Germany had re-established the death penalty after abolishing it at an earlier

16 See the following edited volume: *O smertnoi kazni. Mneniia russkikh kriminalistov. Sbornik s prilozheniem ukazatel'ia literatury na russkom iazyke o smertnoi kazni* (On the Death Penalty. Opinions of Russian Criminologists. Collection with an Appendix that Includes a Bibliography of Works in Russian on the Death Penalty). Moscow (1909, 10–11, 117); and Tagantsev (1906, 8).

stage. Therefore, they said, Russia would be badly advised to abolish this practice approved of in the civilized world.[17] The bill's main proponent in the State Council, the famous criminal law expert Nikolai Tagantsev[18], answered these arguments first by pointing to the progressive reduction of cases in which the death penalty had been applied in the preceding decades in Western Europe. This was, according to him, a reliable sign that the total abolition of the death penalty in Western Europe could be expected in the near future. Tagantsev further pointed to the examples of Italy and Norway, two western European countries that had already abolished the death penalty. According to him, this meant that not all "civilized" countries applied the death penalty. More importantly, it helped demonstrate that that the death penalty did not at all act as a deterrent, given the reduction in the number of formerly capital offenses committed in Italy since the death penalty's abolition there.[19] One of the opponents of the bill in the State Council, Kasatkin-Rostovskii, claimed to have evidence that this was untrue, and that such crimes had risen by 1,000 percent in Italy since the death penalty's abolition. Tagantsev vehemently repudiated this claim in the *Vestnik Evropy* [Messenger of Europe], a well-known liberal journal, shortly thereafter (1906, 14–15).[20] Thus, in the State Council's debate both abolitionists and supporters of the death penalty employed differing accounts of the situation in the West to bolster their claims, a sure sign of the importance of Western reference models in Russian politics at the time.

At the end of the debate, a commission of 15 members of the State Council was elected, which was to deliberate further on the bill.[21] In its report issued ten days later, it stated that, on the one hand, the death penalty was doubtlessly "in contradiction of the principles of Christian love, piety and humanity" and that the majority of criminal experts had proven that "it is not so much acting as a deterrent, but intensifying and not seldom even producing new crime". On the other hand, it asked not to forget that the death penalty continued "to be applied in such cultured

17 *Ibid.*, 8–9; *Gosudarstvennyi Sovet, Stenograficheskie Otchety*. 1906 god. *Sessiia I. Zasedanie Deviatoe*, June 27, 1906, St. Petersburg (1906, 20–21, 34).

18 On Tagantsev, see Shilov (2008).

19 *Gosudarstvennyi Sovet, Otchety* (1906, 14–15).

20 *Ibid.*, 22–23.

21 *Gosudarstvennyi Sovet, Otchety* (1906, 37).

states as England, Germany, Austria, France and the United North American States." This circumstance, according to the commission's report, did not decide the question of the death penalty in general, but cast doubt on "the timeliness and usefulness of a solution to this question in its proposed general formulation". Death sentences in regions under a state of war or emergency were particularly affected: "in most parts of the cultured states there are laws intended just for the case of extraordinary circumstances", that is situations, in which "the whole or even the nature of the state are in danger". This included:

> ...in France, the *état de siège*; in Germany, the *Belagerungs- und Kriegszustand*; and in Austria, the *Standrecht*. The rules about the state of war in Russia should also be counted in this category. The death penalty, in particular, is steadily applied on the basis of the aforementioned emergency laws, as an ultimate punitive measure in the suppression of mutinies, insurrections and similar circumstances.[22]

In conclusion to these considerations, the commission presented a revised draft of the Duma's bill to the State Council's General Assembly. It stipulated, on the one hand, a reduction of the offenses to which the death penalty could be applied under criminal law solely to assassination attempts on the tsar. On the other hand, it left the existing regulations for areas under a state of emergency untouched.[23] Since the vast majority of death sentences in Russia were pronounced under military law in areas under a state of emergency, this revised draft could hardly satisfy the Duma, which boded ill for further negotiations between the two legislative chambers.[24] Before it could come to these, just one day after the State Council's commission drafted its report, the Duma was dismissed by the tsar. Its legislative initiatives, including the bill on the abolition of the death penalty, thus came to an abrupt end.

22 Gosudarstvennyi Sovet, Doklad kommisii, uchrezhdennoi dlia razsmotreniia vnesennago iz Gosudarstvennoi Dumy zakonoproekta ob otmene smertnoi kazni, in: *Rossiia. Gosudarstvennaia Duma. Sozyv I, Proekt zakona ob otmene smertnoi kazni*, St. Petersburg (1906, 7–8, 20–21).

23 *Ibid.*, 22; Ascher's assertion (1992, 169) that the State Council's commission (which he calls a "special committee") never "acted on" the draft bill is therefore incorrect.

24 In fact, the conservative elements of this draft were hardly surprising. The Duma's competency to legislate over military courts *per se* was questionable (according to the Fundamental Laws) and was, in any case, denied by the State Council's majority: see Maklakov (1964, 145–149); Ascher (1992, 169).

In August 1906, one month after the dismissal of the First Duma, the Council of Ministers under the new Prime Minister Stolypin ordered the introduction of martial field courts in all regions under "extraordinary protection" or "martial law" (basically the whole Empire at the time) via Article 87 of the Russian Fundamental Laws.[25] These courts were authorized to judge civilians for all kinds of delinquencies whenever the guilt of the accused was deemed "obvious". Five officers chosen by the Governor-General were to act as judges. They had to pronounce their sentences within 48 hours. No appeals were possible, and death sentences had to be carried out within less than 24 hours (Fuller 1985, 173–176; Rawson 1984, 47–49). As a result, the number of death sentences and executions skyrocketed even further. In the last months of 1906, 558 people were executed (just two less than the number of death sentences), which was more than 70 times the average of the preceding decades. In the first four months of 1907 the number of death sentences reached an historic peak of more than 1,400 (Liessem 1989, 508–509).

In view of these extraordinarily high numbers, the deputies of the Second Duma (predominantly center-left) concentrated on the abolition of the martial field courts that were the root of the soaring number of death sentences and executions. On March 12, 1907, a bill was introduced stipulating the abolition of the military field courts.[26] It was passed unanimously on April 17, 1907.[27] On April 19, 1907, though, before the State Council could deliberate on this law, Stolypin's decree on the establishment of military field courts expired because the government did not put it before the Duma in time for approval.[28] Thus, the martial field courts ceased to exist, and temporarily the number of death sentences and

25 The Fundamental Laws, the *de facto* constitution of the Russian Empire, were promulgated by the tsar in April 1906 (in response to his manifesto of October 17, 1905, which had promised certain civil rights and an elected parliament). Art. 87 allowed the government to issue laws in urgent cases when the Duma was not in session.

26 *Gosudarstvennaia Duma, Sozyv II, Otchety* (1907, 354–358).

27 *Ibid.*, 2278–2285.

28 According to the Fundamental Laws of the Empire, this decree had to be put before the Duma within two months and subsequently approved by majority for it to remain in force. Stolypin had already promised the Duma on March 13, 1907, that he would not ask for its approval. He declared this to be a gesture of good will, expecting the Duma to cooperate (Stolypin 1991, 73–77; Liessem 1989, 516–517; Rawson 1984, 49).

executions in the Empire dropped sharply (Viktorskii 1912, 370; Liessem 1989, 508–509; Fuller 1985, 176).

However, in the following two years the number of death sentences and executions again reached historic peaks, despite the fact that revolutionary unrest had largely subsided by this time (Liessem 1989, 508–509; Rawson 1984, 37, 50). In reaction to this, on June 19, 1908, exactly two years after the passing of the bill on the abolition of the death penalty in the First Duma, 103 (mainly Kadet) deputies introduced a modified version of this bill into the Third Duma.[29] It was clear that this bill had little chance of passing as Octobrists[30] and Rightists now formed a majority in the parliament.[31] Yet the fact that the Third Duma's majority never allowed the bill onto the agenda of the Duma's plenum (Viktorskii 1912, 368–369; Liessem 1989, 518) reflected, in some ways, the continued importance attached to the issue of the death penalty in Russian society at large: the avoidance of parliamentary debate and confrontation was a convenient way to avoid the ire of the Russian electorate. This was the end to serious legislative initiatives for the abolition of the death penalty in the Empire before February 1917.

The Idea of Several "Europes" and Popular Resentment: The Debate in Publications and Petitions (1905–1914)

Outside formal political institutions, however, the debate continued. Particularly since the 1905 Revolution and the subsequent increase in death sentences by military courts, the number of articles in the press and in specialized volumes dedicated to the subject soared to unprecedented levels.

29 *Gosudarstvennaia Duma. Sozyv III. Sessiia I. Stenograficheskie Otchety, Zasedaniia 61–98*, St. Petersburg (1908, 3640); Viktorskii (1912, 368–369).

30 Union of October 17: A right-wing liberal party which considered the tsar's Manifesto of October 17, 1905, as the proper basis for the new political order. It constituted the strongest faction in the Third Duma (1907–1912), but disintegrated in the course of the legislative period partially because of internal disagreements.

31 On several occasions, the Octobrist leader Guchkov had expressed his support for the harsh measures taken by the government to suppress the revolution (Ascher 1992, 247; Pipes 1992, 300; Birth 1974, 125–127).

Newspapers widely covered prominent cases of sentenced and executed people and published calls for mercy and a halt to the bloody punishment with thousands of signatures. A number of academic, professional, women's rights and *Zemstvo* organizations published collective protests against the death penalty (Nethercott 2007, 126–127). The liberal journal *Pravo* (Law) provided a bridge between the professional juridical class and the interested public via its articles on the matter.[32]

Several anthologies specially dedicated to the subject of the death penalty appeared in Russia during the years between 1906 and 1913, providing an overview of the wide range of authors and the prevailing opinion of the time. In 1906, criminal law expert Mikhail Gernet together with O. Gol'dovskii and I. Sakharov published *Protiv smertnoi kazni* (Against the Death Penalty). The volume contained 48 articles, 25 from Russian and 23 from Western European authors (mainly from France, England, Germany and Italy). As the title suggests, all of the authors rejected the death penalty. Several of the Russian contributors made explicit reference to Western European tendencies and experience, using these references in ways that bore striking resemblance to rhetorical strategies previously employed in the Duma.

Using arguments similar to those put forward by Tagantsev in his speech during the State Council's debate in June 1906, Vladimir Solov'ev's posthumously published article, for example, explained to the readers that the use of the death penalty had declined considerably since the late eighteenth century in almost all Western European countries. In several countries, including Italy, Portugal and the Netherlands, it had been completely abolished. Like Tagantsev, Solov'ev saw this as proof of two things: first, since there was no surge in the number or gravity of crimes committed in these countries after abolition, the death penalty obviously had no deterrent effect. Second, the progressive contraction of the death penalty in the Western European countries demonstrated that its global abolition was just a matter of time (Solov'ev 1906, 3–7, 11–15).

N.V. Davydov, in an argument revealing the universalist ideology of mono-linear "development" and "progress", expressed bewilderment at the fact that this "barbaric punishment [...] is [not only] flourishing in

32 See, for example, Berenshtam (1905); Gutman (1906); Nabokov (1906a); Nabokov (1906b).

China, Korea […], among the peoples of Africa and in other uncultured countries, but is allowed in Europe as well." To him it was hardly explicable that "in England, France, Germany and in other cultured countries, every year courts sentence delinquents to death […]" The only explanation he could offer was that "the death penalty is sanctioned by the effective penal codes in Europe by misunderstanding, that it has not been abolished only because of routine and the pressure of the past on the present similar to hypnosis." However, the death penalty contradicted the Christian culture and the laws of moral and "reason, feeling, experience—everything argues against the death penalty". Like Solov'ev, Davydov found hope in the fact that "recently this institution has been progressively dying out in all cultured countries" (1906, 67–70).

P. Krapotkin referred in his contribution, like Kuz'min-Karavaev and Tagantsev in their speeches, to Western European experience (1906). He added that it was well-known that the most horrible murders in England and France were committed by people who had previously assisted at public executions, proof of their demoralizing effect.

For the purpose of our study, Gol'dovskii's article *Smertnaia kazn' pred sudom Evropy* (The Death Penalty before the Tribunal of Europe) is perhaps the most significant contribution in the volume. It served as an introduction to the contributions of the 23 Western European authors. Gol'dovskii posited that there were indeed several Europes. There was, for example, a Europe that had supplied the Russian government with credit just days before the Duma convened and which probably did not care about death sentences. Similarly to Kovalevskii in his speech in the first Duma, however, he then argued: "nevertheless one can say with certainty that before us we have the societal opinion of *all of* Europe, expressed by its acknowledged authorities, [i.e.] well known scholars, authors and politicians." These "best people of our time" from different countries of Europe had rendered their "verdict" with such swiftness and above all with such unanimity (differing only in form) that it was clear that the task given to them [by the editorial staff of the volume] corresponded "to the heartfelt and most profound endeavors of the entire thinking Europe" (Gol'dovskii 1906, 282–283). Thus, more directly than the other authors in this volume and other journalists and writers at the time, Gol'dovskii expressed what many of them suggested implicitly: While Europe had many faces, there was just one "true" Europe. This true Europe was not the one of the majority of Western European states who continued to apply the death penalty; rather, it was the one represented by its best personalities who recognized the barbarity, harmfulness, and uselessness of this form of punishment. Russia should not emulate any old Europe but only the true and ideal one. Therefore it would be well advised to abolish the death penalty completely.

Similar arguments to those used in Gernet's anthology of 1906 can be found in the anthology *O smertnoi kazni* (About the Death Penalty, 1909). It contained articles by 30 Russian criminal law experts, all against the death penalty, reaffirming Tagantsev's argument that Russian legal experts were nearly unanimously opposed to this form of punishment. In 1913, a volume with a whole series of texts against the death penalty by Tagantsev himself utilized Western Europe in its arguments in similar ways.

A different line of argumentation appeared in another study published by Gernet (1913) which focused on the history of the death penalty and its diverse application in various countries. Although written as a scientific work, this publication made it plain that all the facts presented in it spoke against the penalty. In the chapter "The Death Penalty and Societal Opinion" (1–34) he offered a class-based analysis that was clearly influenced by Marxist ideas. By integrating Russia in the European picture, it differed from the account given by most of the other prominent Russian opponents of the death penalty cited so far. Gernet argued that the clergy, nobility, and also partially the bourgeoisie (where it constituted the ruling class), had always and everywhere (that is, in Western Europe and in Russia) been advocates of the death penalty because it served as a means to maintain their privileges. This is why during the "bourgeois" French Revolution a large majority in the National Assembly had rejected the abolition of the death penalty. By contrast, capital punishment had always and everywhere been opposed by most peasants, workers, and left-wing parties.

There was, however, a difference between Russia and Western Europe. In the former, not only peasants and workers, but also most representatives of educated society and the press (except for some extreme-rightist circles and newspapers) took a stand against the death penalty. By contrast, in Western Europe only the socialist press and parties unequivocally spoke out against this form of punishment (28–34). Gernet did not explain explicitly this difference; his class analysis, however, suggests that the different status of the bourgeoisie was a decisive reason for the diverging attitude of this class in Russia and the West (after all, the bourgeoisie formed the "ruling class" in Western Europe, though not [yet] in Russia).

On the whole, statements condemning the death penalty were very common in Russia's learned society (*obshchestvo*). Other opinions, of course, existed. The tsar and his ministers, a majority in the State Council, many Octobrists as well as ultra-rightist and monarchist organizations all favored maintaining the death penalty (*ibid.*, 28–33; Ascher 1992, 145, 168–169, 245–246; Fuller 1985, 173–174). Strikingly, however, very few publications favoring the death penalty appeared, and few persons positioned themselves publically as advocates of capital punishment.[33] Their statements were clearly outnumbered by the multitude and prominence of those who publically opposed it.

Moreover, as Gernet (1913) implied, hostility towards the death penalty was not limited to educated society. Thousands of peasants and workers supported public calls for mercy for specific people convicted to death, as well as for a total abolition of the death penalty. Duma deputies from different parties received many petitions with hundreds of signatures from peasants and factory workers demanding the abolition of the death penalty and amnesty for those sentenced to it.[34] Among those who

33 In *O smertnoi kazni* (1909), the (only) voice skeptical of an abolition of the death penalty in Russia could be found in a footnote to excerpts of N.D. Sergeevskii's *Russkoe ugolovnoe pravo* (Russian Penal Law), published first in 1890. Here, Sergeevskii stated that as long as the people's ethics did not condemn any human bloodshed as barbaric (which was not the case in Russia), an abolition of the death penalty would lead to nothing: either the death penalty would reoccur in the form of self-administered justice (*samosud*) or—even worse—the people would consider this abolition to be a sign of weakness on the part of the authorities. Besides, in one of the few publications critical of the campaign to abolish the death penalty, Smirnova (1906) accused liberals and revolutionaries of hypocrisy and of being against the death penalty only when it was directed against their own people.

34 See, for example, a letter from 1908, with the heading *My nizhepodpisavshchiia-sia prisoediniaemsia k protestu protiv smertnoi kazni* (We, the Undersigned Join the Protest against the Death Penalty), in: Pavel N. Miliukov Collection of the Bakhmeteff Archive (Columbia University, New York), Box 3, Folder VII; *Nakaz v dumskuiu fraktsiu Rossiiskoi Sotsial-Demokraticheskoi Rabochei Partii ot rabochikh Vladivostokskago Porta* (Instructions to the Duma parliamentary group of the Social-Democratic Workers' Party by the workers of the Vladivostok harbor), March 18, 1907, in: Grig-

signed these petitions there were possibly people who had no problem with self-administered justice (*samosud*), which often led to the death of the accused (Frierson 1987, 62–69; Figes 1998, 109–110). However, when imposed and carried out by the state and military authorities, in many cases against rebellious peasants and workers, the death penalty was highly unpopular among the common people. In contrast to the speeches and publications by more educated members of society, peasants and workers mostly did not refer to Western Europe in order to make their point. However, given their opposition to the death penalty, on the one hand, and the claim in Gernet's then standard book (1913) that the death penalty was a repressive instrument of the privileged classes, on the other, they set a notable expectation for any future government claiming to speak on their behalf.

The Short-Lived Russian Exception: The Total Abolition of the Death Penalty and Its Twofold Repeal (1917–1918)

Public opposition to the death penalty and its role as symbol of the arbitrary and oppressive nature of the Imperial state help to explain why the abolition of capital punishment was one of the first legislative acts of the Provisional Government after the February Revolution of 1917. Except for the third article of this law, its wording repeated verbatim that of the draft bill approved by the First Duma eleven years earlier (Browder and Kerensky 1961, 199–200). Articles in the rightist-conservative newspaper *Novoe Vremia* (New Time), the left-liberal *Rech'* (Speech) and the socialist *Rabochaia Gazeta* (Work Newspaper) alike greeted this decision with enthusiasm and relief. Vladimir Nabokov could claim with pride that, "in no other country has moral opposition to this worst type of murder reached such shattering force as with us" (*ibid.*, 200–203). Thus, for him Russia was in this respect at last standing at the forefront of human progress. Indeed, the campaign in Russia for the abolition of the death penalty had been exceptional (in both a European and international context), and so

orii A. Aleksinskii Collection of the Bakhmeteff Archive (Columbia University, New York), Box 7, Folder 11; see also Gernet (1913, 28–34).

was the Provisional Government's decision to abolish the death penalty, even extending to soldiers in wartime.

The Russian exception, however, did not last long. The unusually high number of desertions and lack of discipline among Russian soldiers was attributed by leading generals to the lack of the death penalty. On July 11, 1917, A.A. Brusilov, Commander-in-Chief of the Russian army, asked the new Prime Minister Kerensky to reintroduce the death penalty at the front. His main arguments are familiar. Besides a threat to resign otherwise, he explained that, "the democratic armies of France, Belgium, and America, which are infinitely more cultured than ours, have the death penalty in their legislation". Above all, he referred to the "historical lesson" of the army of Revolutionary France, which (after temporarily giving in to "the principles of humanity and soft-heartedness") came "to the same conclusion" and only then became stunningly victorious. Just one day later, Kerensky's government agreed to the reintroduction of the death penalty for soldiers committing desertion, mutiny and treason (Abraham 1987, 226–227).[35] Without considerably reducing the number of desertions, this measure proved to be one of the bones of contention between the Provisional Government and the Petrograd Council of Workers' and Soldiers' Deputies (which condemned it on the initiative of the Socialist Revolutionaries) in the months to follow (Abraham 1987, 292–293; Browder and Kerensky 1961, 985–986). It thereby contributed to the political instability and unrest during the last months of the February regime. However, for civilians, the death penalty remained abolished until the end of the regime.

After the Bolshevik October coup, the first measure of the Second Congress of Soviets (on October 26, 1917) was to abolish the death penalty without exception, including during wartime and under military law (Adams 1970, 579–580; Berg 1983, 155). In doing so, its members acknowledged the lasting disapproval of the death penalty within Russian society and especially among Russian workers, peasants and soldiers. This was a time when the Bolsheviks had to consolidate their power. They therefore had to be considerate of the wishes of the Left Socialist Revolutionaries (their allies at that time) and of public opinion in general.

35 See Brusilov's letter to Kerensky, Kerensky's explanation and the according law in Browder and Kerensky (1961, 980–994).

However, with the reintroduction of the death penalty and the onset of the Red Terror (Berg 1983, 155; Pipes 1995, 223–224), by September 1918 at the latest other imperatives had begun to dictate the policies of the Bolsheviks.[36]

Conclusion

Between the Revolutions of 1905 and 1917, the death penalty occupied a key place on the political agenda of the Russian people and their representatives. This constituted a Russian peculiarity, rooted in Russian traditions and distinctive legal features (especially the extraordinary laws introduced in 1881). At the same time, the arguments exchanged on this topic by prominent opponents and proponents of the death penalty signaled their desire not to see themselves as legal outliers on this issue. As with other important reform topics at this time, such as the peasant question and worker's legislation, they looked to the West to find reference models and advice on how to act and legislate. This was the "civilized world" they wanted to be part of, and hence they saw no choice other than to follow the path pursued by Western states.

The debates on the death penalty show more clearly than others, however, that elite representations of the West and the "civilized world" were not random. Participants in this debate had clear conceptions of what they meant by "Western" and "civilized". Much to their chagrin, the practice of most Western states regarding the death penalty did not correspond to this vision. At the same time, it did little to change their conviction that the West and Russia should follow the same path of development. Thus they placed themselves in a tradition of "outstanding" Western thinkers and, in view of the contradictory practice of many Western states, saw no

36 Although the decision to abolish the death penalty without exception was not officially repealed until September 1918, the Bolsheviks resorted to summary executions as early as February 1918; the first death sentences by Soviet courts were passed in June 1918 (Berg 1983, 155.) Pipes sees the oblique wording of a "resolution" by Commissioner of Justice P.I. Stutchka as evidence of a reintroduction of the death penalty as of June 1918 (1992, 766). Lenin was always an adherent of the death penalty (Pipes 1992, 754–760; Berg 1983, 155).

choice but to do the exceptional and take the legislative lead on this issue. In their view, they were doing this not only on behalf of Russia but on behalf of the whole "civilized world".

The fact that virtually all well-known Russian penal law experts, and even many military judges, publicly opposed the death penalty sheds light on Russia's legal culture in the late imperial period. The legal initiatives taken by the First Duma, in which many jurists had won seats, were rooted in a widespread abolitionist mood. Thousands of peasants and workers signed petitions against the penalty, which shows that opposition did not emanate solely from learned society. One might be tempted to question the significance of these legal initiatives given the fact that nothing came of them until the end of the Empire. The First Duma's unanimously passed draft bill, however, not only sent a public signal that put pressure on the government but also set a precedent that was used by the Provisional Government in 1917. The fact that the bill was confirmed by both the Provisional Government and the Bolsheviks shortly after seizing power was a sign of the profound enmity against the death penalty in Russia's legal culture and public consciousness. Wherever democratic standards and procedures were applied in early-twentieth century Russia, the death penalty had no chance.

Works Cited

Abraham, Richard (1987). *Alexander Kerensky: The First Love of the Revolution.* New York: Columbia University Press.

Adams, Will (1970). Capital Punishment in Imperial and Soviet Criminal Law. *American Journal of Comparative Law,* 18, 3, 75–94.

Ascher, Abraham (1992). *The Revolution of 1905. Authority Restored.* Stanford: Stanford University Press.

Ascher, Abraham (1988). *The Revolution of 1905. Russia in Disarray.* Stanford: Stanford University Press.

Bendix, Reinhard (1980). *Kings or People: Power and the Mandate to Rule.* Berkeley: University of California Press.

Berenshtam, Vladimir (1905). Smertnye kazni. *Pravo*, N° 38, 3131–3135.

Berg, Ger P. van den (1983). The Soviet Union and the Death Penalty. *Soviet Studies*, 35, 2, 154–74.

Birth, Ernst (1974). *Die Oktobristen (1905–1913): Zielvorstellungen und Struktur.* Stuttgart: Klett.

Browder, Robert Paul and Kerensky, Alexander F. (eds.) (1961). *The Russian Provisional Government 1917. Documents.* Vol. I, Stanford: Stanford University Press.

Daly, Jonathan W. (1995). On the Significance of Emergency Legislation in Late Imperial Russia. *Slavic Review*, 54, 3, 606–629.

Davydov, N. V. (1906). Smertnaia kazn'. In M.N. Gernet, O.B. Gol'dovskii, and I.N. Sakharov (eds.) *Protiv smertnoi kazni: Sbornik statei,* 67–74. Moscow: Tipografiia T-va I. D. Sytina.

Dictionnaire Encyclopédique de la Littérature Française (1999), 2nd ed., Paris: Laffont.

Eliashev, M. (1905). Okolo smertnykh prigovorov. *Pravo*, N° 35, 2868–2870.

Emmons, Terence (1983). *The Formation of Political Parties and the First National Elections in Russia.* Cambridge: Harvard University Press.

Fedorenko, A.L (1993). Vladimir Dmitrievich Nabokov. In Pavel V. Volobuev (ed.) *Politicheskie deiateli Rossii 1917: Biograficheskii slovar'* Bol'shaia Rossiiskaia Entsiklopediia, 226–227. Moscow: Nauchnoe Izdatel'stvo.

Fel'dshtein, G.S. (1909). Protivniki smertnoi kazni v russkoi kriminalisticheskoi literature vtoroi poloviny 18 v. i pervoi chetverti 19 v. In *O smertnoi kazni. Mneniia russkikh kriminalistov. Sbornik s prilozheniem ukazatel'ia literatury na russkom iazyke o smertnoi kazni*, 5–10. Moscow: "Zveno".

Figes, Orlando (1998). *Die Tragödie eines Volkes: Die Epoche der Russischen Revolution, 1891–1924.* Berlin: Berlin-Verlag.

Frierson, Cathy (1987). Crime and Punishment in the Russian Village: Rural Concepts of Criminality at the End of the Nineteenth Century. *Slavic Review*, 46, 1, 55–69.

Fuller, William C. (1985). *Civil-Military Conflict in Imperial Russia: 1881–1914.* Princeton: Princeton University Press.

Gernet, M.N. (1913). *Smertnaia kazn'.* Moscow: Tipografiia "Ia. Dankin i Ia. Khomutov".

Gernet, M.N., O.B. Gol'dovskii, and I. N. Sakharov (eds.) (1906). *Protiv smertnoi kazni: Sbornik statei.* Moscow: Tipografiia T-va I. D. Sytina.

Gol'dovskii, O. B. (1906). Smertnaia kazn' pred sudom Evropy. In M.N. Gernet, O.B. Gol'dovskii and I. N. Sakharov (eds.). *Protiv smertnoi kazni*: *Sbornik statei*, 282–290. Moscow: Tipografiia T-va I. D. Sytina.

Grand Larousse Universel, T. 9 (Journal à Mantes) (1984), Paris: Larousse.

Gutman, I.Ia. (1906). Eshche po povodu smertnykh prigovorov. *Pravo*, N° 8, 673–674.

Hagen, Manfred von (2002). Freedom of the Press after 1861. In Idem (ed.) *Die russische Freiheit. Wege in ein paradoxes Thema*, 98–113. Stuttgart: Franz Steiner Verlag.

Hildermeier, Manfred (1978). *Die sozialrevolutionäre Partei Russlands. Agrarsozialismus und Modernisierung im Zarenreich (1900–1914).* Köln: Böhlau.

Hosking, Geoffrey A. (1973). *The Russian Constitutional Experiment. Government and Duma, 1907–1914.* Cambridge: Cambridge University Press.

Kanishcheva, N.I (2008). Vladimir Dmitrievich Nabokov. In Valentin V. Shelokhaev (ed.) *Gosudarstvennaia Duma Rossiiskoi imperii: 1906–1917 Entsiklopediia*, 390–391. Moscow: Rossiiskaia Politicheskaia Ėntsiklopediia.

Khailova, N. (1996). Maksim Maksimovich Kovalevskii. In Valentin V. Shelokhaev (ed.) *Politicheskie partii Rossii: Konets XIX-pervaia tret' XX veka. Entsiklopediia*, 255–256. Moscow: Rosspen.

Khailova, N.B. (2008a). Maksim Maksimovich Kovalevskii. In Valentin V. Shelokhaev (ed.) *Gosudarstvennaia Duma Rossiiskoi imperii: 1906–1917 Entsiklopediia*, 118–120. Moscow: Rossiiskaia Politicheskaia Entsiklopediia.

Khailova, N.B. (2008b). Vladimir Dmitrievich Kuz'min-Karavaev, In Valentin V. Shelokhaev (ed.) *Gosudarstvennaia Duma Rossiiskoi imperii: 1906–1917 Entsiklopediia*, 308–309. Moscow: Rossiiskaia Politicheskaia Entsiklopediia.

Koselleck, Reinhart (1980). "Fortschritt" und "Niedergang": Nachtrag zur Geschichte zweier Begriffe. In Reinhart Koselleck (ed.) *Niedergang: Studien zu einem geschichtlichen Thema*. 214–230. Stuttgart: Klett-Cotta.

Krapotkin, P. (1906). Nakazanie smertnoi kazni. In M.N. Gernet, O.B. Gol'dovskii and I. N. Sakharov (eds.). *Protiv smertnoi kazni: Sbornik statei*, 230–233. Moscow: Tipografiia T-va I. d. Sytina.

Liessem, Peter (1989). Die Todesstrafe im späten Zarenreich. Rechtslage, Realität und öffentliche Diskussion. *Jahrbücher für Geschichte Osteuropas*, 37, 4, 492–523.

Luhmann, Niklas, and Schorr, K.E. (1988). *Reflexionsprobleme im Erziehungssystem*. Frankfurt am Main: Suhrkamp.

Maklakov, V.A. (1964). The *First Duma. Contemporary Reminiscences*. Bloomington: Indiana University Press.

Morison, John (1999). The State Duma: A Political Experiment. In Anna Geifman (ed.) *Russia under the Last Tsar. Opposition and Subversion 1894–1917*, 137–152. Oxford: Blackwell.

Nabokov, Vladimir (1906a). Otmena smertnoi kazni. *Pravo*, N° 21, 1901–1908.

Nabokov, Vladimir (1906b). Zakonoproekt ob otmene smertnoi kazni. *Pravo*, N° 51, 4015–4028.

Nethercott, Frances (2007). *Russian Legal Culture before and after Communism: Criminal Justice Politics and the Public Sphere*. London: Routledge.

Pipes, Richard (1992). *Die russische Revolution, Vol. 2: Die Macht der Bolschewiki*. Berlin: Rowohlt.

Pipes, R. (1995). *A Concise History of the Russian Revolution*. London: Harvill Press.

Rapp, Friedrich (1992). *Fortschritt: Entwicklung und Sinngehalt einer philosophischen Idee.* Darmstadt: Wiss. Buchges.

Rawson, Donald (1984). The Death Penalty in Late Tsarist Russia: An Investigation of Judicial Procedures. *Russian History/Histoire Russe,* 11, 1, 29–52.

Riasanovsky, Nicholas V. (1952). *Russia and the West in the Teaching of the Slavophiles.* Cambridge: Harvard University Press.

Sergeevskii, N.D. (1909). Russkoe ugolovnoe pravo. In: *O smertnoi kazni: Mneniia russkikh kriminalistov. Sbornik s prilozheniem ukazatel'ia literatury na russkom jazyke o smertnoi kazni,* 33–36. Moscow: Zveno.

Shilov, D.N (2008). Nikolai Stepanovich Tagantsev. In Valentin V. Shelokhaev (ed.) *Gosudarstvennyi Sovet Rossiiskoi imperii 1906–1917. Entsiklopediia.* 269–270. Moscow: Rosspen.

Slonimskii, L. (1905). Narodnoe predstavitel'stvo i pravovoi poriadok. *Vestnik Evropy,* 10, 736–744.

Smirnova, S. (1906). *Smertnaia kazn' pered sudom nashikh revoliutsionerov.* St. Petersburg: Knigoizdatel'stvo "Druzei svobody i poriadka".

Solov'ev, V. (1906). O smertnoi kazni. In M.N. Gernet, O.B. Gol'dovskii, and I.N. Sakharov (eds.) *Protiv smertnoi kazni: Sbornik statei.* 3–23. Moscow: Tipografiia T-va I. D. Sytina.

Stolypin, Petr A. (1991). *Nam nuzhna velikaia Rossiia. Polnoe sobranie rechei v Gosudarstvennoi Dume i Gosudarstvennom Sovete, 1906–1911.* Moscow: Molodaia Gvardiia.

Tagantsev, Nikolai (1913). *Smertnaia kazn'. Sbornik statei N.S. Tagantseva.* St. Petersburg: Publisher: Gosudarstvennaia Tipografiia.

Tagantsev, Nikolai (1906). Zakonoproekt o smertnoi kazni v Gosudarstvennom Sovete. *Vestnik Evropy,* 11, 5–34.

Terebov, A. and Khailova, N. (1996). Vladimir Dmitrievich Kuz'min-Karavaev. In Valentin V. Shelokhaev (ed.) *Politicheskie partii Rossii: Konets XIX-pervaia tret' XX veka. Entsiklopediia,* 288–289. Moscow: Rosspen.

Viktorskii, S.K. (1912). *Istoriia smertnoi kazni v Rossii i sovremennoe eia sostoianie.* Moscow: Tipografiia Imperatorskago Moskovskago Universiteta.

Waldron, Peter (1998). *Between Two Revolutions. Stolypin and the Politics of Renewal in Russia.* London: UCL Press.

Wild, Adolf (1987). Frédéric Passy: der Gründer der internationalen Friedensbewegung. In *Der Friedens-Nobelpreis von 1901–1904*, 126–135. Zug: Ed. Pacis.

A New Legal Order under Discussion: Legal Reform and the *Loya Jirga* in Afghanistan in the 1920s

Benjamin Buchholz

Introduction

The foundations of modern Afghan statehood were laid during the reign of King Amânullâh Khân (r. 1919–1929).[1] Under his grandfather, 'Abdurrahmân Khân (r. 1881–1901), Afghanistan had already become a territorial entity with defined borders and an increasingly centralized state organizational structure. But it was not until Amânullâh Khân's reign in the aftermath of the third Anglo-Afghan War (1919) that the country achieved full independence, followed by its first constitution in 1923. On this basis, Amânullâh Khân initiated a process of modernization designed to reframe the social and political order in his realm.[2] Central to his reform efforts was the introduction of a new legal order. It was meant to replace the existing legal pluralism in Afghanistan and thus provide one law for all.[3]

At the beginning of his reign, Amânullâh Khân was quite successful in the conception, deliberation and implementation of his ambitious reforms. However, the more they appeared to affect the everyday lives of the people and infringe upon the influence of traditional elites, the more he lost the support of the relevant political actors.[4] The king had limited means to implement his reforms by force. As a result, his government had

1 Even though Amânullâh Khân used the title *amir* at the beginning of his reign, in this paper I refer to him as "king", since he chose the title *shâh* in 1927.

2 One of the best overviews of the history of modernization in Afghanistan can be found in Gregorian (1969).

3 A good summary of the reform efforts in the legal system during the Amâni era can be found in Grevemeyer (1990).

4 For an excellent analysis of the tensions that were provoked by Amânullâh's reforms see Nawid (1999).

to pursue a highly conciliatory approach if it had any hope of enforcing them.

Against this background, this chapter analyzes the strategies employed by the Afghan government in the 1920s to promote and legitimize the first Afghan Constitution and its associated set of legal initiatives. In this context, I am primarily interested in the symbolic dimension of the legislative process—its public enactment and negotiation within Afghan society—rather than in particular laws or their application in legal practice. This dimension of the legal reforms of the 1920s is best highlighted using the example of the newly instituted *loya jirga* (Pashto: Great Assembly).

The *loya jirga* was designed as a central political assembly with supra-regional coverage. Its task was to discuss and legitimize government policy in general, and the legal reforms in particular. Each of the three assemblies (summoned in 1923, 1924 and 1928) created a temporary "space of encounter" for face-to-face communication and, thereby, an exchange of representations between representatives of the state and representatives of the people.[5] This forged a link between the center and the periphery and, so to speak, between the initiators and the target group(s) of the reform program. As such, the *loya jirga* became one of the king's most important political instruments for staging, discussing and revising his representations of a modern Afghanistan.

By analyzing the sessions of the three *loya jirga*s against the background of the (legal) reforms of the 1920s, I argue that the acceptance or rejection of certain laws hinged not only on their contents or anticipated effects, but also on their symbolic representations and the way they were communicated between the king and his subjects. It was therefore all the more important for the king to assure the delegates of his personal willingness to uphold the values of Afghan society and to refute arguments that the legal reforms conflicted with "traditional" norms, especially Islamic ones. Hence, Amânullâh Khân's ability to both formally and symbolically reconcile his proposed reforms with the existing array of social, religious and cultural norms became a particular challenge in his attempt to establish a new legal order. I intend to show that he underwent a transformation in

5 On symbolic representations as a concept and point of entry for historical analysis, see Chartier (1989).

his interactions with the traditional elites, switching from an integrative and consensus-orientated approach to one of exclusion and compulsion. I argue that this transformation is of the main reasons for his failure to "modernize" Afghan society and ultimately led to his abdication in 1929.[6] The manifold problems he faced within this process of negotiation become all the more apparent if one considers that "the legal system is both a mirror of society and an authoritative guide for its development. Societies with segmented or plural legal systems face a hall of mirrors that can make legal reform quite difficult" (Suhrke and Borchgrevink 2009, 215). Thus, analyses of disputes over the reform of legal systems shed light not only on competing legal norms but also on different visions of the social order in general.[7]

In this chapter, I trace different and evolving representations of the legal, social, and political order in various ways: by considering their verbal articulation within the assemblies, by taking into account their non-verbal expression by means of the actors' behavior or clothing, and by examining the spatial setting and procedural aspects of the assembly's meetings.[8] In order to highlight these representations from different perspectives, I use a range of sources. Beside the existing literature on the history of law in Afghanistan, this chapter is based on an examination of Afghan newspapers and official documents, including statements, rules of procedure, speeches, resolutions and minutes of *loya jirgas*. These contemporary Afghan sources are supplemented by British archival material from the India Office Records (IOR) in London, including intelligence reports and diaries of British representatives in Kabul. Based on this material, my argumentation is divided into two parts. First, I give a brief overview of the legal system in Afghanistan at the beginning of the twentieth century, the reform program of Amânullâh Khân and the institution of the *loya jirga*.

6 The reasons for the failure of this attempted (legal) modernization are without question multifaceted and up to now still under discussion. Still one of the best summaries of this question can be found in Gregorian (1969, 266–274).

7 For a good overview on the relationship between cultural studies and legal studies, see Conermann (2007).

8 This is inspired by the concept of "*Oratorik*" as it has been developed by Johannes Helmrath in the context of a research project at the Collaborative Research Centre "Changing Representations of Social Order" in Berlin. See, for example, Feuchter and Helmrath (2009).

In the second part, I advance chronologically and focus on the shifting purposes, proceedings and outcomes of the *loya jirgas* as instruments for communicating the legal reforms during the regency of Amânullâh Khân.

Legal Reform in Afghanistan at the Beginning of the Twentieth Century

A Plural Legal Order

At the start of the twentieth century, Afghanistan had neither a written constitution nor a comprehensive statutory law.[9] Legal practice at that time was characterized by a very low degree of formalization and by "legal pluralism", which is understood here as "the presence in a social field of more than one legal order" (Griffith 1986, 1).[10] The legal pluralism, as it existed in Afghanistan around 1900, consisted of three components:[11] first, the Islamic law—officially based on the *Hanafi* jurisprudence but in practice influenced by a much wider spectrum of *Sunni* and *Shi'i* legal traditions—which was applied in local *shari'a*-courts or in the few existing state courts; second, rudimentary statutory laws based on decrees issued by the ruler (Beck and Grobba 1929, 290–291); and third, customary laws based on unwritten tribal codices (for example, the *pashtunwâli*) which were predominantly applied in traditional assemblies (*jirgas*, *shurâs* etc.) to solve local disputes.[12] Sultân Muhammad Khân, former secretary of Amir 'Abdurrahmân Khân, described the legal system in Afghanistan around 1900 as follows:

The law of Afghanistan in the present day may be easily placed under three headings; (1) those of Islam; (2) those of the Amir, which are based upon Islamic

9 There is a wide range of literature on the development of the legal system in Afghanistan. See, for example, Kamali (1985) and Moltmann (1982).

10 For a similar definition, see von Benda-Beckmann (2008).

11 On legal pluralism in the case of Afghanistan, see Barfield (2008) and Meininghaus (2007); Kemper and Reinkowski (2005) discuss legal pluralism more broadly in the context of the Islamic world.

12 For a discussion of the historical role of *jirgas*, see Nölle-Karimi (2005). On the *pashtunwali* in general, see Rzehak (2011), whose analysis also includes a section on the customary legal system.

laws, the opinions of the people, and the Amir's own personal view and ideas; (3) customary laws of the various tribes (Khan 1900, 126–127).

These three components also appear as a feature of legal practice in Afghanistan up to the present day, even though the relationship among them has never been defined unequivocally. In particular, the relationship between customary law and Islamic law remains difficult to grasp. Many ordinary people do not recognize them as distinct from each other and, moreover, often perceive them as one legal system. There has thus always been a mutual penetration of the different legal conceptions in legal practice, even though the relative influence of each has changed over the past century. As in most societies where more than one legal system exists, the different legal conceptions in Afghanistan sometimes complemented and more often contradicted each other, as for example in the domain of family law (Meininghaus 2007, 3). They have often interacted in such a way that a single case could migrate from one legal sphere to another (Barfield 2008, 351), which gave parties to the legal conflict more options but also created uncertainty.

In order to overcome this plural order and create a minimum of legal certainty, since the emergence of a central state in Afghanistan at the end of the nineteenth century successive governments have promoted legal standardization (both legislative and judicial). The overall aim was to model all legal relations on state law and to administer them through state institutions. This in particular had practical repercussions for the complex interplay between Islamic law as interpreted by religious scholars and statutory law.[13] Accordingly, most legal reforms in the twentieth century were aimed at enlarging the purview of statutory law at the expense of Islamic law or, at least, at strengthening the state's influence over Islamic jurisdiction by codifying Islamic law and educating and employing Islamic judges. However, as Barfield argues, "in contrast to most nations where state power has moved all other contenders for legal authority to the margins or eliminated them, in Afghanistan the power of each has waxed and waned" (2008, 351).

By the beginning of the twentieth century, Amir 'Abdurrahmân Khân and his successor, Amir Habibullâh Khân, had undertaken the first steps

13 For the concept of "scholar's law" vs. "ruler's law" in the case of Afghanistan, see Etling (undated).

in this direction.[14] Under 'Abdurrahmân Khân the Islamic judges (*qâzis*) were made employees of the state and several levels of jurisdiction were created across the country. During his regency the treatise *Asâs al-quzât* ("Principles for Judges") was published and distributed as a binding manual for judges. In 136 paragraphs, it codified a set of rules that defined the competences of the judges and laid down a formal framework for court procedures.[15] The compilation of an Islamic law code was also started under his aegis. His son, Habibullâh Khân, then had this monumental work completed and published in four volumes under the title *Sirâj al-ahkâm* ("Torch of the Laws"). As a guide for judges in *shari'a*-courts, it consolidated and translated *Hanafi* Law from the Arabic texts into Dari (Kamali 1985, 35). To be clear, such encroachments of the state into the field of Islamic jurisdiction should not be equated with an intention to secularize the legal order in Afghanistan.[16] Most steps undertaken by the legislator at this stage were not at all meant to challenge Islamic norms. Rather, they should be seen as an attempt to gain authority over legislation and jurisdiction in general, and the interpretation and application of Islamic law in particular.

The legal reforms at the beginning of the twentieth century were, however, rather tentative and had yet made little progress on curbing the pluralist and often arbitrary nature of legal practice in Afghanistan. Nor did these early reform efforts provoke substantial resistance among the traditional elites, as these measures lacked the scope to curtail their relative autonomy or affect local legal practices. During the era of the so-called Amâni reforms in the 1920s, this comparatively peaceful coexistence of state and non-state actors in the field of jurisdiction changed drastically. The state's increasing engagement in the legal sphere bore potential for conflicts between the state and the traditional elites. The latter feared for their relative autonomy in legal matters as well as for the resources they drew from their positions in the jurisdiction. Thus, they began to accuse

14 Still one of the best surveys on the reform efforts under these two regents can be found in Gregorian (1969). On the regency of 'Abdurrahmân Khân, see Kakar (1979); on Habibullâh Khân's reign, see Schinasi (1979).

15 An introduction into the *Asâs al-quzât* is offered in Ghani (1983).

16 Regarding the secular character of the reforms during the reign of Amânullâh Khân, see Olesen (1995, 126–133).

the government of drafting laws that did not conform to the principles of Islam.

The Amâni Reforms: Contested "Modernization"

After Amânullâh Khân's ascension to the throne in 1919 and the achievement of full independence from the British Empire, the so-called "Young Afghans" began to implement their vision for a modern Afghan state and society. Influenced by the modernist and pan-Islamic ideas current in the region, they called for (national) unity/consensus (*ittihâd/ittifâq*), independence (*istiqlâl*) and "progress" (*taraqqi*).[17] Having the new ruler at the head of their movement, they intended to initiate a reform process "from above" with the overall aim to make Afghanistan a model for modernization in the Islamic world. Swayed by the reforms in the Ottoman Empire and the constitutional revolution in Iran, which were both geared towards Western models, the first aim of these Afghan reformers was the adoption of a constitution. The subsequent reform of the whole legal system was meant to become the vehicle of their "modernization" efforts. The codification of law, the (re-)structuring of the judicial system, the training of legal experts, and the advancement of a new legal understanding within Afghan society were the most ambitious tasks on their path to a complete reorganization of the legal system in Afghanistan (Grevemeyer 1990, 173; Olesen 1995, 129–131).

The reform process and the expansion of the influence of state institutions in the legal sphere took place in several phases. The first step was the adoption of a constitution as a starting point for the codification of public and private law. During this phase most of the legal reforms accompanying the constitution targeted public law and thus were aimed at the remodeling of state structures as well as the regulation of the relationship between state and individual. Beside the constitution, perhaps the most important *nizâmnâma* (statute/law)[18] was the *nizâmnâma-yi tashkilât-i asâsiya* (law of [the state's] basic organization) that provided for the establishment and regulation of basic state institutions. In the second phase, the

17 See, for example, the official announcement for the *loya jirga* of 1924 printed in Kushkaki (1925, 10–11).

18 During the Amâni era, most new laws and statutes were passed as *nizâmnâmas* rather than under the more common title of *qânun*.

reforms moved into the sphere of private and penal law.[19] Altogether, during the reign of Amânullâh Khân, over 70 *nizâmnâmas* were issued that affected nearly all parts of social and political life (Grevemeyer 1990, 173; Rafi' 1999).[20] In the field of jurisdiction, in particular, several reforms were implemented in the aftermath of the constitution: a formally independent judiciary was established for the first time in Afghanistan under Article 50 of the constitution and a multi-level system of courts was created. At the same time, newly established legislative institutions like the *shurâ-yi dawlat* (state council) began to draft laws—when possible, on the basis of the *shari'a* (Poullada 1973, 75).

At the time of Amânullâh Khân's ascent to the throne, however, not one legal expert in Afghanistan was trained in western legal norms and only a few experts were available to develop a "western-type" legal code (Grevemeyer 1990, 171–179). Hence, the reformers chose to borrow from the experiences of other countries in the region. From the start, experts from Turkey and Iran were invited to advise the Afghan government in the legislative process.[21] Notwithstanding their enthusiasm for "progress", the Afghan reformers were quite aware of the possibility that their interference might alienate the traditional elites. New laws, such as those for conscription and taxation as well as reforms in the field of jurisdiction, education and family affairs indeed aroused suspicion amongst the clergy and tribal elite over their conformity with Islamic principles. Therefore, the reformers were keen to refute allegations that the new laws might be "legal transplants" from a non-Islamic context.[22] To ensure the conformity of so-called borrowed laws with the *shari'a*, all drafts passed a review by the *shurâ-yi dawlat* (state council) and the *majlis-i wuzarâ* (council of ministers) before they were submitted to the king to be signed (Beck and Grobba 1929, 293–294). Some laws were even drafted in direct coop-

19 A list of almost 70 *nizâmnâmas* promulgated during the reign of Amânullâh Khân can be found in Poullada (1973).

20 Numerous *nizâmnâmas* are available online at the Afghanistan Digital Library (ADL) under http://afghanistandl.nyu.edu/.

21 For example, Bedri Bey, former head of police in Constantinople who became a member of the Afghan state council, has often been called the father of the Afghan constitution. See Beck (1928, 67–157, esp. 71–72).

22 Suhrke and Borchgrevink (2009, 212–214) have applied Alan Watson's concept of "legal transplants" to contemporary Afghanistan. The concept, however, also seems to hold true for the early period of legal reforms.

eration with members of the *hay'at-i tamyiz*, a council of high ranking, state-appointed *'ulamâ*. While this procedure can be seen as a strategy to shore up the legislative process, it was equally essential to promote the intentions of the government. The latter had to demonstrate to the public that the reforms were in no case contrary to the Islamic or cultural heritage of Afghan society. The most striking example of this conflation of law with tradition was the more neutral labeling of most laws and regulations as *nizâmnâmas* rather than as *qawânin*, as the latter term was commonly associated with secular laws. Yet, this was far from sufficient. The government had to explain the contents of its reforms and adjust them in accordance with the demands of the *'ulamâ* and other influential social figures. Campaigns were therefore set up, both in print media and in the form of public speaking tours by the king, to communicate the intentions of the king and government to the population.[23]

The urgency of public consultations became obvious after the first *nizâmnâmas* were announced in 1924, provoking an uprising in the Southern tribal areas, which came to be known as the "Khost Rebellion". Propaganda efforts by the rural clergy fuelled these tensions, as *mullâs* denounced the constitution and other *nizâmnâmas* as contrary to Islamic principles.[24] It is noteworthy, however, that up to then very few of the new laws had actually been put into practice. On the contrary, the crisis showed that even rumors about the state's planned implementation of laws contrary to the *shari'a* could cause severe tensions. It became clear that any serious reform effort would be fraught with symbolically charged arguments.[25]

Communicating the New Legal Order: The Loya Jirga

Faced with the distrust of the traditional elites and an inability to implement his ideas by force, Amânullâh Khân had to find other ways to communicate his ideas for a new legal order. Thus, he set up the *loya jirga*

23 Besides the yearly spring *darbârs* (see below), a good example for such a campaign is Amânullâh Khân's account of his 35-day-journey to Kandahar in 1925. See Rafi' (1999).

24 See India Office Records (IOR)/L/PS/10/1050, P 3289/1924, Enclosure No. 1 to His Majesty's Chargé d'Affaires, Kabul's Despatch No. 84, dated July 3, 1924.

25 For this and other topics relating to the role of the clergy during Amânullâh Khân's reign, see Nawid (1997 and 1999).

as a central political assembly and communicative platform with nearly a thousand delegates from all over the country.[26] Prior to 1919, Afghan monarchs had occasionally convened extraordinary court audiences under the label *darbâr-i ma'âli* (High Court).[27] During certain political crises a large number of local and regional authorities from the provinces were assembled in the capital. Their presence in Kabul allowed the monarch to personally inform them about the state's policy, secure their support for his decisions, and turn them into distributors of his message in the provinces of his realm—as in 1916, when Habibullâh Khân announced Afghanistan's neutrality in World War I.

Even though the *loya jirga* partially drew on the model of these courtly assemblies, its creation in the 1920s symbolized a renunciation of the old courtly tradition of decision-making. Such assemblies had been strictly unidirectional in their communication and had not at all provided for an exchange of arguments between the ruler and his subjects. Within the context of the post-1919 reform process the *loya jirga*, by contrast, was explicitly designed to be a political body for exchanging views and ideas between different social and political groups, supervising the state's activities, and legitimizing the decisions of the king, the government, the ministries, and the state council. To generate this legitimacy, the institution provided the delegates, in accordance with the new *zeitgeist*, with freedom of speech and voting rights. In short, the *loya jirga* enabled the king to engage much more openly than his predecessors with the relevant political and social actors of his realm. Thus, the *loya jirga* became a space for cultural interaction and open negotiation. In that, it was not only an instrument to promote the reform process; it became a symbol of the new order itself.

---

26 In the literature the origins of the *loya jirga* are often located in the tradition of tribal *jirgas*. Thereby, the *loya jirga* is considered a national pendant of a genuine Afghan consultative tradition. Alongside this, the *loya jirga* has been described as a century-old institution. Today we may assume that Afghan rulers did not summon assemblies under the label of *loya jirga* in either the eighteenth or the nineteenth centuries. See Noelle-Karimi (2002), Hanifi (2004), Buchholz (2007). For a classical approach to the history of the *loya jirga*, see Mihrabân (1982).

27 Accounts of these court audiences can be found in *Sirâj al-Akhbâr*, vol. 5, no. 11, pp. 2–3 and *Sirâj al-Akhbâr*, vol. 5, no. 16, pp. 1–3. See also the reports of the British Agent in Kabul, as in IOR/L/PS/10/202, P 2028/1916, Diary of the British Agent at Kabul for the week ending April 7, 1916.

Legal Reform 1923–1928

The Loya Jirga of 1923: New Laws and Local Interests

Amânullâh Khân knew that his steps toward modernization and legal reform bore the risk of alienating him from the tribes and the clergy on whose support his rule depended. Therefore, it was politically opportune for him to have his policies and especially the constitution discussed and legitimized by the Eastern Province's tribal and religious nobility, which was politically the most important and powerful at the time. Lacking a suitable political body that could be used as a constituent assembly for this purpose, he founded a new one: The first assembly labeled as a *loya jirga* was convened in the spring of 1923 in Jalalabad in order to negotiate and legitimize the draft of the first constitution as well as some other *nizâmnâmas*, such as that for the organization of the newly established *shurâ-yi dawlat* (state council).[28]

Amânullâh Khân amalgamated different consultative traditions within the new *loya jirga* to give it legitimacy and make it an example of his integrative approach to reform. The early *loya jirga*, therefore, was a hybrid: Similar to the court audiences of old, the *loya jirga* brought together representatives of the state and delegates who were meant to represent the people, while the king remained the main actor within the sessions of the assembly.[29] The labeling of the assembly as a "great *jirga*" drew on the local tradition of convening consultative councils and thus symbolized the king's intention to locate the law-making process within the framework of the traditional norms of Afghan society. Last but not least, parliamentarian features that addressed the modernistic ideals of the constitutionalists were included in the new concept. The intended combination of old forms of political consultation with new ideas of political representation and participation became most tangible in the elections of local representatives that were held on the first day. Even more significant was Amânullâh Khân's

28 See *Amân-i Afghân*, vol. 3, no. 19, p. 11; *Tulu'-i Afghân*, vol. 2, no. 24, p. 4; *Ittihâd-i Mashriqi*, vol. 3, no. 100, p. 1.

29 The first *loya jirga* especially drew on the yearly spring *darbârs* (court audiences) that were held by Habibullâh Khân in Jalalabad. For an account of such a *darbâr*, see, for example, IOR/L/PS/10/200, P 1563/1912, North-West Frontier Provincial Diary no. 13 for the week ending March 30, 1912.

public announcement that he would discuss his political aims with his subjects and that the delegates should engage in open debate with him.[30] In all of this, Amânullâh Khân tried to prove both his awareness of the need to integrate the traditional elites in the constitution-making process and his own personal willingness to adjust his reforms to their demands. The Afghan people were supposed to become a society on whose behalf and for whose advancement the king claimed to reign, which he made clear with the adoption of the country's first constitution (Grevemeyer 1990, 199–200). The king intended to give the representatives of the people the opportunity to experience the meaning of being a member of this new Afghan society via the consultations of the *loya jirga*. This new form of political consultation was therefore most prominently a signifier of a new political order.

During the sessions of the *loya jirga* the king did everything to win over the representatives of the tribes and the clergy for his constitutional project: The draft of the constitution was read out and explained by him personally, inviting the delegates to criticize it as they saw fit. In order to show his respect for them, he dressed in local clothes and spoke partly in Pashto, the language of the majority of the delegates.[31] How did the representatives of the tribes respond to this novel attitude of the king? Even though the delegates inside the audience hall enthusiastically made use of their right to speak, they had very little to say about the actual topic, the constitution. They neither demanded any essential amendments to the constitutional text nor did they go into the legal texts at all. On the contrary, many of the speakers simply ignored the actual purpose of the assembly and took advantage of being personally received by the king for their own purposes. They broached issues such as local conflicts and had to be reminded by the king of the primary topic: the constitution.[32]

30 In this context it is noteworthy that in his speeches he referred to the delegates as the "representatives of the people" (*wukalâ'-i millat*) who should have a say in the country's future. See *Amân-i Afghân*, vol. 3, no. 19, p. 13.

31 Here it must be stated that the prevailing language at the Court in Kabul was Persian. The king's use of Pashto can be seen as a special reference to the new leverage of the Pashtun culture he intended to assign to the Afghan nation.

32 See IOR/L/PS/10/1085, P 1299/1923, Diary No. 9 for the week ending March 6, 1923.

From a legislative point of view, the assembly can be seen as an overall success for the king: At the end of the sessions the 872 delegates signed and sealed the first Afghan constitution without any amendments.[33] Neither official state publications nor British intelligence reports mention any kind of tensions between the king and the delegates regarding the proposed legal reforms. On the contrary:

> The anniversary of his accession to the throne was celebrated at Jelalabad on February 27 and the following days, and on this occasion the Ameer met for the first time large numbers of Afridis, Mohmands, and other frontier tribesmen. These have returned to their homes considerably impressed with the friendly manner in which the Ameer received them, and by his exhortations to them to keep the peace among themselves and with their neighbors.[34]

That was not surprising. At that time Amânullâh Khân, the liberator of the Afghan nation, had reached the peak of his popularity. The consultations had made clear there was far less potential for conflict surrounding the constitution than the king had feared. The early reforms discussed at the first *loya jirga* admittedly had little obvious impact on the living conditions in the provinces. From the points of view of the clergy and tribal leaders, the constitution seemed to bear little immediate risk of diminishing their relative autonomy in legal matters or in their traditional spheres of influence. Its content was perhaps too abstract to spark the real interest of the delegates or to provoke resistance on their part, which would risk friction between them and the king. The king was therefore able to count his experiment in political participation via the *loya jirga* a success. It is not surprising, then, that Badshah Gul from the *Mohmand* tribe suggested that tribal *jirgas* should be convened as often as possible in the future.[35] Discussions on the upcoming reforms, especially in the field of the criminal and civil law, promised to spark much more critical reactions.

---

33 This is mentioned in the afterword of the constitution. For an English version, see Poullada (1973, 289).

34 *The Times*, March 24, 1923, p. 9.

35 See IOR/L/PS/10/1085, P 1299/1923, Diary no. 9 for the week ending March 6, 1923.

The Loya Jirga of 1924: Reaction and Reactions

Based on the positive experiences of Jalalabad, the *loya jirga* was supposed to be institutionalized as a periodically convened consultative body for the discussion of all further reforms.[36] One year later this *modus operandi* was used again, this time in the city of Kabul. By 1924, however, the political circumstances had changed dramatically. The second *loya jirga* was convened against the background of the first severe crisis Amânullâh Khân's government had to face since the War of Independence in 1919. In response to several legal initiatives, the *mullâs* in the Southern rural areas had begun to agitate against the government in Kabul and spurred the *Mangal* and *Zadrân* tribes to offer armed resistance against the central government. In the following weeks, tribal militias had been organized and government troops were sent to strike down the insurgency.[37] Against this background, the re-convening of the *loya jirga* can also be seen as an attempt by the king to build up an alliance against the insurgents by demonstrating his willingness to negotiate on controversial laws. However, with the enemy at the gates of the capital, the king, who had intended to personally spearhead the negations with the assembled delegates, had little bargaining power (Beck 1928, 74).

The shift of the *loya jirga* from the periphery to the center demanded a fundamental conceptual change of purpose for the body to a communication platform of national importance. Almost 2,200 delegates came to Kabul, of whom nearly 800 were supposed to participate in the sessions of the assembly as representatives of the people.[38] In order to establish the *loya jirga* as a legitimate body and make it a symbol of the new order, formalization was needed: Freedom of speech, voting procedure and the setting of an official agenda were affirmed as rights in written form for the first time.[39] Within this institutional venue, Amânullâh Khân wanted all controversial laws to be discussed and legitimized. He was further able to

36 See *Amân-i Afghân*, vol. 5, no. 3, pp. 7–8.

37 For two brief accounts of the rebellion, see Nawid (1999, 100–104), Olesen (1995, 133–138).

38 See IOR/L/PS/10/1085, P 3203/1924, copy of Military Attaché, British Legation, Kabul's Diary no. 24 for the week ending July 4, 1924.

39 See the published account of the deliberations: Burhânuddin Kushkaki (1925), *Ruydâd-i loya jirga-yi dâr as-saltana*, 45–50.

ascertain the common mood at the peripheries of his realm through the comments of the provincial delegates and use them, in a reverse direction, to propagate his representations of a modern Afghanistan. The *loya jirga* was once again meant to symbolize the willingness of the ruler to share his power with the people and adjust the legal reforms according to their demands. From the state's official point of view, the aim of the *loya jirga* was thus to "raise the edifice of the state upon the Islamic System of consultation (*mashwarat*) and to make it possible for the nation to express views on all vital concerns of the state pertaining to the national wealth" (quoted in Nawid 1999, 106).

In order to achieve this, the delegates were encouraged to actively contribute to the assembly's agenda. Accordingly, the king had all the legislative initiatives of the past four years read out and then the delegates were asked which *nizâmnâmas* they wanted to discuss.[40] Through the delegates' choices the king hoped to gain insight into the needs and sensitivities of his nation.[41] Amongst many issues raised, the delegates demanded another discussion of the constitution and of the penal code, the *tamassuk al-quzât* (a manual for judges concerning criminal cases), the martial and burial law, the law for conscription, and the taxation and commercial laws.[42]

The debates that followed, however, had little in common with the harmonious atmosphere in Jalalabad. After the *loya jirga* had finished its sessions on the review of Afghanistan's bilateral treaties, it entered into the discussion of internal affairs.[43] Here, the weakened king came under severe pressure from conservative *'ulamâ*. They demanded amendments to the constitution that ensured its Islamic character, for example, by adding that *Hanafism* should be the state's official school of religious law (Art. 2) and that the term "freedom" (*âzâdi*) should not include the freedom of religion (Art. 9).[44] The document was then passed after short debate. After that, further obstacles began to surface when the *Nizâmnâma-yi jazâ* (Penal Code) and the *Tamassuk al-quzât* were opposed by several high ranking *'ulamâ*. They protested that these relied on "weak" *hadiths* (*riwâyât-i za'ifa*) and were therefore contrary to the tenets of the *Hanafi*

40 Kushkaki (1925, 113–115).
41 *Ibid.*, 23.
42 *Ibid.*, 115. See also Nawid (1999, 107).
43 Kushkaki (1925, 106).
44 *Ibid.*, 125–149.

school of Islam.[45] Similar problems occurred during the discussion of the marital code, especially concerning polygamy and child marriage, which the king had to withdraw after heated debate.[46] Interestingly, the debates centered only on contradictions between the new laws and Islamic norms while almost entirely omitting the question of customary law. Despite all the criticism, the king fought his way through the debates with a willingness to negotiate and find compromises. Ultimately, he even sacrificed the state-employed *'ulamâ* of the *hay'at-i tamyiz*, on whom he placed responsibility for certifying laws contrary to the *shari'a*. He dismissed them and requested the delegates of the *loya jirga* to elect a new council of *'ulamâ*. This council would then be tasked with reconciling the controversial laws with the interpretations of the *Hanafi* school, including the penal code as well as the *Tamassuk al-quzât*, which, after its revision, was supposed to be published under the title of *Fatâwâ-yi amâni* in Arabic, Persian and Pashto.[47]

These and all the other concessions the king was forced to make are often assessed as a severe defeat for his reform project. And yet, Amânullâh Khân could view the *loya jirga* as a success. During the sessions, he had again and again presented himself as an arbitrator between the multiple interests within Afghan society and the conflicting aims of the traditionalists and modernists. By taking the objections against his law proposals in the field of social reforms seriously, he was able to get the more pressing reforms passed through the *loya jirga*: there was not even a debate, for example, about the *nizâmnâma-yi tashkilât-i asâsiya* that was supposed to lay the foundation for the structure of the new state.[48] He was also able to gain the support of the appeased *'ulamâ* in order to defend his law for conscription.[49] Last but not least, the delegates of the *loya jirga* assured him of their support in the case of the Southern tribal revolt that threatened his sovereignty.[50]

45 For a good analysis of the *loya jirga's* impact on the penal legislation, see Beck (1928) and Nawid (1999, 106–113).

46 See Kushkaki (1925, 112–113, 167–198).

47 *Ibid.*, 210–213, 302–304.

48 *Ibid.*, 165.

49 *Ibid.*, 322–324.

50 *Ibid.*, 363–371.

As a result of the consultations, with all his concessions and the revision of laws according to the demands of the delegates, the king had managed to appease the *'ulamâ* and quelled fears of an impending secularization of the country. Having shown a genuine willingness to negotiate on those reforms that were regarded as an illegitimate intervention of the state into the social order, Amânullâh Khân was finally able to consolidate his image as a preserver of *islâmiyat*[51] and a legitimate ruler (Nawid 1999, 107).[52] The *loya jirga* had therefore again fulfilled its purpose. Its 19 resolutions embodied the perpetuation of the Islamic foundations of Afghan society, and proved the new political self-awareness of the king vis-à-vis his subjects and his respect for the social reality of his realm.[53] He had harmonized the reform process with the differentiated cultural and social framework of Afghan society and assured the conservative *'ulamâ* of their role as preservers of an Afghan Islamic identity. To underpin the consensus-oriented manner in which he had presided over the *loya jirga,* he had an account of the deliberations published and distributed throughout the country.[54] However, this temporary appeasement was by no means a sign of the king's retreat from his overall aim to modernize both Afghan society and its legal order.

The loya jirga of 1928: Staging Modernity

In 1928 Amânullâh Khân made a tour of several European countries as well as Iran, Turkey and India. Impressed by what he saw, he intended to bring pieces of European modernity to Afghanistan:

> I visited Europe not for pleasure, recreation or the purchase of machinery, but in order that I might explore the real road of progress. My sole object was the

51 The term *islâmiyat* was used by Amânullâh Khân as well as by the delegates. See Kushkaki (1925, 52, 249). The preservation of *islâmiyat* in Afghan society has played a decisive role in discussions about the legal system up to the present day. See also Suhrke and Borchgrevink (2009, 211).

52 See also Kushkaki (1925, 112).

53 The resolutions are listed in Beck (1928, 92–94).

54 This was the oft-quoted *Ruydâd-i loya jirga-yi dâr as-saltana* by Burhânuddin Kushkaki.

advancement of my nation. [...] Whatever I learned will shortly be laid before the nation.[55]

After his return he resolved to push the reform process forward in a much more drastic and less conciliatory manner. This became especially clear in his attitude toward the position of women in Afghan society. In 1924 he had withdrawn most initiatives that could have affected the sensitivities of his people, such as the education of girls. Now he made it clear that the time for appeasement had come to an end. The following statement on the role of women in Afghan society may serve to illustrate this: "[...] the women in Afghanistan only know how to sit idly in the houses, and they do nothing more. Why should not then such a country be backward, while countries where women share equally with men be prosperous?"[56]

In order to present his further reform goals to the Afghan public, he called for a third *loya jirga* in August 1928. While he had made the *loya jirga* of 1924 a symbol of consensus-oriented politics, the 1928 assembly was meant to communicate the new position of the king towards the progress of his country and his ideas of a modern Afghan society in a very unambiguous manner. Given the king's new rhetoric, an *éclat* could be expected during the new assembly. This may also have been the reason why the authorities in the provinces faced major problems finding appropriate candidates to be sent as delegates to Kabul. Eventually, several of the candidates tried to avoid getting involved in any of the expected social reforms.[57]

Indeed, the *loya jirga* of 1928 was drastically altered from its previous incarnation. Though its basic mode of operation had not been amended, the body received a new makeup. Based on the experiences Amânullâh Khân had gained during his visits to European parliaments and in line with the progressive reforms he planned to lay before the assembly, the upcoming *loya jirga* was meant to become a symbol of Afghanistan's step

55 Amânullâh Khân, July 21, 1928, in Kandahar, quoted in IOR/L/PS/10/1285, P 4275/1928, Enclosure No. 1, to His Majesty's Minister's Kabul Despatch no. 67, dated July 21, 1928.

56 *Ibid.*

57 See IOR/L/PS/10/1207, P 4878/1928, Diary of the Military Attaché, British Legation, Kabul, for the week ending August 11, 1928, and IOR/L/PS/10/1207, P 4629/1928, Diary of the Military Attaché, British Legation, Kabul, for the week ending July 28, 1928.

towards "modernity". The king intended to make this step visible and tangible for the delegates. First, they were forced by royal proclamation to give away their coats and turbans, dress in modern (*'asri*) clothes, and have their hair and beards trimmed. Second, they were to enjoy the pleasures of Western entertainment, such as female dancers, which led to an early quarrel between the delegates and the king (Ali 1930, 18–19). This all culminated in the attendance of women at the sessions of the assembly, which was without question a provocation in the Afghanistan of the 1920s.[58]

Amânullâh Khân must have known that his new attitude bore some potential for conflict. Therefore, and in order to gauge the temperament of the assembly, he had a party of delegates specially selected to discuss his agenda before the loya jirga meetings started. The agenda was received very coldly and it was reported that the king was strongly advised by his senior officials to modify his program. He finally did so, on the (internally expressed) excuse that the assembly consisted of uneducated and uncivilized people who were unable to give a sound opinion on matters that required special knowledge.[59] This attitude towards the delegates was carried further when he ordered two high clerics to be arrested after they had circulated a manifesto in which they had accused the king of a policy contrary to Islamic principles.[60] With all this, Amânullâh Khân had cleared the way for the upcoming debates on his reforms and had protected himself from unexpected resistance on the part of the assembly.

What followed had very little in common with the past two *loya jirgas*. Though open discussions were still permitted to an extent, the king refused to take criticism of his policy into account (Ghubâr 1996, 1277; Hanifi 2004, 313). He now adopted a hostile attitude, especially toward the clergy, assigning them responsibility for the backwardness of the country (Ali 1930, 19). The time for change had come and the king knew

58 See the special edition of *Amân-i Afghân* on the *loya jirga* printed in Âhang (1999, 278) and IOR/L/PS/1207, P 5311/1928, Diary of the Military Attaché, British Legation, Kabul, for the week ending September 1, 1928.

59 See IOR/L/PS/1207, P 5311/1928, Diary of the Military Attaché, British Legation, Kabul, for the week ending the September 1, 1928.

60 See IOR/L/PS/1285, P 4953/1928, Copy of Telegram, from His Britannic Majesty's Minister at Kabul to Foreign Secretary to the Government of India, dated Kabul, September 11, 1928.

that his ideals of modernity would not be attainable following a consensus approach. He made this clear in sharp terms: "I shall enforce what I like and I shall enforce this unveiling even at the point of the bayonet but not by flattery. Know that I am a revolutionary monarch" (quoted in Ali 1930, 19). Besides the striking change in his attitude, the king confronted the delegates with several critical reforms that he intended to push through the assembly: an exclusive power of the monarch to grant pardons; a yearly account of cattle for taxation, instead of every three years; extension of military service up to three years and enforcement of compulsory service; abolition of most official medals and honors; measures to condemn corruption; monogamy as obligatory for government servants; a state examination for all *mullâs* and expulsion from Afghanistan of religious scholars who represented the *Deobandi* School.[61]

The insurgency that rose several months after the *loya jirga*, culminating in the abdication of Amânullâh Khân, was surely a reaction to these inopportune reforms. The attempt to bring the Islamic judges under the control of the state and the planned expulsion of *Deoband*-trained scholars caused severe animosity amongst the clergy. The enforcement of compulsory military service ensured that they would have strong allies amongst the tribes. Nevertheless it is still implausible that the subsequent uprising was caused solely by these reforms, as their real impact was not yet clear at this stage. And thus, one can assume that the change in the king's attitude towards the clergy as well as his aggressive and "revolutionary" rhetoric had made the traditional elites skeptical that their king was still willing to uphold the traditional values of Afghan society. For the first time, Amânullâh Khân had shown obvious signs of a determination to implement his ideas by coercion. Though he had to that point refrained from seriously proceeding against the *purdah* (female modesty), it seemed only a matter of time until he would break this and further taboos. One can infer that the traditional elites, in light of the events of the *loya jirga* in 1928, lost confidence in their long-term ability to defend the traditional legal, social and political order, including the Islamic and cultural foun-

61 See, for example, the chapter "*muqarrarât-i loya jirga ki ba kasriyat-i mutlaq-i wukalâ' taswib yâfta*" in the official publication "*Ba millat-i 'azizam*", url: http://hdl.handle.net/2333.1/5hqbzkmf [accessed July 21, 2010]. For an English summary, see IOR/L/PS/1207, P 5242/1928, Appendix to Diary for the Week Ending September 8, 1928; or Adamec (1974, 132–137).

dations of Afghan society, against the "modernizers". Whereas the *'ulamâ* had accepted the king's concessions at the *loya jirga* of 1924 by praising his *islâmiyat* in the Friday prayer they now punished him by questioning his true beliefs and thereby the very legitimacy of his rule (Nawid 1999, 158).

Conclusion

"One law for all" would have been an excellent slogan for Amânullâh Khân. This is particularly true when the stress is put on *law*. An emphasis on "one" and "all" would work as a slogan for most legal reforms undertaken in Afghanistan ever since. Naturally, the idea of what might be one law for all Afghans, and how it could mirror the multiple social realities in Afghanistan, has changed since the 1920s according to the ideological agendas of the different ruling classes and their specific conceptions of an ideal legal order. Yet, the set of problems has remained the same: Most governments that have tried to abolish the existing legal pluralism and substitute it with "one law for all" have faced major problems, since the enforcement of one legal system over others has always entailed the disempowerment of those presiding over existing orders. The obstacles the socialist revolutionaries faced after the coup d'état in 1978 in their attempt to replace legal pluralism with a universalistic legal order almost overnight offers one further example of this conflict.[62]

In the Afghan context, the state has seldom had the capacity to implement legal reforms by force. Thus, the success of any reform effort has depended at least partially on its ability to pursue an integrative approach and to present its ambitions as in line with the multiple cultural demands of Afghan society. Therefore, not only the content of legal texts and their potential impact have played a crucial role in the legislative process, but also the image(s) attached to them and the attitude of the reformers towards their targets for reform. Accordingly, the debates that accompanied legal reforms did not concentrate on the question of whether they were

62 For an interesting comparison of the Amâni reforms and the reforms of the socialist party in the 1980s, see Nawid (1993).

superior to Islamic and/or customary law or not. Rather, they centered on whether the reforms were capable of integration into the traditional normative system at all. At the same time it was indispensable for the legislator to present himself and his general policy as guarantors of the traditional system.

By taking the Amâni reforms and the *loya jirga* as an example, I have attempted to show that, in the context of major legal reforms, especially those that bore a high conflict potential, the ways they were communicated and staged played a crucial role for their successful enactment. Here, the examination of the three assemblies convened in the 1920s highlights the importance of this symbolic and communicative dimension of the legislative process. The change in the king's attitude vis-à-vis the traditional elites from a consensus-based approach to compulsion seemed to be one decisive factor for the gradual emergence of a chasm between him and those assigned to legitimate his reforms. Surely, the reforms discussed by the first *loya jirga* in 1923 bore less potential for conflict, making it easier for the king to present himself as preserver of the traditional social order. By contrast, the resistance of the conservative clergy against the social reforms that became the major point of contention at the *loya jirga* in 1924 displayed the limits of the king's agency, especially when he was in a state of political and military weakness. At the same time, the outcome of the assembly made clear that, as long as the king presented himself as an arbitrator between the multifaceted interests in Afghan society and took the concerns of the traditional elites seriously, he was able to sustain his general claim to power and thus continue his policy. The outcome of the 1928 *loya jirga* and the crisis that followed disclosed a truism that is valid to the present day: As soon as the ruler turned from consensus to compulsion, adopted an authoritarian attitude and publicly challenged the canon of cultural values, he immediately faced major resistance. The traditional elites lost their confidence in his determination to uphold the social values of Afghan society, resulting in the erosion of his claim to power. All other reforms proposed by him were then regarded as conceived by an illegitimate ruler and, therefore, as being illegitimate themselves.

Thus, the changing attitude of the king as well as the symbolic representation of his ideas became one major reason for the failure of his modernization project. One may then draw the conclusion that in the short run Amânullâh Khân had failed not primarily because of a general rejection of "modernization" by the traditional elites, but because of his inability to let them participate in the legislative process. In the long run, however, numerous reforms outlived the king's abdication. Decades later, historians and politicians rehabilitated Amânullâh Khân as a notable contributor to the modernization of Afghanistan.

The *loya jirga*'s persistence as an institutional format can be considered an example of the sustainability of Amânullâh Khâns political achievements. As a consultative political assembly with national coverage, convened for the purpose of public consultations in the course of major (legal) reforms and political crises, it has remained one of the most important political tools for Afghanistan's rulers over time. It has remained not only an instrument for the formal discussion and legitimation of political decisions, but also a forum for symbolic politics with all its attendant chances and risks. The *loya jirga* has, as such, been used by governments in the course of major decisions of national importance up to the present day. Most constitutions have had to pass via the debates of a *loya jirga*. With the enactment of the constitution of 1964, the *loya jirga* was itself codified as a constitutional body.

Works Cited

Adamec, Ludwig (1974). *Afghanistan's Foreign Affairs to the Mid-Twentieth Century. Relations with USSR, Britain and Germany*. Tuscon: The University of Arizona Press.

Âhang, Kâzim (1378/1999). *Sayr-i Jurnalims dar Afghânistân*. Kabul.

Ali, Ahmad (1930). *The Fall of Amanullah*. India Office Library.

Barfield, Thomas (2008). Culture and Custom in Nation-Building. Law in Afghanistan. *Maine Law Review*, 60, 2, 348–373.

Beck, Sebastian (1928). Das Afghanische Strafgesetzbuch vom Jahre 1924 mit dem Zusatz vom Jahre 1925. Aus dem Persischen übersetzt und mit einer allgemeinen Einleitung in die afghanische Strafgesetzgebung versehen. *Die Welt des Islams*, 11, 1, 67–157.

Beck, Sebastian and Fritz Grobba (1929). Afghanistan. In Franz Schlegelberger (ed.) *Rechtsvergleichendes Handwörterbuch für das Zivil- und Handelsrecht des In- und Auslandes 1: Länderberichte*, 289–310. Frankfurt am Main: Keip.

Benda-Beckmann, Franz von (2008). Pluralismus von Recht und Ordnung. *Behemoth. A Journal on Civilisation*, 1, 1, 58–67.

Buchholz, Benjamin (2007). Thoughts on Afghanistan's Loya Jirga: A Myth? *Asien*, 104, 23–33.

Chartier, Roger (1989). *Die unvollendete Vergangenheit. Geschichte und die Macht der Weltauslegung*. Berlin: Wagenbach.

Conermann, Stephan (2007). Verfassungen asiatischer Staaten als Ausgangspunkt für die Untersuchung rechtskultureller Spannungsfelder. In Stephan Conermann and Wolfram Schaffar (eds.) *Die schwere Geburt von Staaten. Verfassungen und Rechtskulturen in modernen asiatischen Gesellschaften*, 1–18. Hamburg: EB-Verlag.

Etling, Bruce (undated). *Legal Authorities in the Afghan Legal System (1964–1979)*, accessed: August 21, 2010: http://www.law.harvard.edu/programs/ilsp/research/alhp.php

Feuchter, Jörg and Helmrath, Johannes (2009). Oratory and Representation: The Rhetorical Culture of Political Assemblies, 1300–1600. *Parliaments, Estates and Representations*, 29, 53–66.

Ghani, Ashraf (1983). Disputes in a Court of Sharia, Kunar Valley, Afghanistan, 1885–1890. *International Journal of Middle East Studies*, 15, 3, 353–367.

Ghubâr, Mir Ghulâm (1375/1996). *Afghânistân dar masir-i târikh*. Tehran.

Gregorian, Vartan (1969). *The Emergence of Modern Afghanistan. Politics of Reform and Modernization, 1880–1946*. Stanford: Stanford University Press.

Grevemeyer, Jan Heeren (1990). *Afghanistan: Sozialer Wandel und Staat im 20. Jahrhundert*. Berlin: VWB.

Griffith, John (1986). What is Legal Pluralism? *Journal for Legal Pluralism*, 24, 1–55.

Hanifi, Jamil M. (2004). Colonial Production of Hegemony Through the 'Loya Jerga' in Afghanistan. *Iranian Studies*, 37, 2, 295–322.

Kakar, Hasan Kawun (1979). *Government and Society in Afghanistan. The Reign of Amir Abd al-Rahman Khan*. Austin: University of Texas Press.

Kamali, Mohammad Hashim (1985). *Law in Afghanistan: A Study of the Constitutions, Matrimonial Law and the Judiciary*. Leiden: Brill.

Kemper, Michael and Maurus Reinkowski (eds.) (2005). *Rechtspluralismus in der Islamischen Welt*. Berlin and New York: Walter de Gruyter.

Khan, Mir Munshi Sultan Mohammad (1900). *The Constitution and Laws of Afghanistan*. London: John Murray.

Kushkaki, Burhânuddin (ed.) (1303/1925). *Ruydâd-i loya jirga-yi dâr-as-saltana 1303*. Kabul.

Meininghaus, Esther (2007). *Legal Pluralism in Afghanistan*. Amu Darya Series Paper No. 8, accessed: August 17, 2010: http://131.220.109.9/fileadmin/webfiles/downloads/projects/amudarya/publications/ZEF_Working_Paper_Meininghaus_33.pdf

Mihrabân, 'Abdullâh (1361/1982). *Târikh-i jirgahâ-i milli dar Afghânistân*. Kabul: Majlis-i sana-i shurâ-i milli jumhuri-yi Afghânistân.

Moltmann, Gerhard (1982). *Die Verfassungsentwicklung Afghanistans 1901–1981. Von der absoluten Monarchie zur sozialistischen Republik*. Hamburg.

Nawid, Senzil (1993). Comparing the Regimes of Amanullah (1919–29) and the Afghan Marxists (1978–92): Similarities and Differences. *Critique*, 2, 2, 15–31.

Nawid, Senzil (1997). The State, the Clergy, and British Imperial Policy in Afghanistan during the 19th and Early 20th Century. *International Journal of Middle East Studies*, 29, 4, 581–605.

Nawid, Senzil (1999). *Religious Responses to Social Change in Afghanistan, 1919–29. King Aman-Allah and the Afghan Ulama*. Costa Mesa: Mazda Publishers.

Nölle-Karimi, Christine (2002). The Loya Jirga–An Effective Political Tool? A Historical Overview. In Christine Nölle-Karimi, Conrad Schetter, Reinhard Schlangenweit (eds.) *Afghanistan–A Country without a State?* 37–52. Frankfurt: IKO-Verlag für Interkulturelle Kommunikation.

Nölle-Karimi, Christine (2005). Die paschtunische Stammesversammlung im Spiegel der Geschichte. In Michael Kemper and Maurus Reinkowski (eds.) *Rechtspluralismus in der Islamischen Welt*, 177–194. New York and Berlin: Walter de Gruyter.

Olesen, Asta (1995). *Islam and Politics in Afghanistan*. Richmond: Curzon.

Poullada, Leon B. (1973). *Reform and Rebellion in Afghanistan 1919–1929. King Amanullah's Failure to Modernize a Tribal Society*. Ithaca: Cornell University Press.

Rafi', Habibullâh (ed.) (1999). *Hâkimiyat-i qânun dar Afghânistân ba qalam-i 'alâhazrat Amânullâh Khân Ghâzi*. Peshawar.

Rzehak, Lutz (2011). *Doing Pashto. Pashtunwali as the Ideal of Honourable Behaviour and Tribal Life among Pashtuns*, accessed August 23, 2011: http://www.aan-afghanistan.org/index.asp?id=1567

Schinasi, May (1979). *Afghanistan at the Beginning of the Twentieth Century: Nationalism and Journalism in Afghanistan. A Study of Serâj ul-akhbâr (1911–1918)*. Naples: Intercontinentale.

Suhrke, Astri and Kaja Borchgrevink (2009). Negotiating Justice Sector Reform in Afghanistan. *Crime, Law and Social Change*, 51, 2, 211–230.

Agents of Knowledge Transfer: Western Debates and Psychiatric Experts in Late Imperial Russia

Lena Gautam

"Oh, what a tragedy!" It was a night in May 1909 when the housekeeper of the Skadovskii family was awakened by this cry from her employer. Startled, she ran into the darkened bedroom. The small light next to the icon flickered as the youngest child of the family slept. His mother, Tatiana Skadovskii, lay on her bed—blood seeped from her right cheek. The scream of the housekeeper woke the nanny and the cook. Together, they looked at the lifeless body of the woman. Lev Skadovskii, son of the Marshall of Kherson and husband of Tatiana Skadovskaia, had made a trip with his son to the steamer pier that afternoon. After his return he had sat with Tatiana in the garden. In the evening they had quarreled. Now she was dead. Skadovskii ran around the room excitedly and the nanny was afraid that he might kill himself. She talked to him and tried to appease him. He swore and cursed, tore himself away and finally fled down the road. "No one said anything at that time," the nurse later reported, "but everyone knew that Skadovskii had killed his wife."[1]

Almost a year later, the Kherson Circuit Court in southern Russia initiated the criminal proceedings which put him on trial for murder. Though the Court had no doubt that the accused had killed his wife (in fact, Lev Skadovskii confessed to the murder), the jury acquitted him at the end of the second day of the hearing.

The course and outcome of the Skadovskii trial were heavily shaped by the testimony of psychiatric experts, who pointed to the insanity of the accused. This chapter therefore uses the Skadovskii case to analyze and explain the influence of psychiatric experts on Russian criminal cases in the late nineteenth and early twentieth centuries.

---

1 Ekaterinoslavskii okruzhnoi sud. Ubiistvo zheny. *Pravo*, 16 (1910), 1010.

Straddling the fields of justice and psychiatry, the topic of experts in cases of criminal law is embedded in the history of psychiatry and criminology. Inspired by Michel Foucault's book *Folie et deraison* (Madness and Civilization, 1961), the issues of "madness and badness" (Harris 1991, 9) in general and the legal status of insanity in particular have attracted the attention of historians since the late 1960s and early 1970s.[2] Whereas the general history of Russian psychiatry was discussed by several monographs and papers in previous decades (Brown 1981, 1983; Engelstein 1992), the topic of psychiatric experts in imperial Russia has only recently begun to attract the attention of scholars (McReynolds 2010, Becker 2003).[3]

Unlike earlier work on psychiatric experts and their role in late imperial Russian criminal courts, this study focuses on psychiatric experts as players who successfully forced an alteration in legal practice to their own advantage. It shows how these experts managed to increase their own influence and autonomy by utilizing important changes in legal procedures in the 1860s and new scientific beliefs imported from Western countries. In this way, the chapter identifies the experts' impact as a result of a multidimensional process. Drawing on contemporary psychiatric, neurological and legal publications, the essay emphasizes that the rise of psychiatric experts in late imperial Russia was largely due to the import of Western science and by its subsequent institutionalization and systematic popularization. Physicians and psychiatrists, in particular, instigated the import of Western knowledge and greatly profited from it. I illustrate this process and the role of psychiatric experts in judicial practice by examining the newspaper coverage of a murder case and the records of the psychiatric expert V. M. Bekhterev.

I will now briefly introduce the legal system, which provides the framework for these developments, before moving on to discuss the changing role of medical experts within it. The very fact that Skadovskii, as a member of the hereditary nobility of Kherson, was indicted by the same court as members of the peasantry and that the case was held in public with

2 On experts in French courts, see Harris (1989); in British courts, see Wiener (1999) and Smith (1981); in American courts, see Rosenberg (1968) and Tighe (1983).

3 For examples of older work in this field, see Morozhov and Kalashnik (1967). For examples of early publications on forensic psychiatry in Soviet Russia, see Berman and Hunt (1950); Killian and Arens (1950).

a jury was a result of the Russian Judicial Reform half a century earlier. Before the Reform (1864), the Russian legal system had been dominated by inertia, caprice and a confusing array of different courts. Catherine II had established four corporate courts: one for the aristocracy and the free peasants, one for city residents, one for the servants and the educated urban population, and village courts for the rural population. In addition, there were many extraordinary courts: the orphans' court, the court of conscience, the court of the nobility, the commercial court and the military and ecclesiastical courts.

In practice, however, the peasant serf majority rarely came into contact with the regular courts because the case law of the serfs was the matter of patrimonial jurisdiction of the landlords. Only serious crimes committed by peasants were brought before the regular courts. Where the responsibility of the landowners ended, the peasants often resolved their conflicts independently, according to their own flexible understandings of law that differed across regional, ethnic and religious boundaries. Those people who did end up in regular courts were faced with inquisitorial procedure, a written and highly formalized process of gathering evidence (LeDonne 1974). The launch and discontinuation of the investigation was solely at the discretion of the police authorities, and the accused was not heard personally at any time.[4]

When the Russian government decided to put an end to this form of justice in 1864, it did so as part of a larger reform movement: with the abolition of serfdom, the relaxation of censorship, the reform of education, military reform, and the reform of local administration, the Empire was looking to follow the developments of its European neighbors. The Russian Judicial Reform of 1864 was designed to follow the example of European models (in particular, French, Prussian, and Anglo-Saxon). Oral and public proceedings were established, the penalty was bound to the final verdict, and the newly established courts were, at least in theory, open to all estates. In addition, jury courts were introduced to hear most criminal and some civil cases. Even though the implementation of the reform turned out to be difficult, and parts of it were later reversed, the changes

4 For a detailed description of Russian judicial institutions before and after the Reform, see Baberowski (1996).

that had been achieved were a great source of inspiration for the liberal elite.

The Reform also strengthened the position of the enlightened bureaucrat, a relatively new type of official who helped to spread Western legal ideas within the Empire These bureaucrats, who had been trained at the newly established law schools[5], differed from other Russian officials in expertise and professional ethics (see also Wortman 1976). The Reform further secured jurists an important and increasingly indispensable role in the changing administrative structures. The well-educated elite pinned high hopes on these jurists and were also deeply convinced of their moral quality (Urusov 2009, 410).

The Changing Position of Medical Experts

The Judicial Reform not only changed the position of jurists within the legal system. After 1864, the law also fundamentally altered the role of medical forensic experts who were responsible for determining the frame of mind of the accused at the time of the crime. The reliance on medical experts for granting the mentally ill a special status within criminal proceedings was a long-standing legal tradition in Russia. In 1801, Peter I signed and put into force the first written statement concerning the need to involve physicians in criminal cases when indicated by the circumstances of the case.[6] A modified version of this section can be found both in the Criminal Code of 1845, in its new edition of 1885[7] and also in its revised version of 1903.[8]

5 The Imperial Law School (*Uchilishche Pravovedeniia*) was founded in 1835 in St. Petersburg. The first chair of law in Russia had already been established at Moscow University in the eighteenth century, and further law schools were opened at the universities of Kazan and Khar'kov in the nineteenth century.

6 *Polnoe Sobranie Zakonov Rossiiskoi Imperii*, Volume 26, No. 19846.

7 *Ulozhenie o nakazaniiakh ugolovnykh i ispravitel'nykh* 1845 (ed. 1885), *Svod zakonov Rossiiskoi Imperii,* Volume 15, paragraphs 92 and 95–97.

8 Ugolovnoe Ulozhenie 1903, *Svod zakonov Rossiiskoi Imperii,* Volume 15, paragraph 39.

The Criminal Code of 1845, which remained in force until the early twentieth century, defined two necessary conditions for the existence of a criminal and punishable act: clear proof of the crime's occurrence and convincing evidence that the crime "should be imputed to the defendant or defendants in a state of guilt" (*dolzhno byt' vmeneno podsudimomu ili podsudimym v vinu*)" (Bhat 1997, 88). Bhat describes the changes in the concept of criminal responsibility/competence (*vmeniaemost'*) before and after the Reform as a development towards a narrower definition:

In the pre-Reform era reasons for restricting *vmeniaemost'* included: the defendant's mental state as well as the fortuitousness of the alleged crime's negative consequence, the defendant's mental deficiencies or extreme youth, crimes committed unwittingly or in error, and so on [...] After 1864 the definition of *vmeniaemost'* became more restrictive [...], [its] denotative purview was narrowed, and the defendant's mental state increasingly became the sole subject of the criteria for competence (*ibid.*, 89).

However, these legal changes, which should primarily be regarded as clarifications of terminology, had less of an influence on legal practice and on the changing status of medical experts than other factors. Expert participation in public and oral hearings, as well as new scientific debates on crime and criminals, played a more decisive role.

I now briefly summarize Elisa Becker's recent research (2003) on the changing role of medicine and medical experts in Russian legal practice, as a background for the subsequent analysis on the ways in which Western medical debates and knowledge were perceived and imported into Russia. In the pre-Reform system, determining the mental state and criminal responsibility of the accused was an administrative issue.[9] Under the authority of the Ministry of Internal Affairs a commission of physicians, administrative officials, the governor and the vice-governor determined the mental status of the accused. This procedure remained in place until 1864.[10]

After the Judicial Reform, this process became part of preliminary investigations, which were under the responsibility of the new circuit courts.

9 On the distinction between *vmeniaemost'* (competence) and *vinovnost'* (guilt), see Bhat (1994, 198; 1997, 88).

10 On changing methods and competencies of insanity inquests, see Becker (2003), 322ff.

The prosecution decided whether to consult a medical expert in each case. The defense was also allowed to invite experts on their own initiative. The authority of experts who were invited by defense lawyers, however, was often challenged by the prosecution (*ibid.*, 333). This was particularly true during the first years after the reforms. One of the main changes for medical experts was their new participation in public hearings. Unlike the pre-reform procedure, expert "participation after the reform was highly visible, and subject to challenge" (*ibid.*, 326).

Even as they became ever more subject to criticism, medical experts managed to significantly improve their position within the legal system until the turn of the century. This success was mainly due to the close co-operation between lawyers and medical experts. While sharing "a common interest in extending the role of science within the new judicial system" (*ibid.*, 348), Becker argues, "they jointly sought to enhance their own occupational influence, independence and authority […]" (*ibid.*, 387).

From the mid-1880s, a lively discussion on the role of medical experts in court proceedings developed in newly founded medical journals.[11] The discussion included the participation of jurists who shared and supported the physicians' position concerning the relevance of expert testimony in criminal cases. As a result, by the turn of the century it was a generally accepted notion and legal practice to treat medical experts not as "witnesses", as in the early years after the Judicial Reform, but as "scientific judges" (*ibid.*, 379). This change in terminology reflects the changing role and enhanced status of medical experts within legal proceedings.

Becker examines the effects of the professionalization of medical work that accompanied the formation of a medical association in the mid-1880s[12] with numerous all-Russian medical congresses, growing Russian participation in international conventions, and the founding of several

11 For example, *Arkhiv psikhiatrii, neirologii i sudebnoi psikhopatologii* (1883–1899); *Vestnik psikhologii, kriminalnoi antropologii i pedolog* (1904–1919); *Vestnik psikhologii, kriminalnoi antropologii i gipnotizma* (1904–1912); *Vestnik sudebnoi meditsiny i obshchestvennoi gigeny* (1882–1888).

12 The Society of Russian Physicians in Memory of N. I. Pirogov/Pirogov Society *(Obshchestvo russkikh vrachei v pamiat' N. I. Pirogova/Pirogovskoe Obshchestvo)* was the most influential medical association, existing from 1883 to 1918.

medical journals: these developments increased the impact of experts' testimony on the outcome of legal proceedings.[13]

Focusing on the collective and individual aspirations of physicians and their catalyzing role in the advancement of medical experts, Becker argues that it was mainly social factors that shaped developments in the legal system. Changes in basic scientific assumptions, by contrast, play a secondary role in her reasoning. These new scientific beliefs were strongly inspired by Western debates that had been introduced into Russia by physicians such as V.M. Bekhterev.

These debates, which will be discussed below, attached high importance to the mental condition of the accused, leading the determination of "criminal responsibility" to become a central issue in criminal cases. This scientific shift—strongly connected with the so-called Criminal Anthropological School—must be seen as a necessary pre-condition for the advancement of medical experts during the last three decades of the Russian Empire.

Importing Western Thought: The End of the Free Will

One of the most famous Russian psychiatric experts at this time was Vladimir Mikhailovich Bekhterev (1857–1927). He finished his studies in 1878 at the Military Medical Academy in St. Petersburg, writing a dissertation on the relationship between body temperature and mental illness in 1881. He then became an influential pioneer of the introduction of Western medical thought to Russia and also profited from this development. Focusing on this subject, he positioned himself in the center of contemporary scientific discussions, since both humanist and natural scientists were concerned with the explanation of human behavior. [14]

In contrast to conventional psychology, to which Bekhterev referred as *subjective psychology*, he saw the task of his *objective psychology* not in dwelling on subjective "feelings, imaginations, concepts and so on"

13 On the medical professionalization in Russia since the mid-nineteenth century, see also Frieden (1981).

14 See Sully (1976) on the development of this field of research in Germany.

(Bekhterev 1913, 21). Rather, he sought to uncover those neuropsychological processes that could "be analyzed and studied by objective methods" (*ibid.*, 20) because "any neuropsychological process is accompanied by material or nervous processes in the brain" (*ibid.*, 21).

The assumption that both normal psychological phenomena and mental diseases were due to physiological processes or defects won more and more adherents. Out of this conviction grew not only the Italian criminal anthropological school, surrounding Cesare Lombroso (1835–1909) and his widely read work *L'uomo delinquente* (1876), but also experimental psychology, which gained currency in Europe from the 1870s onward.

Bekhterev left Russia for a journey to Europe in 1884, after several years of clinical work in St. Petersburg Psychiatric Hospital. On this trip, he visited famous scientists all over Europe, including the German physician and psychologist Wilhelm Wundt (1832–1920) in Leipzig. A few years earlier, Wundt had founded the world's first experimental psychological laboratory in order to study human behavior using natural-scientific methods. According to the assumptions of the nascent experimental psychology, if psychic phenomena were rooted in physical processes, they could be examined via scientific methods.[15]

Wundt would be regarded by future generations as the "father of experimental psychology" (Boring 1950, 317) and as a man who "exerted enormous influence on the development of psychology as a discipline" (Stanford Encyclopedia of Philosophy 2011).[16] He was already hailed his contemporaries for his book "The Basic Traits of Physiological Psychology" (Gründzüge der physiologischen Psychologie) (1873–74): "The recent work of Professor Wundt may be said to have defined the boundaries of a new department of research" (Sully 1876, 20). In the following years his experimental-psychological laboratory became a "working tool" and symbol of the experimental oriented psychology and also an international export hit. By the end of the nineteenth century, such laboratories had mushroomed, as a contemporary scientist suggested: "[...] there is, I think, no country now contributing to the general stock of scientific

15 On Bekhterev's distinction between normal psychology and experimental psychology and on the question of whether psychology is a science, see Franz (1907), 656.

16 Wilhelm Wundt, Article in: Stanford Encyclopedia of Philosophy (http://plato.stanford.edu/entries/wilhelm-wundt), accessed May 22, 2011.

knowledge that does not possess at least such foundation" (Titchener 1898, 27).

When Bekhterev returned to Russia in 1885, he became Professor of Psychiatry at the University of Kazan. Following the example of Wundt, he established the first psychological laboratory in Russia.[17] At this time, Lombroso's theory that criminal behavior was caused by biological predisposition had already been the subject of heated debate in Russia. Referring to Darwin's theories, Lombroso claimed that "born criminals" could be identified by physical characteristics such as the distance between their eyebrows, the position of eyes, or the size of their ears: "Nearly all criminals have jug ears, thick hair, thin beards, pronounced sinuses, protruding chins and broad cheekbones" (Lombroso 2006 [1876], 53). In founding the criminal anthropological school of thought, Lombroso applied the broadly shared scientific assumption that physical and mental processes, including criminality, were linked.

This debate stirred the interest of various scholars, especially lawyers and physicians. Soon, a flurry of articles in Russian law journals began to discuss possible reasons for criminal behavior. In Russia, the criminal anthropologist Dmitrii Dril' played a particularly prominent role in spreading and popularizing Lombroso's ideas in the 1880s and 1890s, writing various books on the causes of youth crime and on the "psycho-physical" categorization of criminals (for example, Dril' 1884, 1890). Although he was critical of Lombroso's undervaluation of the social causes of crime, in 1895 he introduced his own book "Crime and Criminals" (*Prestupnost' i Prestupniki*) by acknowledging Lombroso's scientific output:

> [...] The Italian psychiatrist and professor of forensic medicine [...] Cesare Lombroso [...] has given a powerful impetus to the study of crime. [...] His work moved this topic away from the sphere of metaphysical theory and relocated it in the working rooms of the scientist. This is unquestionably the merit of Professor Lombroso. [...] Though he made mistakes and errors [...], his famous work *L'uomo delinquente* has to be regarded as the starting point of a new era in the science of criminal law (Dril' 1897, 16).

As Dril' was both lawyer and physician, he can be seen as an intermediary between the legal and medical professions. While he was one of the

17 On V. M. Bekhterev's Psycho-Neurological Laboratory, see Shereshevskii and Akimenko (2000).

most active discussants of contemporary medical-legal topics, he seems to have been part of a minority. The majority of the scientific community rejected Lombroso's biological determinism (Mill 2010, 61; Becker 2003, 373). A considerably larger number of Russian scientists and lawyers were followers of the so-called criminal sociological school.[18]

This school developed at the beginning of the 1880s in reaction to Lombroso's biological determinism (Nethercott 2007). Criminal sociologists did not fundamentally deny the importance of anthropological and biological factors in the development of delinquent behavior; however, they criticized the criminal anthropologists' emphasis of this point and paid greater attention to the social environment and education of the criminal. The best known adherents of this school among Russian jurists were Ivan Foinitskii and Mikhail Gernet.

While their explanations for delinquent behavior differed, both groups were convinced that there are limits to human free will. This debate encouraged research into the causes of criminality that linked anthropological, biological, sociological, psychiatric and pedagogic knowledge, attempting to explore criminal motivation from an interdisciplinary perspective. As a consequence, views on crime and the personality of the delinquent changed: Under certain conditions the offender came to be seen as a non-responsible victim of his or her social environment, of education, or of his or her biological predisposition.[19] Crime thus came to be perceived as a potential result of these circumstances.

The import and local adaptation of these views were preconditions for the quick advancement of medical experts in Russian imperial courts. These views attached importance to the defendant's mental capacity vis-à-vis criminal responsibility, making it a central issue in criminal cases. Of equal importance for the growing status of experts was the broader community's acceptance of scientific beliefs as facts. This process helped to establish the experts' new role and was closely connected with the institutionalization and popularization of scientific discourse.

18 The emergence of the criminal sociological school is usually associated with the "Marburger Programm" of the criminal lawyer Franz von Liszt. See von Liszt (1882).

19 For a list of the circumstances that could lead to defendant's insanity (dating back to 1835), see Becker (2003, 335–336).

Institutionalization and Popularization

Bekhterev was intrigued by the impact of social environments on people's behavior. He was a well-known advocate of progressive education, convinced that pedagogy could and should be used to promote the social reintegration of juvenile offenders (Mill 2010, 227). He was also a proponent of the psychiatric concept of "degeneration" (see below), which explains mental disease not only in terms of hereditary predispositions, but also with reference to social experiences. At the same time, his studies and expert testimonies in court bear witness to the fact that, in the tradition of the criminal anthropological school, he attached the greatest importance to a person's anatomy.

In his laboratory, founded in 1885 at the University of Kazan, Bekhterev experimented with human reactions to visual, optical and acoustic stimuli as well as with hypnosis and other methods of suggestion. Simultaneously and in constant competition with Ivan Pavlov (1849–1936), he carried out influential research in the field of conditioned reflexes.

In 1892 he founded the Society of Neurologists and Psychiatrists (Obshchestvo Nevropatologov i Psikhiatrov), the first of its kind in Russia, and two years later the first Russian journal of psychiatry (Nevrologicheskii Vestnik). When appointed to a professorship at the St. Petersburg Military Medical Academy in 1894, he returned to his alma mater to replace his former teacher Mierzheevskii. His work linked various disciplines, such as pedagogy, biology, medicine, neurology, sociology and law. The lectures given at Bekhterev's St. Petersburg-based Psycho-Neurological Institute (Psikhonevrologicheskii Institut), founded in 1908, reflected this interdisciplinary approach. This institute brought together medical, legal and educational science and attracted many students (Pines 1928, 678).

His contemporaries considered him to be one of the most influential and one of the most active scientists, at least through his time in St. Petersburg (Engelstein 1993, 351 *et seq.*). This was true for learned society in the Russian Empire as well as for the scientific community beyond the Empire's boundaries. Publishing an amazing array of papers in German and French journals, contemporaries jokingly called Bekhterev a "typewriter with a steam engine" (Weygandt 1927, 6). His research attracted the attention of major international scientists such as John B. Watson, the founder of the American school of behaviorism, and left an imprint on Russian society. In his autobiography, Maxim Gorky writes about the impression Bekhterev's lectures had made on him. As a young man, Gorky attended these weekly lectures in Kazan's "Mad House" where Bekhterev presented mentally disabled people to his audience. In this way, the famous physician explained mental disease patterns to his students. In Gorky's memories a fascination with the ill is mixed with disgust and fear (Gorky 1976, 638–639).

The social fascination with the mentally ill at this time was also reflected in literature: In Fyodor Dostoyevsky's "Crime and Punishment", the impoverished and mentally ill student Razkolnikov (the Russian verb *razkolot'* meaning "to disrupt, to decompose") becomes a murderer. In court, the question of how Razkolnikov became a criminal and the question of his criminal responsibility play a central role. Dostoevsky's book was so influential that several articles appeared in late nineteenth-century Russian scholarly journals that discussed Razkolnikov's case and its meaning for the Russian legal system.

It is therefore safe to say that Bekhterev, as the leading figure in the fields of experimental psychology and psycho-neurology (and probably the most famous medical expert in Russia), had played an important role in transferring Western discourse to Russia. This discourse questioned the boundaries of the free will, and subsequently constrained popular perceptions of individual responsibility. These new ideas were a precondition for the rise of psychiatric experts in the last third of the nineteenth century. By founding institutes in Kazan and St. Petersburg, and by establishing scientific societies and journals, Bekhterev significantly contributed to the institutionalization and scientization of this discourse. Institutionalization, scientization, and popularization helped to unify the discourse and to increase its persuasiveness and sphere of influence. Bekhterev was therefore both an important promoter of this discourse and, in his role as a scientist and psychiatric expert, personally profited from this development.

In the Courtroom: the Application of Scientific Beliefs

The import of Western knowledge did not only change the role of experts, but also the course and character of criminal court proceedings. On the basis of a murder case that took place under participation of Bekhterev, the following part shows the practical application of this discourse and the position of psychiatric experts in court.[20]

The trial against Lev Skadovskii, for a murder that took place on April 5, 1910, was an event of high interest at its start.[21] Aside from the members of the court, the jury, numerous witnesses and five experts, a large audience was present in the courtroom. Public interest in the new courts was great; this was especially true for criminal cases. Some reformers interpreted this as public interest in the practice of law (Dzhanshiev 1907, 482–492). This interest may, however, have had more to do with a public craving for sensation. Public trials constituted an unprecedented, interactive space of communication for citizens and officials. While burglary cases sometimes attracted no more than three spectators (Ivanovich 1891, 580), interest in court spectacle was significant when the accused were either well-known figures (Pipes 2010, 51), or members of the privileged estates, as in Skadovskii's case.

The reading out of the indictment, the hearing of witnesses, the testimony of the defendant, the assessment of the jurors and the verdict and pronouncement of the sentence turned criminal trials into social events.[22] By discussing the character and circumstances of the accused, the experts, in particular, helped to turn the courtroom sometimes into a type of public

20 He worked as an expert already during his stay in Kazan. See, for example, NART (*Natsional'nyi arkhiv Respubliki Tatarstan),* 51–4-1851, pp. 58–62. Reproduction and discussion of this case can be found in Usmanova (2009, 240–247). The most famous case in which he participated as an expert was the Beylis trial in 1913. See, for example, Retsnik (1999).

21 Bekhterev's personal notes on this case as well as a resolution (*postanovlenie*), expert testimony (*zakliuchenie*), the decision of the court (*opredelenie*), a police report (*politseiskii raport*), minutes of witnesses' statements (*protokol' doprosa svidetelei*) and other documents connected to this case can be found in TsGIA (*Tsentral'nyi gosudarstvennyi istoricheskii arkhiv Sankt-Peterburga*), 2265–1-550, pp. 115–252.

22 See also McReynolds (2010, 636) on Russian jury courts as sites for the performance of "social dramas" heavily covered by the boulevard press.

theatre, a place where peoples' souls were bared to the public.[23] Another consequence of experts' participation was the circulation of "specialized knowledge well beyond the limited readerships of professional journals" (McReynolds 2010, 624). Courtrooms, in other words, served as sites for the circulation of, and popular engagement with, imported scientific insights.

Skadovskii sat on his bench while the indictment was read out. From time to time he flinched, looked around for the guards and cried. He was charged with murder. The preliminary investigation had already provided a sketch of the sequence of events leading to the deed. Shortly after their wedding, the young couple had moved from Warsaw to Kherson, Skadovskii reported. Their marriage was a happy and cordial one. However, shortly after they had moved house, Tatiana began to have arguments with her husband's family. These arguments seem to have had a detrimental effect on their marriage. On the night of the murder, the couple had yet another fight about this issue. The nanny testified that she had heard them discussing a serious topic. Lev Skadovskii demanded that his wife should take the first step towards reconciliation, but she rejected this. Both were very upset, Skadovskii reported. Finally, his wife insulted his family in such a harsh manner that he angrily pulled out his gun and fired. The autopsy showed that the shot was fired at close range and that the victim was killed instantly.[24]

Shortly afterwards, a police officer and the prosecutor arrived. Skadovskii confessed to the crime and reported the dispute that had taken place. When asked by the prosecutor which words the victim had used to insult his family, he stated that he could not remember. The prosecutor stayed until daybreak. The youngest child of the family lay in his crib and cried, said the prosecutor. The victim's mother was sitting by her daughter's dead body. She was crying, too, and bemoaning her daughter's miserable life, prompted by her marriage. At the same time, the murderer who had caused this tragedy lay on the sofa and slept.[25]

23 Michel Foucault argues that the new penal systems established in Europe from the eighteenth century onward brought "the soul to the stage of justice". He explains that "a complex of scientific knowledge" was included in court practice as part of this process (Foucault 1976, 34).

24 Ekaterinoslavskii okruzhnoi sud. Ubiistvo zheny, *Pravo*, 16 (1910), 1011.

25 *Ibid.*, 1013.

While the court had no doubt that the accused had killed his wife (in fact, Lev Skadovskii had confessed to the murder), at the end of the second day of the hearing the jury acquitted him. The reason for this was that the court treated the question of whether Skadovskii was guilty of committing the crime (*vinost'*) separately from the question of his personal responsibility (*vmeniaemost'*). Determining the personal responsibility of the offender required consideration of the psycho-physical circumstances surrounding the act. This led to a detailed consideration of the offender's psyche that became part of the public proceedings after the Judicial Reform: Was the offender sane at the time of the act or had he lost control? What was his state of mind? What motivated him to commit the crime? In which environment had he grown up? Did he suffer from a mental disease, or was there a genetic predisposition towards crime in the family?

To answer these questions, numerous witnesses were heard in the course of the trial. They provided information about the character of the accused and of the victim, about their family situation, and the relationship between the accused and his wife. At the same time, it had to be determined whether the defendant had a mental illness or was genetically predisposed to violence. In addition to the testimony, the correspondence between defendant and victim was examined, and previous convictions of the defendant were discussed. The final assessment of his mental state was left to the psychiatric experts.

The statements of the witnesses on the character of Lev Skadovskii were consistently negative. Only the father of the accused described his son in a more positive light while giving an explanation for the murder. His son, the father reported, loved his family very much: his parents, his sisters and brothers. He was sensitive, understanding and helpful to strangers. However, in his youth, he had developed a short temper. He sometimes behaved insolently and in a rude manner, the father told the court. The close ties to his family, the father indicated, were the reason for his violent reaction to Tatiana's insult. The mother of the victim, however, called Skadovskii an "intolerable human being". He was "despotic, nervous, and would tolerate no opposition and [demanded] unconditional submission from everyone."[26] The teacher who had educated Skadovskii as a child seconded this opinion. A priest, who had known Skadovskii since childhood,

26 *Ibid.*, 1012.

also described him as an unrestrained man who tolerated no opposition. He sometimes allowed himself to commit wicked acts, was vengeful and hard to calm down.[27] Only a few years prior to the murder of his wife, the priest recalled, Skadovskii's bad character had sealed another person's fate. One day in 1900, Skadovskii felt so provoked by the "cynical smile" of a student that he shot him, causing serious injury. He was subsequently charged by a military district court for shooting on the streets of Kherson and for attempted murder while in a state of excitement.[28]

He was born a hundred years too late, another witness judged. He should have lived in the era of serfdom, because he tended to insult the weak. In contrast, he always behaved submissively towards his superiors.[29]

The witnesses also addressed the character of the victim at great length: She was a happy, cheerful and dove-like girl and the incarnation of the old aristocracy, old school friends reported.[30] Skadovskii had often insulted and abused his wife while Tatiana suffered and endured it all with Christian humility. She had taken an entirely subordinate role to him and did everything he asked of her, Tatiana's sister testified.[31] When asked about the relationship with his wife, the defendant expressed his love for the victim and late remorse for the act:

> My wife was wonderful, an angel, a saint. [...] I loved her, I still love her and will love her all my life. Right after the deed, I felt no remorse, I did not suffer. There was nothing. But as the dawn broke, I realized the horror. I knew I would be jailed and hoped it would be easier there. But there it was terrible. If you knew what I had to endure in solitary confinement. [...] The shape of my dead wife appeared to me every day, from morning to evening. I recalled the happy moments of our joint life, I remembered her words. [...] At night I had nightmares. That's the way I lived and am still living. I have lost everything.[32]

After this statement he sank into the dock, crying. Many witnesses confirmed the tight bond between the couple. The servants, Skadovskii's father, the priest and the governor (who was a friend of the accused), answered with slight hesitation when asked by the prosecutor if they had

27 *Ibid.*, 1011.
28 *Ibid.*, 1011
29 *Ibid.*, 1014
30 *Ibid.*, 1014.
31 *Ibid.*, 1012
32 *Ibid.*, 1011–1012.

the impression that the defendant was of sound mind: "Yes, he seemed healthy to me. The only strange thing about him," so the Governor added, seemingly amused, "was the love for his wife."[33] After the witnesses' interrogation was completed on the second day of the trial, the court turned to the personal correspondence between defendant and victim. Parts of the letters were read out to the court, and both the contents and the way they were written supported the statements of the witnesses who had stressed the great attachment of both.[34]

The statements of five psychiatric experts, based on a two-hour examination of the defendant, followed. Under the direction of Bekhterev, the group of experts came to the following conclusion:

> All data which the court has collected concerning the person of Skadovskii lead to the conclusion that Skadovskii has to be seen as an abnormal human being. Independently of the fact that Skadovskii has killed his wife, he seems to be a person with a deeply broken psychic individuality (*chelovek s rezko narushennoi psikhicheskoi individual'nost'iu*).[35]

The experts saw the cause of the psychological illness in a biological predisposition. Thus, they followed the criminal anthropologists' thesis that criminal behavior was rooted in hereditary factors:

> Since birth Skadovskii has been loaded with a hereditary disposition to psychological illness. His maternal ancestors show heavy psychic abnormalities (*nenormal'naia psikhika*). The mother herself was treated several times by psychiatric experts.[36]

According to the experts, this predisposition showed itself during his childhood in "anxiety at night, hallucinations, an excessive sensitiveness and an abnormally quick temper."[37] In the course of his life, "these traits became worse and led to great impulsivity, which was mixed with agonizing moods, which the defendant tried to fight in vain." Among these "obvious abnormalities", according to Bekhterev, heavy impulsivity dominated, which drove "Skadovskii's personality to heavy action". All of these phenomena, according to the diagnosis, "lead to a psychic illness—*psychas-*

33 *Ibid.*, 1014.
34 *Ibid.*, 1015.
35 *Ibid.*, 1016.
36 *Ibid.*
37 *Ibid.*

thenia, which is an intermediate state between a nervous and a psychic dysfunction. Skadovskii is not mad, but without a doubt, he is a degenerate man (*degenerat*) and, in addition, dangerous for his environment."[38]

The experts saw Skadovskii's illness as confirmed by the results of the medical examination which showed "an organism with all signs of degeneration".[39] The concept of degeneration, as used in Russia at the time, posited that individual bio-psychological disorders could be acquired by individuals over their lifetime, and then be transmitted to each successive generation with increasingly acute manifestation (Beer 2007, 31). Similar to Lombroso's concept of the "born criminal", degenerate people "are people who have malformed ears, a squint, bad teeth and, in short, can be recognized as abnormal by certain outward defect" (Ballet 1905, 202–203).

In conclusion to this expert testimony in court, Bekhterev thus explained that like all human beings who take action in a state of frenzy:

> Skadovskii lost self-control and consciousness during and after the criminal act. As a result, his whole behavior became automated. Characteristic for human beings who act in a state of frenzy is the dreamy state in which Skadovskii found himself after the offense for several hours and the complete loss of memory, so that he even forgot the fatal insult spoken by the victim, which made the accused kill her.

Consequently, they assessed Skadovskii's murder of his wife as a "strong emotional act committed in a kind of psychic convulsion."[40]

The experts' conclusions were clearly rooted in the convictions of the criminal anthropological school. Starting with the medical history of the defendant's maternal ancestors, they diagnosed a hereditary predisposition to mental illness. The defendant's father, probably with ulterior motives, had already reported familiar cases of "psychic abnormality, suicide, alcoholism and general degeneration" in his family. Skadovskii's developmental history, which described him as being an unusually sensitive child who later turned out to be impulsive and short-tempered, was viewed as the result of this predisposition.

38 *Ibid.*, 1016; the concept of degeneration is traced back to the Franco-Austrian physician Bénédict Augustin Morelsee (1857).

39 Ekaterinoslavskii okruzhnoi sud. Ubiistvo zheny, *Pravo*, 16 (1910), 1016.

40 *Ibid.*, 1017.

The diagnosis of *psychasthenia* referred to a mental state that had only recently been defined as an illness. A few years prior to the case, the French psychiatrist Pierre Janet (1903) had classified it as a "neurotic disorder" that leads to weak volition, anxiety and reduced self-esteem.[41]

The experts concluded that the murder had to be seen as an emotional act committed in a state of frenzy and unconsciousness. This conclusion denied the defendant's criminal responsibility and strengthened the position of the defense. The prosecutor, however, strenuously objected to this assessment with a three-hour speech. The behavior of the accused was not a sign of a mental illness or the consequence of degeneration, he argued, but was more simply the bad behavior of an aristocrat. Only the alcoholism of the mother's grandfather was relevant, in his view, but this fact was not sufficient to conclude that the defendant was degenerate. "Skadovskii acted in a state of mental excitation, but with the deliberate intention to kill his wife."[42]

When the prosecutor had finished his plea, the defense attorney again turned to the jury. He referred to experts' evaluation of the murder as the act of a madman, and denigrated the assessment of the prosecutor as the opinion of a layman. This argument is significant in that it illustrates the authority attributed to experts at the time. In contrast to early post reform criminal cases, the defense attorney left determination of responsibility solely to the experts. The defense attorney pleaded for the accused to be handed over to the care of his family. "The family," the attorney promised, "will protect society from this mentally ill individual who has destroyed with his own hands his entire fortune."[43] The jury retired to deliberate and reached their decision within ninety minutes. They found the accused guilty, but conceded that he had acted in a state of madness. The court therefore decided to release the accused into the custody of his father. The prosecutor protested against this decision and announced that he would launch an appeal. The defense attorney, however, had successfully convinced the jury of the defendant's lack of criminal responsibility,

41 At this time, the diagnosis of *psychasthenia* was only of minor relevance in psychology. In the International Classification of Mental Disorders (ICD) by the World Health Organization, it is classified under the code F48.8 as "other, closer to designated neurotic disorder". See also Dilling (2000), 195.

42 Ekaterinoslavskii okruzhnoi sud. Ubiistvo zheny, *Pravo*, 16 (1910), 1016.

43 *Ibid.*, 1017.

totally sidestepping the prosecution by employing the assessment of medical experts against it.

Conclusion

The import, adaptation and implementation of Western medical and legal ideas in the late tsarist Empire changed legal practice, particularly in criminal cases. Psychiatric forensic experts, in particular, both facilitated and profited from this process.

New theories about the causes of criminal behavior, imported from Italy, Germany and France, formed the scientific basis for this advancement. The utilization of discourses of criminality enabled psychiatric experts to strengthen their own authority and influence in legal proceedings. Both the criminal anthropological school, promoted in Russia particularly by Dril' and Bekhterev, and the social anthropological school questioned the boundaries of the free will. The assumption of limited human agency raised the importance of the sanity question in criminal cases. As a result, psychiatric experts became crucial in criminal proceedings, since these experts were the primary judges of the defendants' mental states and therefore criminal responsibility.

Seen from historical perspective of science, the story of this discourse is a classic success story. Within a few years, the idea of the social and biological relativity of human action became widely accepted. This acceptance, moreover, was not limited to the narrow area of science, but also seemed common among the population.

The success was, to a considerable degree, the result of the personal and collective efforts of a group of physicians. Establishing research institutes such as the Psycho-Neurological Institute in St. Petersburg and chairs at various Russian universities, physicians like Bekhterev helped to institutionalize and popularize the discourse.

At the same time, the success of the discourse is also the story about the rise of the experts. While late imperial physicians were offered only badly paid jobs in the public service sector (Frieden 1981, 210–221), psychiatrists now received more public attention and acceptance.

The concomitant professionalization of medical-legal work enhanced the experts' position in court proceedings. They were suddenly the keepers of expert knowledge, to which the prosecution and defense had only limited access. This undermined the authority of jurists while strengthening the position of experts in court.

Works Cited

Baberowski, Jörg (1996). *Autokratie und Justiz: Zum Verhältnis von Rechtsstaatlichkeit und Rückständigkeit im ausgehenden Zarenreich, 1864–1917*. Frankfurt am Main: Klostermann.

Ballet, Gilbert (1905). Traitment à appliquer aux délinquents à responsabilité limitée. *Revue pénitentiaire*, 29, 202–203.

Becker, Elisa M. (2003). *Medicine, Law and the State: The Emergence of Forensic Psychiatry in Imperial Russia*. PhD diss., Department of History and Sociology of Science, University of Pennsylvania.

Beer, Daniel (2007). Blueprints for Change: The Human Science and the Coercive Transformation of Deviants in Russia, 1890–1930. *Osiris*, 2, 26–47.

Bekhterev, Vladimir M. (1913). *Objektive Psychologie oder Psychoreflexologie, die Lehre von den Assoziationsreflexen*. Berlin, Leipzig: Teubner.

Berman, Harold J. and Hunt, Donald H. (1950). Criminal Law and Psychiatry: The Soviet Solution. Stanford Law Review, 4, 635–663.

Bhat, Girish N. (1994). *Trial by Jury in the Reign of Alexander II: A Study in the Legal Culture of Late Imperial Russia, 1864–1881*. PhD. diss., University of California, Berkeley.

Bhat, Girish N. (1997). The Moralization of Guilt in Late Imperial Russian Trial by Jury: The Early Reform Era. *Law and History Review*, 1, 77–113.

Boring, Edwin G. (1950). *A History of Experimental Psychology*. New York: Appleton-Century Crofts.

Brown, Julie V. (1981). *The Professionalism of Russian Psychiatry, 1857–1911.* PhD diss., University of Pennsylvania.

Brown, Julie V. (1983). Psychiatrist and the State in Tsarist Russia. In A. Scull and S. Cohen (eds.) *Social Control and the State,* 267–287. New York: St. Martin's Press.

Dilling, H. et al. (eds.) *Internationale Klassifikation psychischer Störungen* (ICD-10). Bern: Huber.

Dril', Dmitrii (1884). *Maloletnie prestupniki: Etiud po voprosu o chelovecheskoi prestupnosti, eia faktorach i sredstvach bor'by s nei.* Moscow: A.I. Mamontova.

Dril', Dmitrii (1890). *Psikhofizicheskie tipy v ikh sootnoshenii s prestupnost'iu.* Moscow.

Dril', Dmitrii (1895). *Prestupnost' i Prestupniki. Ugolovnogo-psikhologicheskie etiudy.* St. Petersburg: Ia. Kantorovich.

Dzhanshiev, G. (1907). *Epokha velikikh reform. Istoricheskiia spravki.* St. Petersburg: B.M. Volfa.

Engelstein, Laura (1992). *The Keys to Happiness: Sex and the Search for Modernity in Fin-de-Siècle Russia.* Ithaca, NY: Cornell University Press.

Engelstein, Laura (1993). Combined Underdevelopment: Discipline and the Law in Imperial and Soviet Russia. *The American Historical Review,* 98, 338–353.

Foucault, Michel (1976). *Discipline and Punish: The Birth of Prison.* Frankfurt am Main: Suhrkamp.

Franz, Shepherd Ivory (1907). Psychology at Two International Scientific Congresses. *The Journal of Philosophy, Psychology and Scientific Methods,* 24, 655–659.

Frieden, Nancy M. (1981). *Russian Physicians in an Era of Reform and Revolution.* Princeton: Princeton University Press.

Gorky, Maxim (1976). *Autobiographische Romane.* München: DTV.

Harris, Ruth (1991). Murders and Madness. *Medicine, Law, and Society in the Fin de Siècle.* Oxford: Oxford University Press.

Ivanovich, I. (1891). V zale suda i v soveshchatel'noi komnate. Iz vospominanii prisiazhnogo zasedatelia. *Vestnik Evropy*, 26, 12.

Janet, Pierre (1903). *Les Obsession et la Psychastenie.* Paris: Felix Alcan.

Killian, Frederick W. and Arens, Richard (1950). Use of Psychiatry in Soviet Criminal Proceedings Part I. Journal of Criminal Law and Criminology, 2, 136–149.

LeDonne, John (1974). Criminal Investigations before the Great Reforms. *Russian History*, 1, 101–118.

von Liszt, Franz (1882). *Der Zweckgedanke im Strafrecht.* Marburg: Pfeil.

Lombroso, Cesare (1876). *L'uomo delinquente: In rapporto all'antropologia, alla giurisprudenza ed alle discipline.* Turin: Fratelli Bocca.

Lombroso, Cesare (2006). *Criminal Man.* Durham: Duke University Press.

McReynolds, Louise (2010). Witnessing for the Defense: The Adversarial Court and Narratives of Criminal Behavior in Nineteenth-Century Russia. *Slavic Review*, 69, 3.

Mill, Tatjana (2010). *Zur Erziehung verurteilt: Die Entwicklung des Jugendstrafrechts im zaristischen Russland 1864–1917.* Frankfurt am Main: Klostermann.

Morelsee, Bénédict Augustin (1857). *Traité des dégénérescences physiques, intellectuelles et morales de l'espèce humaine et des causes qui produisent ces varitétés maladives.* Paris: Bailliere.

Morozhov, G. V. and Ia. M. Kalashnik (eds.) (1967). *Sudebnaia Psikhiatriia.* Moscow.

Nethercott, F. (2007). *Russian Legal Culture before and after Communism.* London and New York: Routledge.

Pines, L. (1928). Nekrolog Bekhterev. *European Archives of Psychiatry and Clinical Neuroscience*, 83, 677–686.

Pipes, Richard (2010). The Vera Zasulich Trial. *Russian History*, 37.

Retsnik, G. M. (1999). *Delo Mendelia Beylisa.* St. Petersburg: Bulanin.

Rosenberg, Charles E. (1968). *The Trial of Assassin Guiteau: Psychiatry and the Law in the Gildet Age*. Chicago: University of Chicago Press.

Schattenberg, Susanne (2008). *Die korrupte Provinz? Russische Beamte im 19. Jahrhundert*. Frankfurt am Main: Campus.

Shereshevskii, M. and Akimenko, M. A. (2000). *Istoriia Instituta imeni V. M. Bekhtereva na dokumental'nykh materialakh*, vol. 1. St. Petersburg: Nauchno-issledovatelskii psikhonevralogicheskii institut imeni V. M. Bekhtereva.

Smith, Roger (1981). *Trial by Medicine: Insanity and Responsibility in Victorian Trials*. Edinburgh: Edinburgh University Press.

Sully, James (1876). Physiological Psychology in Germany. *Mind*, 1, 20–43.

Tighe, Janet A. (1983). *A Question of Responsibility: The Development of American Forensic Psychiatry, 1838–1930*. Ph.D. diss., University of Pennsylvania.

Titchener, E. Bradford (1898). A Psychological Laboratory. *Mind*, 27, 311–331.

Urusov, Sergei D. (2009). *Zapiski tri goda gosudarstvennoi sluzhby*. Moskva: Novoe Literaturnoe Obozrenie.

Usmanova, Dilyara (2009). *Musul'manskoe "sektanstvo" v Rossiiskoi Imperii*. Kazan': Fen.

Weygandt, W. (1927). Nekrolog Bekhterev. *Journal of Neurology*, 105, 3–8.

Wiener, Martin J. (1999). Judges v. Jurors: Courtroom Tension in Murder Trials and the Law of Criminal Responsibility in Nineteenth-Century England. *Law and History Review*, 3, 467–506.

Wortman, Richard S. (1976). *The Development of a Russian Legal Consciousness*. Chicago: The University of Chicago Press.

Gatekeepers to the Legal System: The Role of Legal Intermediaries

Tinterillos, Indians, and the State: Towards a History of Legal Intermediaries in Post-Independence Peru[1]

Carlos Aguirre

Introduction

The study of law and legal institutions in Latin America is currently undergoing significant change, which promises to shed light on a number of quite important historical and contemporary issues. Anthropologists, historians, political scientists, and legal scholars are engaged in lively debates about the law and its connection to power, hegemony, culture, and politics. Scholars are showing increasing awareness about the many layers and dimensions of legal systems, the need to look beyond the institutional settings and the normative aspects of the law, and the importance of incorporating culture and politics into the analysis of legal phenomena (see, for example, Aguirre and Salvatore 2001).

Generally speaking, however, scholars have not paid sufficient attention to some of the most critical agents in the actual operation of the law, i.e. those who interpret, apply, and disseminate legal norms and who, in fact, play the role of mediators between state law and ordinary people: judges, magistrates, lawyers, scribes, legal clerks, and others. Although important research has been done about the highest echelons of the justice system—magistrates, high courts and the communities of lawyers, for example—very little has been written on less prominent judicial instances such as justices of the peace. Even more obscure formal and informal legal practitioners—*escribanos* (legal clerks), *tramitadores* (facilitators or legal

1 A number of friends and colleagues commented upon earlier versions of this paper and helped me refine some of my arguments. I want to thank in particular Ricardo Salvatore, Alejandro de la Fuente, Rebecca Scott, Charles Walker, Juan Manuel Palacio, Carlos Ramos, José Gálvez, Marc Becker, Stefan Kirmse, and José Ragas for their criticism, encouragement, and assistance with different types of materials. None of them is certainly responsible for the limitations and errors that readers may identify.

assistants), notaries, and *tinterillos* or *leguleyos* (pettifoggers or informal attorneys)—have received even less attention.[2]

The importance of studying these legal intermediaries can not be exaggerated. Understanding their social and cultural background, interests, tactics, and political and social networks could shed light on a number of issues. First, it would help us understand the actual ways in which ordinary and disenfranchised people experience, understand, and use state law. Second, it will help us comprehend the mechanisms of dissemination, appropriation, and refashioning of notions of justice, rights, and legality among the lower classes. Third, it would allow us to analyze the creation of networks of power at the local level, the forms and nature of intermediation and struggle between elites and subalterns, and the connections between national, regional, and local clusters of power. Finally, such a study would improve our understanding of the complex negotiations between oral and written cultures, white/*mestizo* and indigenous groups, and the urban and rural worlds. In sum, it will make it easier for us to understand the formation and transformation of what have come to be called "legal cultures," especially among those whose access to state law was greatly hindered by differences of language, location, and social and economic status.

One of the most conspicuous of these legal intermediaries in Peru, especially for the period between the mid-nineteenth and mid-twentieth centuries, was the *tinterillo* or pettifogger (also known as *leguleyo, papelista, papeluchero, picapleitos,* or *chupatintas*). A *tinterillo* was a legal practitioner who lacked a diploma–and in most cases, did not have any kind of formal professional schooling—but still performed the duties of an attorney, advising and representing litigants. He was, in short, a fake lawyer. There must be very few characters that have been more vilified than *tinterillos* in literary, political, and historical accounts. And yet, we actually know very little about them. This article poses some questions about the place of legal intermediaries in social, legal, and political struggles in post-independence

2 For valuable social and political histories of lawyers in Latin America, see Uribe-Uran (2000) and Pérez Perdomo (2006). For Peru, see the multi-volume, encyclopedic study by Ramos Núñez (2000–2012). *Tinterillos* have been the subject of a few studies, including Lira (1984) and Becker (2010). On other forms of legal intermediaries, see Palacio (2004) and Scardaville (2003). A masterful account of legal intermediaries in China is Macauley (1998).

Peru and suggests some directions for research about their role in the making of legal cultures.

Understanding legal intermediaries in post-independence Peru also addresses some of the issues that preoccupy this volume as a whole. The formation of a national, state-centered legal system based on the universality of the law was a process shaped not only by inherited colonial notions of race, status, and power/knowledge, but also by newly-acquired liberal concepts about the rule of law and citizenship rights. As a result of this, the Peruvian legal system was "notoriously fractured," to borrow a term that Lauren Benton has used to describe the situation in post-independence Spanish America (2002, 211). The difficulties that Peruvian state-makers encountered in creating a solid institutional basis for the republic (economic limitations, constant political stability, *caudillo* struggles, foreign wars, and regional and ethnic fragmentation) were widely amplified when it came to building a national legal system. First, there was the issue of developing an entirely new set of codes and norms with which to replace the colonial legislation. That would only begin to take place in the 1850s and 1860s, more than three decades after gaining independence. Second, state officials had a difficult time creating the network of institutions and agents that would fulfill the needs of the new legal structure (tribunals, courts, local magistrates, schools for the training of lawyers, and others). And finally, there was the complicating factor that the majority of the population belonged to different ethnic and linguistic indigenous communities that were considered inferior and unworthy of citizenship rights by those in charge of administering the state. This created a post-colonial quandary as well as a terrain for the contestation of legal and political boundaries. After all, the law, as anthropologist John Comaroff has put it, "may serve those who contest authority as well as those who wield it" (1994, x). It is at this juncture that the role of legal intermediaries becomes very significant. They played a central role not only in bridging the gap between the state and ordinary people (and, by doing so, helping to cement a relationship that would otherwise have been much more disconnected) but also in shaping a culture of contestation using the very instruments that were put in place to maintain order and domination. They were the "lubricators" of the legal system, to borrow a term used by Gilbert M. Joseph (2001, xvii).

One Law for All? Post-Independence Legal Systems in Peru

From very early in the colonial period, indigenous peoples learned how to "work the system to its minimum disadvantage" and began to litigate on all kinds of issues before different types of Spanish courts (Hobsbawn 1973). As Steve Stern has suggested (1993, 115), by the 1600s indigenous groups "had developed legal forms of struggle into a major strategy for protecting individual, *ayllu*, and community interests;" they "earned a reputation as litigious peoples." They litigated on issues of land, labor, and the administration of local affairs, including suits against abusive authorities. They lost time, money, and many of their cases, but still "won important local victories" (*ibid.*, 116). Some indigenous people "master[ed] the art of defending themselves in alliance with appropriate bureaucrats or colonial powers" and even went on to display a "more aggressive manipulation of the juridical system to sabotage the colonials" (*ibid.*, 119, 121). The law became, in effect, a contested arena where indigenous people attempted to limit colonial abuses and defend their autonomy. According to historian David Cahill, "the main form of indigenous resistance during the colonial period was not public protest in riots, rebellions, or land invasions; it was, instead, litigation through the corrupted judicial system, basically at the local level" (1988, 115).

The Spanish colonial legal structure, in congruence with the official separation between the "Republic of Spaniards" and the "Republic of Indians," included not only special legislation but also separate courts for "Indians" (*juzgados de indios*). These were created only in Cusco and Lima, which meant that Indians who wanted to bring their cases to these special courts had to travel to one of those two cities.[3] The law also mandated that Indians were to be "favored and defended by ecclesiastical and secular courts," a stipulation that undoubtedly encouraged Indians to pursue justice by all means possible and before all types of judicial and ecclesiastical authorities.[4]

3 To my knowledge, there is no study of these courts.

4 *Recopilación de leyes de los reynos de las indias* (1774, 188). This *Recopilación*, first issued in 1680, was a compilation of the body of Spanish legislation enacted to administer colonial affairs. Its Section VI included all the norms related to indigenous peoples, their rights, and especially their obligations. Not surprisingly, the more benevolent elements of this legislation tended to be ignored in real life and indigenous persons

For indigenous peoples and communities to engage in such massive legal effort, assistance was needed from Indian and non-Indian intermediaries such as notaries, lawyers, scribes, and others. The specific dimensions, conditions, and effects of this intermediation have not yet been studied in great detail, so we know very little about the actual negotiations and maneuvering that accompanied indigenous litigation. Informal legal counseling by *tinterillos* most likely happened, but we lack any studies about it for colonial Peru.[5] What is most remarkable is that individuals from within indigenous communities became highly skilled in the arts of litigation and promoted a very active legal campaign in defense of indigenous rights.

Alcira Dueñas has reconstructed in detail the extraordinary case of Vicente Morachimo, who claimed to be a descendant of the Chimu lords in Northern Peru, and who appeared as "diputado general" and "procurador de naturales" before courts not only in Lima but also in Madrid in representation of several indigenous individuals and communities (Dueñas 2010, 62). Morachimo was well trained in both law and judicial procedures and became "an intermediary between the upper officials and the Indian elites and communities under the jurisdiction of the Audiencia of Lima" (*ibid.*). Morachimo's duties included "a substantial amount of writing, typically judicial *memoriales*, lawsuits, and reports to the King." In these documents, Morachimo denounced abuses against Indians—the *mita* or forced rotary labor, the expropriation of communal land, the *repartimiento de mercancías* or forced sale of goods, the unjust imprisonment of Indians, and other forms of mistreatment (*ibid.*, 62–3). His denunciations were not limited to his own communities in Northern Peru but included cases from as far as Azángaro, in the southeastern corner of the viceroyalty. His most famous document, filed in 1732, was the "Manifiesto de agravios y vejaciones," a damning report on the abuses against Indians and a powerful defense of the rights of native elites. This *manifiesto*, writes Alcira Dueñas, not only constitutes "an important document for the study of Andean legal culture and discursive formation," but it "helped shape other writings of the period as it circulated among rebels,

and communities were generally left at the mercy of abusive authorities, landowners, and other powerful Spaniards.

5 For references to *tinterillos* in colonial New Granada, see Uribe-Uran (2000, 28).

providing a legal foundation others could use to demonstrate the legitimacy of rebellion as a means to achieve justice when the colonial system failed to redress Indian subjects" (*ibid.*, 63, 65). Morachimo is but one example of what must have been a large group of native intermediaries operating in the interstices of the colonial legal system and helping promote indigenous rights.

There was also a group of state-appointed intermediaries named *Protectores de indios* (Protectors of the Indians), a type of ombudsman whose function was "to protect the Indians, alleviating them from abuses, promoting their conversion to Catholicism, and trying to enforce the laws that mandated their good treatment." They were in charge of shepherding Indians' cases through the appropriate bureaucratic and judicial channels (Ruigómez Gomez 1988, 29, 32). The *Protectores* were expected to provide legal counsel and help Indians litigate before courts, but their duties were not restricted to the legal arena since they also included assisting Indians in their attempts to make state authorities change norms or practices they deemed particularly unfair. Not surprisingly, many *Protectores* took advantage of Indians or did not adequately defend them from abuses. *Protectores* generally resided in the capital or in major provincial cities, and only occasionally in rural and remote areas of the viceroyalty, which limited their effectiveness. Still, there is evidence that some of them took their job very seriously. A *Protector* named Don Francisco de Valenzuela reported in 1650 that he had processed twelve thousand cases in his ten years in that position (*ibid.*, 109).

After Peru obtained its independence in 1821, the colonial legal system—which included, as we have seen, norms based on ethno-racial distinctions—was replaced by a new legal structure in which all "Peruvians" were considered citizens regardless of their ethnic background. Equality before the law was invoked as an ideal although, as is well known, there were plenty of exemptions to and restrictions on these principles.[6] At the same time, the laws, codes, and procedures inherited from colonial times continued to inform the day-to-day administration of justice until at least

6 Most constitutions written in the aftermath of independence restricted citizenship rights to literate male adults, thus leaving out women and a large segment of the indigenous population, who were not literate in Spanish.

the 1850s and 1860s, when the first republican Codes were enacted.[7] Thanks to the accumulated experience with colonial legal procedures, institutions, and agents, Indians were able to navigate the intricate labyrinths of a new legal system that, in theory, accorded them the same rights that any other Peruvian enjoyed but in practice treated them as inferior and marginal. For that, they had to count on the help of legal counselors, that is, professional lawyers.

The lawyers' guild (*Colegio de Abogados de Lima*, founded in 1808) was one of the most powerful corporations of the time and had a decisive role in state and public affairs in the aftermath of independence. Lawyers had a visible presence not only in the juridical realm, but more generally as members of what Angel Rama has called "the lettered city" (Rama 1996).[8] According to Rama, "the corpus of laws, edicts, and codes swelled further in the independent countries that emerged from Spanish and Portuguese colonialism, conferring an important role on lawyers, notaries, court clerks, and bureaucrats" (*ibid.*, 30). A *Manual del abogado americano* (Handbook for the American Lawyer) published in Paris in 1827 and reprinted with corrections and updates in Peru in 1830 and 1834, offers an interesting if indirect window into the doctrinal formation and practical training of lawyers in the immediate aftermath of independence.[9] Although little is known about the author (who signed only with his initials, D.J.E. de O.), the Peruvian editions, as Carlos Ramos Núñez has emphasized, "reflect an effort to adapt the original version to the still incipient Peruvian legislation" (Ramos Núñez 2000, 77). The Manual essentially followed the Spanish codification and juridical concepts, but the Peruvian editors inserted a few significant modifications, in particular a decidedly republican rhetoric and a few comments about the more egalitarian nature of the Peruvian legal system when compared with the Spanish colonial one (*ibid.*, 84). When describing the legal sanction of the distinction between nobles and plebeians, for example, the Peruvian editors noted: "This distinction has been abolished among us" (*ibid.*, 87).

7 Although there were various earlier projects, the first Civil Code was issued in 1852 and the first Penal Code in 1862.

8 It is not a coincidence that the term *letrado* designated both a "man of letters" and more specifically a lawyer. See also Mignolo (1989, 73).

9 The two Peruvian editions were printed in Arequipa (Imprenta del Gobierno, 1830) and Lima (Imprenta de Pascual Ramírez, 1834).

Although still forced to work under the colonial legal procedures, lawyers were thus beginning to receive training under a different framework, one in which republican and liberal ideas began to gain visibility. The *Manual* was the standard text used to train future lawyers until at least the 1850s and 1860s, when other authors (and new codes) offered additional instruments for legal practitioners in Peru.

During the early post-independence period most lawyers graduated from the University of San Marcos in Lima and, like their counterparts in most of Spanish America, belonged to Spanish or Creole families of relatively high social status (Mirow 2004, 121). In 1833, there were 127 lawyers registered in the membership roster of the *Colegio de Abogados de Lima,* 89 of which (70 percent) lived and practiced in the capital. The other 38 had their domicile registered in other departments.[10] We do not have reliable figures for the number of lawyers serving each department and even less each city or town, but it is clear that in rural areas and small villages, where the majority of indigenous peoples lived, no or very few certified attorneys were available. Local residents thus had to rely on an increasing number of skillful but informal legal practitioners, the ubiquitous *tinterillos.*

The role of the *tinterillo* in the early years after independence needs to be linked to a larger process of the privatization of power at the local level, wherein functions such as the legal defense of the Indian, formerly considered an obligation of the colonial state, fell into the hands of private individuals. As Andrés Guerrero has noted for the case of Andean Ecuador, the process involved a paradox: the growth of the national state was paralleled by the increasing centrality of local forms of power and expertise. In Guerrero's words, "the administration of the indigenous population in the Republic was no longer a function of the central state" (Guerrero 1996, 200). There was a growing disconnection between the state and indigenous peoples, who were now much more vulnerable to powerful local authorities and landlords. This in turn created a situation in which, according to historian Mark Thurner (1997, 141), "Indians would have to

10 The rest were distributed as follows: 6 in other parts of the Department of Lima, 14 in Arequipa, 4 in Cusco, 10 in La Libertad, and 4 in Junín. This list does not include those lawyers who were acting as "dignitaries" in various positions such as Supreme Court Justices (*Matrícula del Ilustre Colegio de Abogados de esta capital,* 1833).

rely increasingly upon non-Indian intellectuals and literates for the realization of supralocal political goals and for the defense of their interests." They were, Thurner added, "significantly more dependent on non-Indian intellectuals in their dealings with the state" (*ibid.*). Needless to say, *tinterillos* were among those "non-Indian intellectuals". In this context, the national network of courts, tribunals, justices of the peace and other agents of state justice became, at once, ever more important. They were, however, increasingly shaped in their day-to-day application by local agents, including the *tinterillos*, who had become almost always the first and necessary instance in the process of seeking justice by the indigenous population, through litigation but also through other forms of negotiation with the state.

Lauren Benton (2002, 211–213) has called our attention to the way in which a culture of legality shaped the emergence of Spanish American republics in the early nineteenth century. Law and legal institutions, Benton argues, were made central to the process of nation- and state-formation: "Even before the borders of the new republics had been fixed, political leaders embraced strong legal institutions as a nationalist project." This project was "national" only on paper (and even then, not fully inclusive): rural and indigenous groups were kept on the margins of the hegemonic national project. "Legal rhetoric," according to Benton, "was central to emerging, contrastive images of urban and rural cultures" in the early post-independence era in Spanish America. What this means is that the distance between, and the differing status attributed to, urban and rural populations were in part constructed through legal discourses and practices. Legal authority was "notoriously fractured" and litigation, especially on the part of subaltern agents, "quickly revealed the weaknesses of legal orders that remained decentralized and fragmented."

Simultaneously, post-independence state-makers embraced the notion that citizenship rights should be contingent on literacy. In an important book about writing and other recording practices among indigenous peoples, Frank Salomon and Mercedes Niño-Murcia (2011, 292–293) emphasize that independence added a new political function to literacy, namely "literacy as a 'national' project leading toward the transformation of Indians into citizens." They add: "Alleged illiteracy and ignorance of the language in which official literacy had been vested made 'Indians' seem poor prospects for this sort of citizenship." And yet, "by this era a lot of the culture usually styled Andean or traditional or indigenous was already being mediated and reproduced by writing."

Thus, on the one hand, the law—with its institutions, norms, procedures, and agents—was made central to the process of ordering society and building a national project. On the other hand, writing and literacy were adopted as defining elements of the allocation of full citizenship rights. Access to both, while certainly not impossible or unprecedented, was clearly challenging for indigenous peoples. It is at the very intersection of legal and writing practices, understood as arenas of contestation around rights and power, where *tinterillos* and other legal intermediaries came to play a crucial role.

Tinterillos thus filled an important gap: the legal mandate to create a national structure of justice was not met by the existence of a community of lawyers able and willing to operate over the entire national territory. University-trained lawyers were simply not available in smaller villages and towns, especially in the highlands. Pettifoggers had existed since colonial times and, following independence, the law actually allowed them to represent litigants in towns and villages where no (or very few) certified attorneys existed.[11] When lawyers *were* available, they were not always affordable (or even perhaps approachable, given the existing social and linguistic distances) to the poorer members of the local society. *Tinterillos* made legal representation possible for them, thus fulfilling a role that would not have been satisfied otherwise. Without them, a large sector of the population would have been even more deprived of legal (and political) representation. In addition, the highly formalized and potentially confusing rhetoric and theatrical display of the justice system could intimidate ordinary individuals, indigenous or not, unfamiliar with them. As de Trazegnies noted with a bit of hyperbole, "it is possible to imagine the psychological distance that an indigenous peasant could feel inside the courtroom, when he saw attorneys eloquently arguing and elegantly dressed; and then found judges and magistrates in public official events,

11 A decree of April 27, 1848, had established that in places with less than six lawyers, litigants were not required to hire a certified lawyer to be defended before judges and tribunals. Later, in 1854, the *Reglamento de Tribunales y Juzgados* increased the minimum to ten. See Ramos Núñez (2002, 366).

dressed with a black jacket, embroidered with silk, and wearing a little sword, a cane, and a high hat" (1980, 192). *Tinterillos* helped to connect these two worlds in some way, and by doing so became agents of mediation between indigenous peoples, the state, and local elites; between the oral and the written world; and between urban and rural spaces.

Defensa Libre, or the Mother of All Evils

In June 1855, President Ramón Castilla, who had recently abolished Black slavery and would soon do the same with the Indian head tax—a remnant from colonial times—enacted a much less well-known reform: he decreed *defensa libre* ("free defense"), that is, "the right given to litigants to defend themselves before judges and tribunals, without the need of a lawyer that can promote their cases" (Fuentes and de la Lama 1877, 371).[12] Predictably, an avalanche of protests and denunciations was launched by the established community of lawyers, especially in Lima. Legal journals published dozens of articles and editorials against such reform. They blamed the government for creating chaos in the administration of justice, failing to guarantee a fair trial to every citizen and, ultimately, putting at risk the very legal foundations of the Peruvian republic. Although a thorough analysis of both the motivations and ultimate effects of Castilla's decree is beyond the scope of this article, it seems clear that it marked, if not the beginning, certainly an occasion to reinforce and magnify the bad reputation of *tinterillos* and other informal legal practitioners. Sporadic attacks against *tinterillos* appeared on the pages of Lima newspapers in the years after independence, but it was only after the enactment of *defensa libre* in 1855 that the legal establishment saw their profession in real jeopardy. By attributing to the *tinterillo* exclusively negative traits and by blaming him for all the problems that marred the operation of the judicial system, lawyers tried to convince public opinion that only established and professional lawyers could guarantee a fair application of the law and, more importantly, protect the legal foundations of the Peruvian republic.

12 An earlier proposal to adopt *defensa libre* had been presented and discussed at the National Legislature in 1849, but was not approved. See Labarthe (1958, 16).

Manuel Atanasio Fuentes, one of the most prolific writers in nineteenth century Peru and author of numerous legal treatises, used one of his sarcastic *Aletazos del Murciélago* ("The Bat's Wing Flaps") to condemn the *defensa libre* reform. He argued that it brought a more dilatory administration of justice, higher costs for litigants, and a system that only benefited the rapacious *papelistas* or *tinterillos*.[13] Another prominent lawyer, Ramón Gutierrez, also criticized the effects of this reform, focusing on the *juzgados de paz* (district courts), which he called *palenques de rateros* ("nests of thieves").[14] There, he wrote, clients were abused by those that "not having a profession and lacking, many of them, any notion that could enable them to exercise good judgment, can never deal with questions of legal importance, and nonetheless, exercise as defenders of laws that they don't know." In these courts, he added, "a disgraced mob is accustomed to exploiting its miserable clientele, who seek them as counselors, when they are just leeches."

Defensa libre was revoked in 1862, but in localities with less than eight certified lawyers litigants were still allowed to use non-professional counselors.[15] Although we do not have statistics about this, the number of towns and cities where there were less than eight lawyers must have been significant, and thus *tinterillos* still had plenty of opportunity to exercise their trade "legally." Because of that, and also because lawyers wanted to make sure that *defensa libre* would not be legalized again, their aggressive campaign against *tinterillos* continued. In July 1865, for instance, attorney Antonio Iturrino, writing in *La Gaceta Judicial*, suggested that neither honor nor property should be placed in the hands of a "miserable leguleyo." Without proper representation by established lawyers, he added, "juridical disputes would become a marketplace discussion" (*una polémica de verduleras*). *Tinterillos*, he concluded, were "moths that rot the established order of trials."[16] Manuel Atanasio Fuentes and Miguel Angel de

13 Fuentes even wrote some verses about them: "Such *tinterillos* /As San Andrés said/Have claws in their hands/Have claws in their feet." See Fuentes (1866, 28).

14 Ramón Gutierrez, "Abusos y reformas del poder judicial," published in several issues of *La Gaceta Judicial*, June/July 1861.

15 The decree of October 30, 1862, set at eight the minimum number of certified lawyers required to make it obligatory the participation of one of them in the legal defense. See de la Lama (1873, 65).

16 Antonio Iturrino, "La defensa libre," *La Gaceta Judicial*, July 18, 1865.

la Lama insisted on the same point years later: "When *defensa libre* was decreed, a horde of *tinterillos* took over as defenders," and in their hands, the Civil Code became "the cadaver of the law" (1877, 4). *Defensa libre*, they insisted, introduced chaos and discredited the administration of justice. In opposition, they described certified lawyers as "men of enlightened consciousness [and] jealous of their honor and reputation."

The virulent campaign to discredit *tinterillos* and portray them in the most negative way reflects the efforts by the established community of urban lawyers to defend their privileges. Any shortcomings in the administration of justice were attributed to the presence of *tinterillos* or to the corrupt practices of justices of the peace. The protection of the lawyers' corporate interests was not the only motivation behind these allegations, however. As Fernando de Trazegnies has suggested, *defensa libre* empowered intermediaries, most conspicuously the *tinterillo*, who "served other social classes (even when he also profited from them) or, at least, represented an obstacle to the interest of the dominant groups with the purpose of obtaining personal gain" (1980, 123–4). This is indeed a critical issue, one that would be even more central in the latter part of the nineteenth century and the first few decades of the twentieth century, when the social and political oligarchic structures were shaken by a wave of indigenous mobilization, as we will see below.

There was at least one dissenting voice from the lettered community, however, and a very significant one. Francisco García Calderón, a prominent lawyer and the author of the very influential *Dictionary of Peruvian Legislation,* was a critic of *defensa cautiva* (literally, "captive defense," the name given to the obligation to have a certified lawyer in order to litigate). He suggested that the limitations of the Peruvian legal system could not be attributed to *defensa libre*, that it had not caused the ruin of lawyers, and that the campaign against it was motivated by lawyers trying to protect their turf and economic interests. García Calderón's position was framed by his overall defense of *libertad de industria* (freedom of industry) and his critique of monopolies; all economic and productive activities, García Calderón thought, should be free for everybody to exercise. "Anybody that works to make a living, no matter what type of activity it is, has the right to enjoy the same freedom given to the rest" (Ramos Núñez 2002, 369). As legal historian Carlos Ramos Núñez has inferred, García Calderón's position, which reflects his "authentic liberal convictions," constituted an implicit defense of *tinterillos*' right to exercise their trade (*ibid.*, 366–372).

Tinterillos, Indians, and the State during an Era of Mobilization

The images of the *tinterillo* offered by prominent Limeño lawyers that I have summarized above would reverberate powerfully decades later among intellectuals, state officials, and social and political elites, especially during the period from 1885 to 1930. One particular group, *indigenista* intellectuals, can be credited with shaping and disseminating the most widely accepted images of *tinterillos. Indigenismo* was a literary, cultural, and political trend among non-Indian urban intellectuals, artists, and activists that aimed at redeeming Indians from oppression, incorporating them into the nation, and helping them preserve or recover their traditions, culture, and languages.[17] *Tinterillos* are featured in prominent novels such as Clorinda Matto de Turner's "Birds without a Nest" (1889), Ciro Alegría's "Broad and Alien is the World" (1941), and José Maria Arguedas' "Yawar Fiesta" (1941). They are also portrayed in numerous Indigenista works of social analysis such as those written by Luis E. Valcárcel (1972), Luis F. Aguilar (1922), Hildebrando Castro Pozo (1924), or the Mexican Moisés Saenz (1933). Not surprisingly, *indigenismo* also influenced new generations of jurists who embraced the critique of the exploiter *tinterillo* and promoted the cause of redeeming the Indian through paternalistic legislation and education (see Ramos Núñez 2006, 207–274).

In these works, the *tinterillo* was generally depicted as a totally unscrupulous male character, a real master of legal trickeries who responded only to his own personal greed.[18] He particularly (but not only) abused indigenous people, semi- or illiterate peasants, who knew very little Span-

17 The literature on *indigenismo* is enormous. See especially Deustua and Rénique (1984), Lauer (1997), de la Cadena (2000), Coronado (2009).

18 *Tinterillos* were overwhelmingly male, and were portrayed as such in most of the literature reviewed in this article. Only by exception does one read about women practicing the trade. In Puno in the 1920s, a local intellectual reported that "if the husband is weak, or when he has vices, the woman tirelessly works in the fields, in commerce and in all activities of life…even as *tinterillos*" (Castillo 2009, 159).

ish and even less so the intricacies of legal jargon and procedure. He would initiate or foster legal complaints not for the purpose of seeking justice or repairing inequities, but for personal gain alone. He repeatedly and endlessly asked for money from his clients, and when cash was not available, he would seize chickens, potatoes, land, or anything else he could take away from peasants. He usually had a close relationship with various types of legal personnel—judges, scribes (*escribanos*), public defenders (*fiscales*), and others—and would often use them as accomplices.

Tinterillos were particularly scorned in *indigenista* literature for serving the interests of *gamonales*, large landowners that exercised enormous political, economic, and social power in the Andean highlands and imposed quasi-feudal mechanisms of control and labor exploitation over their indigenous laborers.[19] *Gamonalismo*, as Marxist intellectual José Carlos Mariátegui suggested, was not just a social or economic phenomenon, but also one that involved multiple dimensions, including cultural and legal mechanisms of domination. It was forged not solely by the *gamonal*'s personal ambition as it also involved "a long hierarchy of officials, intermediaries, agents, parasites, *et cetera*" (1971, 30). The *gamonal*'s unjust but usually "legal" appropriation of communal land, these critics posited, was almost always carried out with the help of a *tinterillo*, who deceived naïve peasants into signing documents that would eventually give *gamonales* legal and effective ownership of the land. The ensuing trial, which was inevitably won by the *gamonal*, would include all sorts of tricks and maneuvers by the *tinterillo* in order to convince Indians that he was helping them in their *asunto* (case) while, in reality, he was making it easier for the *gamonal*/judge partnership to pillage them.

The moral and political depiction of the *tinterillo* in *indigenista* literature was usually accompanied by physical descriptions of him. These writers, influenced by nineteenth-century physiognomic and anthropological theories in vogue by the final decades of the nineteenth century, seemed to want to establish an association between physical appearance and moral character. In Alegría's "Broad and Alien is the World", the *tinterillo* Bismarck Ruiz—who betrays the community in their struggle against the landowner—is described as follows:

19 For an early analysis and critique of *gamonalismo* see Mariátegui (1971). See also Burga and Flores Galindo (1980); Manrique (1988).

He was a pudgy little man with a red nose, who called himself "juridical defender." Rosendo had found him sitting at a table heaped with papers, holding a dish of stewed meat and a bottle of corn liquor (1941, 17).

On another occasion, the same character is thus depicted:

The lawyer wore a greenish suit, heavy rings on his fingers, and across his stomach, from one vest pocket to another, stretched a chain of gold. His eyes were bleary with drink and he reeked of brandy as though he had been soaked in it (*ibid.*, 73).

In the same novel, another *tinterillo*, Iñiquez, aka "araña" (spider), is portrayed as follows:

He was small and skinny… He spent his time in his office surrounded by sheafs of stamped paper, on which he and his two aides scribbled assiduously in the thick fog of the strong tobacco he smoked. His skin was yellow and drooping mustache and gnarled fingers were still more yellow from tobacco stain (*ibid.*, 163–4).

Because of his "scrawny body sunk between his long legs and his skinny arms he really did look as though he belonged to the spider family" (*ibid.*). This image of the *tinterillo* as an "arachnid" was indeed quite pervasive.[20] One of the first writers to use it was Abelardo Gamarra, otherwise known as "El Tunante," one of the most acid critics of turn-of-the-century Peruvian society. In his book *Cien años de vida perdularia* he described the *tinterillo* or *papeluchero* as "a spider that was tireless in weaving webs to trap all the flies that would fall" (1921, 176).[21] Prominent Cuzqueño indigenista writer Luis E. Valcárcel called the *tinterillo* "law's arachnid" (*el arácnido de la ley*) (1927, 39).

These motifs appeared not only in works of fiction, but also in books written by *indigenista* social critics. Hildebrando Castro Pozo, another classic *indigenista* author, described the *tinterillo* as follows:

20 There is an old tradition of equating the law with a spider web. Anacharsis is quoted by Plutarch as saying to Solon that "laws resemble spiders' webs, and would, like them, only entangle and hold the poor and weak, while the rich and powerful easily broke through them" (Langhorne and Langhorne 1801, 202).

21 One of the stories in this book offered the same plot that *indigenistas* would reiterate over and over again: a litigant named *Justo* ("Just") falls in the hands of the *tinterillo*, named *Sanguijuela* ("Leech"). After so much pain and cost, Justo loses the trial.

He's a white, *mestizo*, or Indian individual, not very well dressed, with a briefcase full of papers under his arm, a purpled face due to the signs of alcohol consumption, and always followed by a delegation of Indians, or even the whole village (...) [H]e lives a life of permanent drunkenness and cynicism (1924, 38).

It is worth mentioning here that local judges, particularly those operating in the highlands, were also portrayed in very similar terms by social critics.[22] According to the standard portrait, the local *juez de paz* (justice of the peace) was not interested in dispensing justice but was instead a highly corrupt individual. He was usually portrayed as one of the members of the *trinidad del Indio* ("the Holy Trinity of Indians"), the infamous exploitative trio of authorities who exercised power and abuse in rural villages throughout the Peruvian Andes: the *gamonal*, the priest, and the justice of the peace (or, alternatively, the *subprefecto*).[23] One of Abelardo Gamarra's stories was that of Juan Pichón, a mediocre lawyer from Lima who managed to get appointed justice of the peace in an Andean town. He brought along an assistant, a "come-tinta" also called *Sanguijuela*, and together started the usual chain of abuses via which Pichón became wealthy and powerful. Gamarra describes Pichón as "a man of wide body, powerful lungs, good stomach, and a better bladder; his eyes are always injected with blood, his voice is throaty (*ronca*), his nose is reddish, his hair is long and without care, his beard disheveled, and always has the appearance of having been partying" (1921, 187). In his study on liberal professions in Peru, Manuel Vicente Villarán commented that there were 2,000 justices of the peace in the country, "almost all of them professional *leguleyos*," a contradiction in terms and an exaggeration that nonetheless illustrates the very low reputation enjoyed by local judges (1900, 15).

The targets of *indigenistas*' attacks, it is worth highlighting, were usually the lower-ranked agents of state justice: justices of the peace, *escribanos*, and *tinterillos*. They operated in geographical and social spaces that were

22 In fact, the legal profession in general was a favorite target of satirical writers and social critics such as Manuel Atanasio Fuentes, Abelardo Gamarra, and Manuel González Prada. Ernest Stowell (1942) found two hundred references to legal issues in the "Peruvian Traditions" written by noted nineteenth-century satirical author Ricardo Palma, most of them containing "invectives" against lawyers, *tinterillos*, and other legal practitioners.

23 See, for example, the novel by José T. Itolararres (José T. Torres y Lara), *La Trinidad del Indio o costumbres del interior* (Lima: Imprenta Bolognesi, 1885).

distant from the centers of economic and political power, and were blamed for all the iniquities that Indians and other subaltern groups suffered.

The inevitable companion to the standard portrait of the *tinterillo* was that of the ignorant Indian, the eternal victim of the *tinterillos*' trickery. In these narratives, indigenous persons and communities appear as childish litigants who, despite the fact that *tinterillos* and other legal agents abused them and that they very rarely won their cases, persisted nonetheless in seeking "justice" through lengthy and costly litigation efforts. Indians, according to this portrait, did not understand how the justice system worked, had a blind faith in lawyers, *tinterillos*, and judges, and did not quite understand what was at stake at any stage in the trial. They were almost "inborn litigants" (*""" pleitistas*). In the highlands, wrote Manuel Vicente Villarán, "there is no book that is more widely read than the Code" [of Civil Procedure], and added that "even Indians, when they come to Lima, buy a copy of it" (*ibid.*). *Indigenista* writer Luis F. Aguilar offered this essentialist and derogatory portrait of "the Indian":

> Not just his ignorance, but also the organic shyness of the Indian are the reason why he can not defend himself against oppressors, and thus his faith in justice and his tendency to litigate. He blindly believes in the efficacy of such social mechanism, organized for the common good (…) [S]quatted before the entrance of the courts and other offices, begging, imploring everybody, he awaits patiently and resignedly to receive news about the status of his *asunto*… [E]ternal victim of the exploitation of unmerciful *tinterillos*, serving for months as servants for the attorney or even the judge, working hard during his free hours to make a living, his fate as an indigenous litigant is to wait: that is the news, the consolation, the counsel, and the command that he receives from everybody: wait! And the Indian sighs, elevates his hands to heaven, and waits… (1922, 29–30).[24]

24 See also Sáenz (1933, 200, 202, 285). This interpretation of Indian litigiousness has been somehow refashioned in what we can call a "fetishist" explanation. According to legal historian Fernando de Trazegnies, for example, it was the Indians' sort of fetishist faith in the judicial system and their "irrational" tendency to litigate which allowed for the advent of the *tinterillo*. There was, he argues, a "farfetched" diffusion of liberal ideology, which "contaminated" indigenous mentality with the idea of individual rights and of a state whose duty was to protect them. Gradually, though, this "social faith" turned into a "magical ingredient" in the "political-ritual" battle that the indigenous peasant carries on. And this was so because "the magical and the ritualistic correspond to the Andean cultural matrix" (1980, 185).

Although it could be argued that *indigenistas* were simply reproducing the nineteenth century urban lawyers' stereotype of *tinterillos* referred to above, there is an important difference: this time the terms of the debate were framed not by the dispute, triggered by *defensa libre,* between professional lawyers and informal practitioners, but by early twentieth century racialized discussions about the "Indian" question in Peru.

As a number of studies have demonstrated, most intellectuals in early twentieth century Peru, including *indigenistas,* tended to offer a very negative portrait of the Indian "race." Indians were presented as submissive, hypocritical, lazy, alcoholic, reluctant to civilization, degenerate, and so forth. Unlike previous versions of anti-Indian racism, however, *indigenistas* offered a sort of "optimistic" prospect: Indians were indeed redeemable through a civilizing process that included, among other things, the spread of education and the enacting of paternalistic legislation (Portocarrero 1995). Under this scheme Indians were to be treated as minors and their crimes judged and punished with special consideration to their uncivilized status. Suitable legislation would help them overcome the many defects attributed to their "race" (Encinas 1920; see also Poole 1990). In the same vein, and unlike extreme, "scientific" versions of racism, this new approach emphasized the role exploitative structures (such as colonialism) and agents (such as local authorities and landlords) had had in shaping the Indians' state of prostration. Within this framework, many of these writers took issue also with cultural (and racial) intermediaries, who were accused of serving the interests of those exploiters. One of those intermediaries was of course the *tinterillo,* who was usually literate, politically savvy, fluent in Spanish, and connected to local networks of political and economic power. "Defending" the Indian thus implied for *indigenistas* a critique of this intermediary, who was often presented in racialized terms: the *tinterillo* was almost always described as an opportunist *cholo* or *mestizo,* that is, a person of mixed racial background. Valcárcel, for instance, stated that "the *leguleyo* is the best product of our *mestizaje,*" thus implying that racial mixing produced degenerate and morally low characters (1927, 39).

The purely negative depiction of *tinterillos*—with its racist undertones against both Indians and *mestizos*—was a motif that permitted lettered and upper-class *indigenistas* to present themselves as the "authentic" defenders of Indians and to construct them as eternal and powerless victims of all types of abuses. What most of these *indigenistas* failed to recognize was that a powerful wave of indigenous mobilization and protest was taking shape right before their eyes, and that some *tinterillos* and other legal and political intermediaries had a critical role in its development. Historian Alberto Flores Galindo called this massive mobilization of peasants "a seismic wave," which shook especially the southern and heavily indigenous departments of Cusco and Puno (2010). In only four years, between 1919 and 1923, fifty rebellions took place in this area. This "veritable social earthquake" included attacks on haciendas and land occupations. There were also protests against "heavy or unscrupulous fiscal burdens, arbitrary political demarcations, pressure to move provincial or district capitals, merchant usury, and broken political promises" (*ibid.*, 161, 167–8). More importantly, rebellions "called peasant servitude—the very foundation of *gamonalismo*—into question" (*ibid.*, 169). As Mark Thurner wrote, "the negation of the historical agency of republican Indians opened an ideological space that would be filled by an early twentieth-century indigenism which ultimately essentialized Indians as prepolitical, indeed prehistorical" (1997, 152). The image of the passive and subservient Indian disseminated by *indigenistas* does not hold. The trope of the *tinterillo* as a purely negative and exploitative character must be subjected to scrutiny.

Red Tinterillos

Although far from denying that there were in fact cases of *tinterillos* that match the unflattering portrait offered by the *indigenistas* and literati, there is enough evidence to suggest that, especially in the period between 1885 and 1930 (that is, between the end of the War of the Pacific and the end of the authoritarian and modernizing administration of Augusto B. Leguía), *tinterillos* played a much more active and positive role in promoting the rights of indigenous peasants and communities and helping them navigate the intricate layers of national and local political and judicial structures of power.

Despite the rarity of *tinterillos* in the written records—which can be explained by the informal nature of their trade and the fact that they had to work almost always in the shadows—a few examples will illustrate their role in helping Indians and peasants foster their agendas. In the aftermath of the 1885 Atusparia rebellion, one of the most violent of the post-independence period, a series of "remarkable petitions" written by *alcaldaes ordinarios* (local indigenous authorities) were presented to state authorities, including the President of the Republic. Thurner emphasizes the importance of these documents as they can illuminate some of the motives of the peasant rebels that are otherwise very difficult to discern given the lack of documents containing their own "voices." These petitions reveal an astute appropriation of the legal rhetoric and discourse of liberalism to promote a defense of peasants' land rights. (*ibid.*, 144, 150) One question remains: who wrote these petitions? Thurner does not offer a definite answer but hints at the existence of a group of scribes that he deems as "radical red *tinterillos* with long experience as defenders of Indians in the local courts" (*ibid.*, 144).

Other studies about peasant politics in nineteenth century Peru have highlighted the importance of the legal battles peasants fought against state authorities, landowners, or other rural agents. *Tinterillos* do not usually appear in these accounts, but we can almost "see" them operating in the shadows.[25] From the 1920s, we know of the case of José Carmona, a *tinterillo* who offered legal support to *ayllus* (indigenous communities) in the province of Vilcabamba in Southern Peru (Flores Galindo 2010, 178). In this and other areas, communities had established a type of cooperative scheme, known as the *rama*, to collect funds that were used, among other things, to procure legal advice and promote litigation against landowners (*ibid.*, 177; Mayer 1917). Communities used these resources to pay for *mensajeros* (messengers) and *personeros* (legal proxies) that would accompany or represent them before state and judicial authorities. In a recent dissertation, Victoria Castillo refers to this as representing an "explosion of formal petitions to the state" by indigenous *mensajeros* (2009, 1). Relatively affluent indigenous families in Puno used their own resources to sue local *gamonales* (Rénique 2004, 96). In the Cusco region, *tinterillos* were

25 Cecilia Méndez, personal communication, June 11, 2001. See, in particular, Méndez (2005); Jacobsen (1993).

hired by Indian communities to prepare *memoriales*—petitions sent to authorities, including those in Lima, to request protection against abuses by *gamonales* (Rénique 1991, 39).[26] "These traveling petitioners interacted with *indigenista* activists (generally white or *mestizo* pro-indigenous intellectuals, feminists, artists, and journalists) to pressure government officials to respond to specific complaints and even implement pro-indigenous legislation" (Castillo 2009, 1). Although there were *tinterillos* and messengers that betrayed the communities' trust, others sided with Indians to the point that landowners considered them "agitators" (Rénique 1991, 39).

The best-known case of a "red *tinterillo*" is that of Ezequiel Urviola, a *mestizo* from Puno who became "Indianized" and embarked on a tireless political and legal defense of Indians during the 1910s and 1920s. He was the son of an impoverished landowner who had apparently lost his land to a powerful *gamonal*. Ezequiel was a very sensitive young student in the early 1910s, when a series of massacres of Indians took place in Azángaro, the province in which he had been born in 1895.[27] In 1914 he moved to Arequipa to study law at the University of San Agustín. He became deeply interested in social and political issues. During his vacations he frequently returned to Puno, where he began to denounce in local newspapers the abuses against Indians and promoted the formation of a committee to improve the social conditions in the department. Around 1920 he was already working as a local organizer in haciendas, where he formed *núcleos de la libertad* (freedom cells) and began to discuss taking concrete actions to protect Indians. He spoke Quechua and gained the trust of indigenous peasants. Furthermore, he actually began to "act" as an Indian, dressing like one and even learning what a witness described as "the subtle art of mimicry, duplicity, and pretense," the alleged features of indigenous behavior (Rengifo 1977, 193). Contemporary observers testified that Indians "looked at him with superstitious respect" and "blindly obeyed him" (*ibid.*, 192). The next step was almost predictable: he decided to drop out of law school because, as he explained to a friend, he did not want to get a

26 Peruvian citizens, according to the 1867 Constitution (article 28), had the right to submit petitions, either individually or collectively, to different branches of the government.

27 Most of the biographical information on Urviola presented here comes from Rengifo (1977). See also Arroyo (2004).

degree in a profession that "has been used to deprive Indians of their land and to annihilate them" (*ibid.*).

Urviola became a peasant agitator and organizer as well as a legal defender of indigenous communities. Accurately speaking, he was a *tinterillo*. He also wrote petitions to the Peruvian Senate in Lima advocating the cause of indigenous peasants. Because of all this, he was the target of accusations and threats by local authorities and landlords, which forced him to leave Azángaro and move to Lima, where he joined the *Comité Pro-Derecho Indígena Tahuantinsuyo*, an organization that fought for the rights of Indians. Urviola continued working as a legal advocate for indigenous peasants who went to Lima to present their cases before the courts and other state offices. In October 1922, for example, he wrote a petition to the president of the Chamber of Deputies complaining that, while Indians were received in Lima by the highest authorities, in the provinces, "because of the intimate complicity of *gamonales* and authorities—who are *gamonales* themselves—all our complaints are dismissed and the legal mandates are disobeyed" (Rénique 2004, 93–94). He wrote numerous such *memoriales* in which, as José Luis Rénique has suggested, the tone was far from submissive and appeared rather threatening. Urviola was not alone in this. A "memorial" presented by messengers from the province of Lampa (Puno) warned President Leguía that "we came for the last time to demand justice, and in case we do not receive it, Mr. President, we will have to achieve it by ourselves in order to save our family from hunger, shame, and dishonor, or emigrate to some other Republic, where the constitutional guarantees are not meaningless." Furthermore, "if we had wanted to take justice into our own hands, as we were resolved to do, and did not because of the observations, promises, and advice of Dr. Rubin, what would four to five hundred *gamonales* and eight to ten sub-prefects achieve against four hundred thousand indigenous people?" (Castillo 2009, 99). As Castillo has written, "even within a framework of paternalism, the indigenous messengers expressed a sense of entitlement, recognizing their rights to appeal to government officials for the protection of their rights and livelihoods. They were unwilling to accept the injustices they faced because they knew they were citizens, even though they were often not treated as such" (*ibid.*, 14).

While in Lima, Urviola lived a very frugal life and his health began to deteriorate. He died of tuberculosis in January, 1925 at the age of thirty. His funeral was a massive demonstration of grief for someone who had acquired an almost legendary status. At least twenty speeches were given at the cemetery during his burial ceremony, which included representatives from labor unions, peasant federations, and groups of radical intellectuals. José Carlos Mariátegui, who had met him in person in 1923, called Urviola "the Indian from Puno" and offered the following portrayal of him: "This encounter was the greatest surprise Peru offered me when I returned from Europe. Urviola represented the first spark of a coming fire. He represented the revolutionary Indian, the socialist Indian. Sick with tuberculosis and hunched, he fell down after two years of indefatigable efforts. Today, it does not matter that Urviola is no longer alive. It is sufficient that he has existed" (1927, 10).

Urviola was one of many such legal and political intermediaries who played a key role in fostering peasant and indigenous agendas during the early decades of the twentieth century. Such mobilization included both peaceful actions (litigation, *memoriales*) and episodes of rural violence (riots, rebellions). The aftershocks of this "seismic wave" reached Lima at a time of intense political activism, both in support of the Indian and in favor of revolutionary social change (Flores Galindo 2010, 152–196). José Luis Rénique notes that there was a well-developed network of Indian and non-Indian activists and organizations (committees, leagues, federations), an "interconnected leadership" of people who were "well-read and well-spoken" and who bridged the legal efforts in both local courts and Lima's tribunals with the social battles taking place on the ground against abusive landlords and authorities (Rénique 2004, 97). These intermediaries did not threaten the livelihoods of indigenous peoples or communities. They did not belong to the "trinity of the Indian." They joined Indians in their attempts to "work the system to its minimum disadvantage." What is worth highlighting is that these "red *tinterillos*" built upon a long tradition of legal intermediaries who effectively worked as "hinges" between rural and indigenous peasants and the state, and whose role was not as negative as the standard, hegemonic narratives about them would have us believe.

Conclusion: Towards a Social History of Legal Intermediaries

By questioning the standard interpretation of *tinterillos* this article advances elements to refine our understanding of subalterns' views of the legal system and its agents. As decades of social and political history "from below" have amply demonstrated, indigenous peasants were not unaware of national or local political debates, were capable of appropriating and reshaping notions of liberalism, justice, rights, and republicanism and, most importantly, were creative and active pursuers of their own agendas.[28] With this understanding, it would have been quite incoherent to expect that those same subjects were so blind and even stupid when it came to their relationship with the law. Peasants' approaches to law and legal intermediation were much less naive than what the standard literature portrayed. In the 1980s, Peruvian legal scholar Luis Pásara conducted a survey of peasants' attitudes towards lawyers. According to the results, peasants consider lawyers necessary, for they could really make a difference and help them foster their cases. However, peasants also believe that lawyers can be abusive: they may delay trials and overcharge them, for instance (1988, 95–104). This poll showed that peasants' views about the judicial system and its agents are not necessarily naive or blind but quite pragmatic, proactive, and lucid. They realize what is at stake, what their chances are, who is on their side, and what can be accomplished. Lawyers (as well as *tinterillos*) could be allies as well as foes. Though they can not be always trusted, *tinterillos* were usually available when needed, while lawyers were not. Novelist Ciro Alegría, a harsh critic of the *tinterillo*, recognized nonetheless that he could represent a "formidable arsenal of defense within its fortress of stamped paper" (1941, 163).

The study of *tinterillos* and other such legal practitioners sheds light on a number of issues. In particular, it illuminates one of those "contact zones" that current historiographical trends consider key to understand processes of historical and cultural change. Intermediation—in this case, legal, but also cultural and political— is critical in particular in countries such as Peru, where different racial, cultural, regional, and linguistic groups coexist in almost permanent tension. This re-thinking of legal in-

28 A representative sample of this scholarship on the Andean region can be found in Jacobsen and Aljovín de Losada (2005).

termediation also strikes at the heart of debates about subaltern representation. Both Thurner and Guerrero address this issue in relation to local intermediaries in nineteenth century Andean societies. Thurner (1997, 144), after wondering who those "red *tinterillos*" were, posed a pertinent question: "What was the process of translation and approbation? In what sense do these petitions speak for the subaltern who cannot speak in the juridical 'republic of letters' for historical reasons of marginalization?"

Addressing a similar quandary, Andrés Guerrero (1996) has come up with the image of the "ventriloquist" to refer to these intermediaries who made the subaltern speak, as he says, mostly in *papel sellado* (stamped paper). These intermediaries, Guerrero argues, "re-wrote" the peasants' transcript, thus critically altering it in that process: "A scribe not only writes down what he hears, what others want and can tell him, and what he can infer. His activity is not constrained to the passive role of writing on official paper what others tell him, even translating that from Quichua to Spanish (…) In that process, he surpasses the confines of the mere transcription, converts the demands of the Indians into strategies founded upon juridical codes and adequate to the political-bureaucratic correlation of forces." In other words, he, like any other ventriloquist, "makes the Indians speak…in the language of the white-*mestizo* Republican state" (*ibid.*, 202–203).

These are important reflections that help make us aware of the complexities behind the relationship between indigenous people (and, more generally, subaltern groups) and the state. I am not sure that the *tinterillo* voice would necessarily mute that of his clients: the ventriloquist image implies that the other voices do not exist or are never heard, an assumption that I would like to question. But can we hear, in the end, the subaltern's "voice" in legal contestation? On the one hand, there is a truth that we must face: except for isolated instances of accused individuals presenting their cases before criminal judges and tribunals (and even these are quite problematic, since they are influenced by the oppressive environment, if not by direct coercion and even torture), the subaltern's "voice" is almost totally erased from the written legal record. What we hear is what others—the judge, the police, the prosecutor, the witnesses, the counselors, the messengers, or the *tinterillos*—say (or write) about them. Does this mean that the subaltern's "point of view" is impossible to recover? Not necessarily. Despite some scholars' agonizing reflections on the impossibility of "recuperating" the subaltern's voice, I still believe that historians can reconstruct—though always imperfectly—the point of view of the subordinate, as decades of research in social history demonstrate (Guha 1983, 2009; Mallon 1994).[29]

The study of legal intermediaries must be a critical step in the reconstruction of the operation of legal systems and the formation of legal cultures, in particular in societies with persistent social, ethnic, and linguistic fractures such as post-colonial Peru. As this article has demonstrated, beyond the written norm and underneath the surface of legal procedures laid a highly complex network of legal and political agents engaged in myriad forms of negotiation without which the legal system would not have worked. Legal intermediaries were the lubricators of the judicial machinery. They had their own agency and worked to advance their own interests, but they were often quite instrumental in helping subaltern litigants work through the complex and frequently hostile theaters of the legal system. At the very least, they facilitated access to litigation, which was a very important form of contestation, especially for disadvantaged groups. As Melissa Macauley wrote in relation to China, "litigation-masters cases thus reveal that resorting to the formal courts empower weaker actors as well as those ideologically favored in the law codes and society" (1998, 6). The latter (the power wielded by the ruling classes) was a given due to structural forms of cultural and political domination; the former (the empowerment of weaker agents) was the result of persistent individual and collective efforts. Indigenous people in Peru systematically engaged in such efforts. They were not powerless victims of landowners, state officials, and judicial authorities; neither were they always blind prey of unscrupulous *tinterillos*. This article has shown that the relationship between indigenous groups and individuals, intermediaries, and the state, was much more complex than what standard accounts suggested, and that the Peruvian legal culture has been crucially shaped by the agency of both indigenous actors and legal intermediaries.

29 Ranajit Guha's now classic methodological suggestion of "reading against the grain" (1983) is quite pertinent here.

Works Cited

Aguilar, Luis F. (1922). *Cuestiones Indígenas*. Cusco: Imprenta de El Comercio.

Aguirre, Carlos, and Salvatore, Ricardo D. (2001). Writing the History of Law, Crime, and Punishment in Latin America. In Ricardo D. Salvatore, Carlos Aguirre and Gilbert M. Joseph (eds.) *Crime and Punishment in Latin America. Law and Society since Late Colonial Times*, 1–32. Durham: Duke University Press.

Alegría, Ciro (1941). *Broad and Alien is the World*. Translated from the Spanish by Harriet de Onís, New York, Toronto: Farrar & Rinehart.

Arguedas, José Maria (1985). *Yawar fiesta*; translated by Frances Horning Barraclough. Austin: University of Texas Press.

Arroyo, Carlos (2004). La experiencia del Comité Central Pro-Derecho Indígena Tahuantinsuyo. *Estudios Interdisciplinarios de América Latina y el Caribe*, 15, 1, 185–208.

Becker, Marc (2010). In Search of *Tinterillos* in Ecuador. Paper presented at the American Historical Association Convention, January 2010, in San Diego, California.

Benton, Lauren (2002). *Law and Colonial Cultures. Legal Regimes in World History, 1400–1900*. New York: Cambridge University Press.

Burga, Manuel and Alberto Flores Galindo (1980). *Apogeo y crisis de la república aristocrática*. Lima: Rikchay Peru.

de la Cadena, Marisol (2000). *Indigenous Mestizos: The Politics of Race and Culture in Cuzco, Peru, 1919–1991*. Durham: Duke University Press.

Cahill, David (1988). Una visión andina: el levantamiento de Ocongate de 1815. *Histórica* (Lima), XIII, 2. 133–159.

Castillo, Victoria (2009). *Indigenous 'messengers' petitioning for justice: Citizenship and indigenous rights in Peru, 1900–1945*. PhD diss., University of Michigan.

Castro Pozo, Hildebrando (1924). *Nuestra comunidad indígena.* Lima: Editorial El Lucero.

Comaroff, John (1994). Foreword. In Mindie Lazarus-Black and Susan F. Hirsch (eds.) *Contested States: Law, Hegemony, and Resistance.* New York: Routledge.

Coronado, Jorge (2009). *The Andes Imagined. Indigenismo, Society, and Modernity.* Pittsburgh: University of Pittsburgh Press.

Deustua, José and José Luis Rénique (1984). *Intelectuales, indigenismo y descentralismo en el Perú, 1897–1931.* Cusco: Centro de Estudios Rurales Andinos Bartolomé de las Casas.

Dueñas, Alcira (2010). *Indians and Mestizos in the "Lettered City." Reshaping Justice, Social Hierarchy, and Political Culture in Colonial Peru.* Boulder: University Press of Colorado.

Encinas, Jose Antonio (1920). *Contribución a una legislación tutelar indígena.* Lima: Casa Editora Villarán.

Flores Galindo, Alberto (2010). *In Search of an Inca. Identity and Utopia in the Andes.* New York: Cambridge University Press.

Fuentes, Manuel Atanasio (1866). *Aletazos del murciélago.* Vol. 2. Paris: Imprenta de A.D. Laine y J. Havard.

Fuentes, Manuel Atanasio and de la Lama, Miguel Antonio (1877). *Diccionario de jurisprudencia y de legislación peruana.* Vol 1. Lima: Imprenta del Estado.

Gamarra, Abelardo (1921). *Cien años de vida perdularia.* Lima: Tipografía Abancay.

Guerrero, Andrés (1996). De protectores a *tinterillos*: la privatización de la administración de poblaciones indígenas (dominadas). In Heraclio Bonilla and Amado Guerrero (eds.) *Los pueblos campesinos de las Américas: Etnicidad, Cultura e Historia en el siglo XIX.* Bucaramanga: UIS.

Guha, Ranajit (1983). The Prose of Counterinsurgency. In Ranajit Guha (ed.) *Subaltern Studies* II, 1–42. Delhi: Oxford University Press.

Guha, Ranajit (2009). *The Small Voice of History.* Delhi: Permanent Black.

Hobsbawm, Eric (1973). Peasants and Politics. *Journal of Peasant Studies*, 1, 1, 3–22.

Jacobsen, Nils (1993). *Mirages of Transition. The Peruvian Altiplano, 1780–1930.* Berkeley: University of California Press.

Jacobsen, Nils and Cristóbal Aljovín de Losada (eds.) (2005). *Political Cultures in the Andes, 1750–1950.* Durham: Duke University Press.

Joseph, Gilbert M. (2001). Preface. In Ricardo D. Salvatore, Carlos Aguirre and Gilbert M. Joseph (eds.) *Crime and Punishment in Latin America. Law and Society since Late Colonial Times.* Durham: Duke University Press.

Labarthe, Manuel (1958). Colegio de Abogados de Lima, 1808–1958. *Revista del Foro*, XLV, 1, 1958.

de la Lama, Miguel Antonio (1873). *Suplemento de los códigos en orden alfabético.* Lima: Imprenta del Estado.

Langhorne, John and William Langhorne (eds.) (1801). *Plutarch's Lives.* Vol 1. London: T. Gillet.

Lauer, Mirko (1997). *Andes imaginarios. Discursos del indigenismo 2.* Lima: SUR and Centro Bartolomé de las Casas.

Lira, Andrés (1984). Abogados, *tinterillos* y huizacheros en el México del siglo XIX. In *Memoria del III Congreso de Historia del Derecho Mexicano*, 383–384. Mexico City: Universidad Nacional Autónoma de México.

Macauley, Melissa (1998). *Social Power and Legal Culture: Litigation Masters in Late Imperial China.* Stanford: Stanford University Press.

Manrique, Nelson (1988). *Yawar Mayu. Sociedades terratenientes serranas, 1879–1910.* Lima: Desco.

Mariátegui, José Carlos (1927). Prólogo. In Luis Valcárcel (author). *Tempestad en los Andes.* Lima: Editorial Minerva.

Mariátegui, José Carlos (1971). *Seven Interpretive Essays on Peruvian Reality* [1928]. Austin: University of Texas Press.

Matrícula del Ilustre Colegio de Abogados de esta capital (1833). Lima: Imprenta de José M. Masías.

Matto de Turner, Clorinda (1996). *Birds Without a Nest.* Translated by J.G.H. and emended by Naomi Lindstrom. Austin: University of Texas Press.

Méndez, Cecilia (2005). *The Plebeian Republic. The Huanta Rebellion and the Making of the Peruvian State, 1820–1850.* Durham: Duke University Press.

Mignolo, Walter (1989). Literacy and Colonization: The New World Experience. In René Jara and Nicholas Spadachini (eds.) *1492/1992: Re/Discovering Colonial Writing.* Minneapolis: The Prisma Institute.

Mirow, M.C. (2004). *Latin American Law. A History of Private Law and Institutions in Spanish America.* Austin: University of Texas Press.

Palacio, Juan Manuel (2004). Aves negras: abogados rurales y la experiencia de la ley en la región pampeana, 1890–1945. *Desarrollo Económico*, 44, 261–288.

Pásara, Luis (1988). El campesino frente a la legalidad [1982]. In *Derecho y sociedad en el Perú.* Lima: El Virrey.

Pérez Perdomo, Rogelio (2006). *Latin American Lawyers. A Historical Introduction.* Stanford: Stanford University Press.

Poole, Deborah (1990). Ciencia, peligrosidad y represión en la criminología indigenista peruana. In Carlos Aguirre and Charles Walker (eds.) *Bandoleros, abigeos y montoneros. Criminalidad y violencia en el Perú, siglos XVIII–XX*, 335–367. Lima: Instituto de Apoyo Agrario.

Portocarrero, Gonzalo (1995). El fundamento invisible: función y lugar de las ideas racistas en la República Aristocrática. In Aldo Panfichi and Felipe Portocarrero (eds.) *Mundos interiores. Lima, 1850–1950*, 215–259. Lima: Universidad del Pacífico.

Rama, Angel (1996). *The Lettered City.* Durham: Duke University Press.

Ramos Núñez, Carlos (2000–2012). *Historia del Derecho Civil Peruano.* Lima: Pontificia Universidad Católica del Perú.

Ramos Núñez, Carlos (2000). *Historia del Derecho Civil Peruano.* Vol. I, "El orbe jurídico ilustrado y Manuel Lorenzo de Vidaurre." Lima: Pontificia Universidad Católica del Perú.

Ramos Núñez, Carlos (2002). *Historia del Derecho Civil Peruano.* Vol. III, "Los jurisconsultos: El Murciélago y Francisco García Calderón." Lima: Pontificia Universidad Católica del Perú.

Ramos Núñez, Carlos (2006). *Historia del Derecho Civil Peruano.* Vol. V, "Los signos del cambio", part 2, "Las instituciones". Lima: Pontificia Universidad Católica del Perú

Recopilación de leyes de los reynos de las indias (1774). 3rd. Edition, Vol. II. Madrid: Antonio Pérez de Soto.

Rengifo, Antonio (1977). Esbozo biográfico de Ezequiel Urviola y Rivero. In Wilfredo Kapsoli et al. (eds.) *Los movimientos campesinos en el Perú, 1879–1965*, 179–209. Lima: Delva Editores.

Rénique, José Luis (1991). *Los sueños de la sierra.* Lima: CEPES.

Rénique, José Luis (2004). *La batalla por Puno.* Lima: Instituto de Estudios Peruanos, SUR and CEPES.

Ruigómez Gomez, Carmen (1988). *Una política indigenista de los Habsburgo: el protector de Indios en el Perú.* Madrid: Ediciones de Cultura Hispánica.

Sáenz, Moisés (1933). *Sobre el indio peruano y su incorporación al medio nacional.* Mexico City: SEP.

Salomon, Frank and Niño-Murcia, Mercedes (2011). *The Lettered Mountain. A Peruvian Village's Way with Writing.* Durham: Duke University Press.

Scardaville, Michael (2003). Justice by Paperwork: A Day in the Life of a Court Scribe in Bourbon Mexico City. *Journal of Social History*, 36, 4, 979–1007.

Stern, Steve J. (1993). *Peru's Indian Peoples and the Challenge of Spanish Conquest. Huamanga to 1640.* 2nd Edition. Madison: University of Wisconsin Press.

Stowell, Ernest (1942). Ricardo Palma and the Legal Profession. *Hispania*, 25, 2, 158–160.

Thurner, Mark (1997). *From Two Republics to One Divided. Contradictions of Postcolonial Nationmaking in Andean Peru*. Durham: Duke University Press.

de Trazegnies, Fernando (1980). *La idea de derecho en el Perú republicano del siglo XIX*. Lima: Fondo Editorial dela Universidad Católica.

Uribe-Uran, Victor (2000). *Honorable Lives. Lawyers, Family, and Politics in Colombia, 1780–1850*. Pittsburgh: University of Pittsburgh Press.

Valcárcel, Luis (1927). *Tempestad en los Andes*. Lima: Editorial Minerva.

Villarán, Manuel Vicente (1900). *Las profesiones liberales en el Perú*. Lima: Imprenta La Industria.

The Ties that Bind: Sovereignty and Law in the Late Russian Empire

Jane Burbank

What significance did the legal system have for subjects of the Russian Empire? Was the law in action primarily punitive and arbitrary, as the Russian intelligentsia has led us to believe? Was the law an imperial tool for oppressing non-Russian subjects, as nationalist histories suggest? Was the law just ineffective, one more flailing arm of bungling bureaucratic rule? Or, as many of Russia's critics, past and present, insist, was there no "real" law in Russia anyway, because law and autocracy are incompatible, because Russia was not "western", and/or for any number of other high principles?

Rather than beginning with these multiple, self-contradicting, but nonetheless widespread conceptions, this essay looks at Russian law from a different, middling, and practical setting—from the desks of Russia's officials charged with carrying out administrative duties and thereby putting legal governance into practice. A focus on the actions of those empowered to implement laws and to enforce their observance can open up a window on law in action—on the ways that both subjects and their rulers in ordinary circumstances put law to work in their lives and made it function in their polity. I argue that use of the legal system by subjects and officials expressed and reinforced imperial sovereignty. The making of laws and the provision of procedures to apply them were obligations incumbent on the ruler; the deployment of the laws by subjects and officials recognized the state's sovereignty and gave it life. The law was more than a "representation" of the Emperor's power; administrative and judicial implementation of laws made sovereignty matter—to policemen, official secretaries, local administrators, of course, but also to vast numbers of litigants, accused people, and petitioners.[1]

1 On representation and political power, see Baberowski (2008).

The questions of my inquiry concern connections between governed and governors in the Russian Empire. My assumptions are that the "middle" levels of government were critical to the operation of imperial rule in Russia, as in other states,[2] and that a focus on the actions of judicial, administrative and police institutions at the provincial level can help us tease out habits of mind and action that linked subjects and their state. My query is: did subjects (Orthodox Christians, Muslims, Russians, Tatars, others) share a political imaginary with their superiors at work in the web of administrative and legal institutions? What kind of sovereignty was extended and communicated through the actions and communications of middle-level civil servants—judges, prosecutors, governors, investigators, policemen—as they dealt with claims, complaints, and testimony of the people they were assigned to govern?

The setting of this chapter is the Kazan judicial district, with its headquarters in Kazan on the Volga River. My sources are administrative records from the early twentieth century, generated by provincial, district, and county level institutions—the governor's chancery, the provincial gendarmes, the district police—as well as township administrations and village assemblies. Judicial-administrative records of this kind offer glimpses of how subjects deployed the law and how administrators wielded their authority.

While the cases discussed below involve specific individuals and communities, their topics and their treatment by administrators are by no means exceptional.[3] With regard to ethnicity—the hegemonic focus of today's studies of imperial governance—the actors in these cases are representative of the populations in this area.[4] Officials, plaintiffs, and accusers

2 On the importance of middle-level actors ("intermediaries") in empires generally, see Burbank and Cooper (2010, 13–14).

3 This observation is based on my research in the National Archive of the Republic of Tatarstan (hereafter NART), where I am exploring questions concerning law and Russian sovereignty.

4 While many scholars assume that the defining characteristic of empires is their governance and usually repression of subordinate nationalities, ethnicity did not in itself always create a problem for imperial rulers or subjects. Moreover, rulers of the Russian Empire recognized and tried to manage multiple kinds of distinctions within the polity: region, religion, personal status as well as ethnicity were matters of attention for governance. On the multiplicity of imperial distinctions—*mnogovariantnost'*—in Russia, see Burbank and von Hagen (2007, 17–21).

come from the three largest ethnic groups in Kazan Province—Russians, Tatars, and Chuvash; the individuals whose actions are called into question are all peasants, as were the vast majority of Kazan's people.[5]

From the thousands of cases processed every year by officials in the Kazan judicial district, I have chosen two well-documented matters that involve surveillance of local officials, prosecution of political dissidence, and enforcement of laws. My account considers the processing of these cases in detail, in part because it was through the various stages of official action that law was made tangible for those concerned, and in part because the workings of what is pejoratively described as the "bureaucracy" in Russia have been so little studied, yet so often criticized as sub-standard.[6] I argue that the governed both assumed the state's authority and appealed to it for their own ends, that non-Russians were active in the lower-middle level apparatus of rule, and that the political imaginary of elites was both communicated to and exploited by ordinary subjects. The web of legal connectivity and the cases that traveled up, down, and around it display practices and beliefs about law, governance, and sovereignty shared by governors and governed.

Russian Law and Empire

Although many people think that Russian law is an oxymoron, legal institutions were fundamental to governing imperial Russia. The Emperor's ultimate power was set forth in law, and subjects possessed rights of vari-

5 In 1913, the officially counted population of the province was 2,850,101; of these, 1,940,630 were Orthodox; 853,715 were Muslim. Seven other religious groups accounted for the rest. Fifteen different national groups, plus a residual category for "others," were counted in the province. The four biggest ethnic categories were Russians (1,108,085), Tatars (898,653) Chuvash (649,940) and Cheremis (145,550). Here as elsewhere, peasants constituted by far the largest estate: 2,461,179 people or 86 percent of the total. See *Obzor Kazanskoi gubernii* (1915), *vedomosti* 2, 3, 4.

6 Inefficiency has become accepted as a characteristic of Russian bureaucracy, even by those who advocate more study of officials. See, for example, Velychenko's provocative article (2000) in which "administrative shortcomings" are both assumed and examined as important openings for nationalist activities (pp. 76–77). For a different, unconventional, and helpful view, see Schattenberg (2008).

ous kinds, defined in legal codes and enforceable at courts. Administrators issued their decisions within the framework of a legal order; litigators took cases to courts legitimated by imperial authorities; investigators followed protocols determined by official rules. Russia's legal system had to deal with problems faced by all empires—how to gain and keep authority over distinct populations with an array of unlike religious, social, and regulatory practices. The answer to the challenge of governing over long distances and many peoples was to devolve many administrative and judicial functions to local authorities. Both in Russian and non-Russian areas, low-level legal matters—family conflicts, small suits, or misdemeanors—could be resolved at village, county, or other regional institutions. The judges for such matters were individuals, often selected by local communities themselves, who were familiar with local norms and religious practices. Far from being a lawless realm, the Russian Empire in the early twentieth century was a place filled with judicial fora, where subjects could have their cases settled by people who knew local habits and expectations (Burbank 2006).

The assignment of governing tasks to local authorities meant that the Empire's legal system was not uniform. Peasants in most areas of the Empire had the right to have some property and family matters decided at administrative institutions according to local custom. This legitimation of custom as a basis for legal decisions was expressed in the Empire's legal codes, as were legal procedures for deciding whether a custom existed or not.[7] The legal system could adjust to new challenges and requirements on an *ad hoc* basis, and reforms could be implemented in some areas, not others. Imperial governance, operating over a long time and changing space, did not make rules uniform for everyone. Instead, the Empire established a variety of institutions empowered to make legal decisions and thereby drew courts and similar institutions in under an "umbrella" of legal authority and control.

The practice of differentiated jurisprudence meant that legal decisions were made in many kinds of legal settings in different parts of the Empire: "rural oral courts" (*sel'skie slovesnye sudy*), "*shariatskie*" (using

7 *Ustav grazhdanskogo sudoproizvodsta* (hereafter UGS), sts. 10^1, 10^2 (Tiutriumov 1916, 210). The UGS is in volume 16, part 1 of the 1914 edition of the *Svod Zakonov Rossiiskoi Imperii* (Digest of Laws of the Russian Empire). I am using an edition compiled by I. M. Tiutriumov (1916).

shari'a) courts, mullah's ordeal instances (*po proizvodstvu ispytanii na zvanie mulli*), township courts (with peasant judges), and "people's (as in native peoples) courts".[8] This framework meant that subjects of all ethnicities and confessions had access to legal ways to resolve conflicts and legitimize property transactions. This widespread network of legal institutions should be borne in mind when considering the significance of the Empire in the lives of both Russian and non-Russian subjects. Most of the questions historians pose about minority populations assume that non-Russians were hostile to imperial rule and engaged in efforts to subvert it. But most of the Empire's peoples were usually not concerned with rebellion, revolution, or resistance. They had to get things done in their immediate settings, and this could mean going to court or another authority perceived to be useful. Our investigations of "law and empire" in Russia need to take account of this address to the law, and not just of actions against it. Just as the facts of ethnic, religious, status, and regional differences were givens for Russia's leaders, imperial rule was a reality for Russia's subjects. Living in an empire was a normal, not aberrant, experience (Burbank and Cooper 2009), and non-Russian subjects, like Russians, could try to use the Empire's legal institutions in their own interests (see also Kirmse in this volume).

The ongoing practice and accessible structures of legal rule in Russia were often ignored by contemporaries, even by professionals active in judicial and administrative institutions, not to mention hostile activists in the intelligentsia (Tissier 2007).[9] The notion that the "rule of law" was something that existed in Western Europe and the United States, but not in Russia, has been a commonplace assumption among Russia's elites from the nineteenth century to the present. But if Russian governance did not add up to "rule of law" for the Empire's critics in and outside Russia, the legal system and its workings had meaning for the ways that ordinary people regarded the state and their place in it.

8 For studies of these various kinds of courts, see on the Caucasus: Agishev and Bushen (1912); Bobrovnikov (2002, 98–204); Jersild (2002, 89–109); Babich (1999, 31–137). On nomad steppe courts, see Martin (1997); on township courts, Burbank (2004).

9 Lenin, exceptionally, paid attention to legal decisions and regulations, the better to castigate both the Empire's governance and moderates' demand for what they understood as western-style law (Burbank 1995).

One effect of the differentiated legal system was the enhancement of local authority, in that most low-level cases were decided, officially, by legally empowered institutions at the village, township, or other regional level. The power of local elites, of many kinds, was a fact well recognized by users of legal instances and a delectable subject for literary and other artistic narratives about corruption, incompetence, and other human foibles. The imperial government knew only too well that devolved power could be abused, and devised various mechanisms for dealing with this problem. Periodic inspections, special investigators, centrally filed dossiers, and disciplinary hearings were part and parcel of decentralized rule. In addition, the umbrella of imperial law offered ordinary subjects ways to go beyond or around their most local authorities, and to call the legality or other aspects of their actions into question.

A second consequence of the network of legal institutions was that an array of intermediary officials, above the village but below the central state, were involved in interpreting and enacting the law on a regular basis. For most subjects, the way the law worked depended not on the tsar and his ministers, but on middle-range authorities of various kinds. In the cases examined below I look at this "middle" level of legal process—not at lawmaking in institutions of the central administration, not decision-making by the Senate, Russia's supreme court, or even at the verdicts of the circuit courts created in 1864—but at the activities of supervisory instances at the district, county, and provincial levels.

At these instances, it was middling sorts of officials who were responsible for interpreting, enacting, and communicating the justice of the state. When a subject appealed the decision of a lower-level court or reported a crime to the authorities, both the address to supervisors and the legal process that ensued reveal beliefs and practices of sovereignty. By reaching to state authorities for official resolutions of contested issues or for punishment of harm, subjects implicitly displayed their understanding of the state's power both to make laws and enforce them. And just as petitions to officials express subjects' assumptions about the state's authority and how to address it, the records of officials' responses offer a glimpse of practices of sovereignty that were both routine and vital for officials. Their communications enforced for themselves and for the people with whom they interacted the state's expectations for how subjects should behave in their relations with each other and with their governors.

A Village Leader under Suspicion

Let us begin with the kind of case that on the surface reeks with colonialism and resistance—the investigation of Zainulla Fazullin, the village leader of Aiukutergin, Tetiushi County (*uezd*) "accused of opposition to the enactment of the law of June 14, 1910."[10] This accusation against Fazullin came to the attention of two institutions critical to the Empire's supervisory functions—the provincial office of the gendarmes (the security police) and the governor's private chancery with its own "secret" department. The law cited in the case against Fazullin was a major element of the now infamous Stolypin Land Reform, expressed in rules issued in 1906 and 1910. These laws—concerning the transformation of land allotments from village into personal property and consolidation of family plots—had initiated a flurry of legal claims on the part of peasants.[11]

The accusation against Fazullin potentially exposed this village official, a Muslim and a Tatar[12],to serious consequences.The case reached the governor's secret department on March 22, 1912, as a report from Colonel Kalinin, the head of the Kazan Province Office of Gendarmes. Kalinin informed the governor that his office had received a request to carry out a political investigation of the "reliability" (*blagonadezhnost'*) of village leader Zainulla Fazullin. The basis for this inquiry was a communication from Shafigulla Fatkullin, a policeman (of Tatar ethnicity) in the city of Perm, as well as information gathered from various local police author-

10 The case at the Kazan governor's secretariat is preserved in NART, 1–4-5207. Fazullin's file processed by the provincial gendarmes is NART, 199–2-1297. Spellings of Fazullin's name vary between and within both files.

11 On the Stolypin reforms, see Macey (1998), and on the disruptions these policies entailed, see Gaudin (2007, 169–206).

12 On Fazullin's religion and other personal attributes, see the report filed with the provincial gendarmes, NART, 199–2-1297, p. 15. The village in question was in a region where Tatars and Muslims predominated. On the population of districts within Kazan province, see *Obzor Kazanskoi gubernii* (1915), *vedomost'* 4.

ities. According to these sources, Fazullin had denounced the Stolypin rules, saying that "this law was not the Tsar's but the nobles', that this law did not exist and that it wasn't necessary to secure [land]." Furthermore, the village leader had "told his co-villagers not to give their mullah the declaration [necessary] for securing a land allotment, since the law was the [land]lords' decree."[13]Colonel Kalinin observed that he had received the correspondence on this matter from his assistant for Tetiushi County, Captain (*Rotmistr*) Kirsanov, and that he would investigate further and report back.[14]

Here we apparently have an ideal case of opposition to the Stolypin Land Reform: a Muslim Tatar who declares the law invalid and instructs his co-religionists not to take part in the process necessary for legalizing families' possession of plots of land. Note, however, that the language of Fazullin's purported speech concerns legality: he does not challenge "law" itself, but the origins of what is said to be a law. The reason offered for not registering land in a new way is that "this law did not exist," and it did not exist because it was "not the Tsar's." This was not the only complexity of this case.

Constable Fatkullin had drawn up his disturbing declaration on January 30, 1912, in the city of Perm.[15] On February 2, the chief of the Office of Gendarmes for Perm Province had sent a report on the matter to his analogue Colonel Kalinin in Kazan.[16] Colonel Kalinin began investigations early in February. His subordinate, Sergeant Shafranov submitted a dispatch on his questioning of villagers on February 14.[17] The police chief for the district of Fazullin's village reported to Kalinin on March 8.[18] All these materials ended up in the case file about Zainulla Fazullin, opened on Colonel Kalinin's orders at the Kazan Province Office of the Gendarmes on March 20, 1912. The dossier at the Gendarmes' Office eventually con-

13 NART, 1–4-5207, p. 2v.

14 *Ibid.*

15 NART, 199–2-1297, pp. 38–38v. More than 500 kilometers separated Perm and Kazan if one had to travel between the two cities.

16 *Ibid.*, p. 19.

17 *Ibid.*, pp. 40–43.

18 *Ibid.*, p. 19.

tained 61 double-sided pages—reports, letters, receipts, communications, summonses, inventories, decisions, and protocols of testimony.[19]

Kalinin's investigation of Zainulla Fazullin was concluded a month after his first report to the governor's office. The file of correspondence "on the investigation of the degree of political reliability" of Fazullin was 25 pages long, and some of its contents appeared to be devastating for the village leader. Constable Fatkullin's "declaration" (*zaiavlenie*) of January 30—the letter that had begun the case—not only charged Fazullin with calling the Stolypin law an "old wives' tale" and refusing to support villagers' requests to legalize their land allotments, but also with opening a "new school for the new teaching in 1909 or 1910" and, after it was shut down, with trying to get the "whole village to reopen the school."[20] This accusation referred to the controversial issue of revised educational methods advocated by Muslim modernizers. The "new method" was considered dangerous by many imperial administrators and threatening by Muslim conservatives (Khalid 1998, 156–183; Yemelianova 1999). Constable Fatkullin's missive thus struck a double blow at official sensitivities: Fazullin was both an opponent of the Stolypin law and an activist in the cause of Muslim reform.

Constable Fatkullin's communications revealed the source of his charges—a mullah, Makhamed-Riza-Zamaldinov, from Fazullin's village. Makhamed-Riza-Zamaldinov had written to him with the complaint that Fazullin was "again disturbing the whole village about re-opening the school" and that he, mullah Zamaldinov, was trying to stop this. Constable Fatkullin explained in his declaration that when he advised Zamaldinov to write to the gendarmes himself, the mullah had said he feared the consequences for himself and his co-villagers if the village leader found out about such an action. Earlier, Zamaldinov claimed, he had submitted a complaint to the land captain (*zemskii nachal'nik*)—the official in charge of administrative oversight of a region—but that the land captain had done nothing. "One can assume," Fatkullin continued, perhaps unwisely, "that he [the land captain] and village leader Fazullin are on friendly terms and the land captain is often a guest of this village

19 *Ibid.* The entire file is the original of the case, as filed at the Office of the Kazan Province Gendarmes. For Kalinin's order to open the inquiry, see pp. 36–36v.

20 *Ibid.*, pp. 33, 38–38v.

leader." Fatkullin concluded his declaration with names of villagers who could confirm Fazullin's refusal to assist those who wanted to claim title to their land allotments, and noted that the letter from mullah Zamaldinov was in his possession.[21]

It was these inflammatory charges that sent Colonel Kalinin, his assistants from the gendarmes, and police officers of various ranks into a flurry of investigative activity. This included the dispatch of Sergeant Shafranov to the village on February 14, the recording of testimony from villagers, a deposition from Fazullin signed by Colonel Kalinin, interim reports from the precinct police chief, the county sheriff, and Kalinin's assistant Captain Kirsanov, and multiple communications among the local police, provincial gendarmes, and the governor's office. The "secret" case against village leader Fazullin, who turned out to be a "self-taught", 55-year-old Muslim with no prior judicial record, was concluded when Captain Kirsanov completed his investigation a month after it had begun. Colonel Kalinin submitted a 25-page report on the case, with his conclusions and recommendations, to the governor's office on April 21, 1912.[22]

Colonel Kalinin based his decision on the Fazullin case on six points. First, it was true that ten peasants had accused Fazullin of opposing the application of the law of June 14, 1910, but one of these witnesses, Abdul Nafiz Khabirov, bore "spite" (*zloba*) against Fazullin "because of a [his, Khabirov's] poor fulfillment of [Fazullin's] orders as village leader." Second, the initial witnesses had brought a false accusation. Support for this conclusion was Fazullin's provision of a copy of a decision of the Bol'she-Toiabinskii township court about a property that had already been conveyed into individual possession on April 30, 1909. With this document Fazullin demonstrated that he had overseen property transfers under the first round of Stolypin decrees. Third, after Fazullin had asked the authorities to question more witnesses, all these new witnesses testified in his favor.[23] Fourth, Captain's Kirsanov's report, based on "personal, completely reliable information," had evaluated the village leader's performance as follows:

21 *Ibid.*, pp. 38–38v.

22 *Ibid.*, pp. 5, 15, 18, 19, 22, 33–36v, 40–43; NART, 1–4-5207, pp. 2–4v.

23 *Ibid.*, p. 4.

Peasant Zainulla Fazullin, as village leader, is distinguished by an unusual level of fulfillment of his duties, is highly demanding of his co-villagers, such actions of his are not at all liked by part of the population of the village Aiuktergin.[24]

Fifth, the report from the Captain continued, "almost the whole of the population of the village Aiukutergin is divided into two parts, one is for the aforementioned Fazullin and the other is against him, therefore the latter presented their hostility under a political cover." Sixth, and finally, Fazullin had never appeared in any matters of the kind "entrusted" to Colonel Kalinin, and "there was no unfavorable information about him related to political matters."[25]

Based on this information, Kalinin asked the governor to agree to end this investigation of political reliability "with no consequences of any kind" for Fazullin. This request, drawn up on April 21, 1912, was acted upon promptly. In the name of the governor, the vice-governor replied to Kalinin on April 25 that, "in accord with your conclusion," the case was ended "with no consequences of any kind for the person in question."[26]

A number of characteristics of this case suggest a set of expectations about governance shared by Tatar peasants, a village mullah, a village leader, the gendarmes, and the governor's office. First, peasants who for one reason or another wanted to get their village boss into big trouble were able to attract the attention of authorities. Makhamed-Riza-Zamaldinov's relation to Abdul Nafiz Khabirov and the "half" of the village that had problems with Fazullin is not clear, but the villagers understood that charges such as opposition to the Stolypin rules expressed by a rural official would be taken seriously by their rulers and punished, or at least that was what they hoped. Mullah Zamaldinov had also appealed to what he imagined to be officials' sensitivity on the "new schooling" issue, but these charges fell out of sight in both Captain Kirsanov's and Colonel Kalinin's reports.[27] In any case, Fazullin's opponents knew how to make their accusations known: Makhamed-Riza-Zamaldinov brought

24 *Ibid.*, p. 4.

25 *Ibid.*, pp. 4–4v.

26 *Ibid.*, pp. 4v-5.

27 It is not clear why this happened. It is possible that both Kirsanov and Kalinin, or one of them, did not consider this matter worthy of attention or did not want to call attention to it.

his complaint to the "right" instance—a policeman (Shafigulla Fatkullin, also a Tatar, and possibly an acquaintance) in a distant city.[28]

Second, the police and administrative authorities acted quite rapidly in response to the complaint. As discussed above, the initial complaint was dated January 30; Colonel Kalinin at the Kazan office began inquiries on February 8; the formal investigation resulted in Kalinin's conclusion on April 21. The Vice Governor accepted the conclusion and ended the case with the appropriate communications three days after receiving Kalinin's final report. People involved directly in this matter received a response—disappointing for the denouncers, possibly satisfying for the village leader—from the state's authorities less than three months after the reception of the first complaint.[29]

Third, the various institutions of the administrative, policing, and legal systems cooperated with each other smoothly. Officials used established routines that followed accepted chains of command; correspondents employed forms of civility that reinforced this hierarchy and identified each person's place in the web of governance. The gendarmerie, the regular police, the governor, and the township courts were not closed off in separate spheres of authority, but worked efficiently together to produce outcomes for litigants. The proof of Fazullin's loyal behavior with regard to land registration was a township court document, along with the testimony, from the gendarmes, that there had been no reports of a "political" nature against him. Colonel Kalinin, and the governor or his representative, considered both kinds of testimonials in their decision.

Fourth, chains of "reliable" individuals who fulfilled their tasks were another crucial feature of this functionality. The police proceedings depended on a constable, a precinct police officer, a district chief of police, a captain in the gendarmes, and two heads of provincial gendarme offices, each reporting or responding to their superiors. Once Colonel Kalinin received the denunciations that opened the case from his colleague in the Perm provincial office of the gendarmes, he relied on his own assistant,

28 Villagers had the right to bring complaints against their leaders to the land captain, but as Makhamed-Riza-Zamaldinov explained, he feared that the village leader and the land captain were too close to each other. He wrote to a policeman in a distant city instead.

29 See the inventory of documents in Colonel Kalinin's report: NART, 199–2-1297, p. 19, and pp. 22, 20, 36–36v, 38–38v, 40–43; NART, 1–4-5207, pp. 1–5.

Captain Kirsanov, to carry out the investigation. In the end the case "for" Fazullin expressed the critical role that loyal servitors played in the system: Fazullin's "unusual level of fulfillment of his duties" was made part of his defense. This was the language of vertical relationships, of reports to superiors, of reliance on individuals who fulfilled their duties.

Fifth, we should note the various kinds of communications that played a part in the investigation. A communication to a policeman in the Perm city police, "investigations" (*razvedki*) from the constable of Tetiushi County and from unnamed members of the Kazan Provincial Gendarmes began the case. The follow-up investigation carried out by Captain Kirsanov involved interviews with witnesses, an official copy of a court decision, evidence— negative—that Fazullin did not have a police record and was not under political suspicion, and finally the Captain's "completely reliable information" about Fazullin's exemplary service. Both documents and oral testimony counted, as did a superior's written testimony to an inferior's reliable service.

These communications suggest the interconnectedness that made governance through legal channels possible, efficient, and available to subjects. Those who addressed their governors to seek retribution against a local boss, the boss himself, and all the officials in the ensuing case appear to play by rules familiar to all—rules that set a premium on witnesses' testimony to the authorities, legal documentation, and reliable performance of duties. The idea that loyal service required enforcing the law was shared widely, even by the denouncers.

Villagers against the Law?

A century's worth of historical investigation about the significance of the Stolypin regulations—whether they were in peasants' interests or not, how many peasants accessed the law and why, the actual and potential consequences of the reform—has not been able to clarify the effect of the law at the time.[30] Administrative and legal records from the period in Kazan

30 Recent and divergent views can be found in Pallot (1999), Williams (2006), and Gaudin (2007, 168–296).

province do make one thing clear—peasants knew about the law, and they knew that denouncing a law was a criminal action that could be punished by the authorities. In the Fazullin case, peasants who had a gripe against their village leader fabricated the charge that he had rejected the law. But this sword could cut two ways.

In February 1912, just before he opened the Fazullin investigation, Colonel Kalinin had been dragged into another accusation of peasant agitation against the Stolypin law. The case involved a Chuvash village, and this time it was a village official—its appointed "delegate for land affairs"—who denounced his co-villagers for opposing his efforts to "put into effect the Land Reform."[31]

On February 16, 1912, Mikhail Petrov, the "peasant delegate of the Imbiurt rural society"[32] produced an elegantly penned petition to "The Honorable Chief of Police of Cheboksary County." Petrov wrote that he had been called to a meeting of the rural assembly of Imbiurt village on February 13, and that there, although he had been the delegate for land matters of this village society for twelve years, the peasants had "demanded that I could not appear in any institution for land conversion matters, and demanded [...] the delegation document back from me, and beat me up, threatening to disfigure me."[33]

Petrov went on to describe this incident in ways that were sure to push buttons with the authorities. According to his account, the villagers were obstructing the enactment of the Land Reform. Furthermore, he asserted:

> Such threats are not isolated events and not only in regard to me but also to others even a little inclined toward the implementation of the Land Reform [...]. In recent dark times, the accused were in communication with political leaders [who] allowed themselves to spread various sermons, [...] and now they are again starting to display their political activity (maybe known to the township administration).[34]

31 NART, 1–4-5190, p. 6.

32 A "rural society" (*sel'skoe obshchestvo*) was the smallest administrative unit in the provinces. All peasants in post-emancipation Russia were members of a rural society that controlled common economic resources and performed many tasks of local administration (Burbank 2004, 3–4).

33 NART, 1–4-5190, p. 17.

34 *Ibid.*

Petrov also appears to have communicated his complaint to the administrative leader (*volostnoi starshina*) of the township in which Imbiurt village was located. Two days later, on February 18, the township leader wrote to his superior, the Cheboksary County Chief of Police, that

> it has come to my knowledge that peasants in Imbiurt village have recently been holding almost daily assemblies, at which they discuss not allowing their co-villagers who want to convert their land allotments into personal property to convert, and in general [not allowing] conversion to the new land usage.[35]

The township leader reported that he "personally" had been in the village with "two local police guards" on February 16 to follow up on this information. His investigations showed that the villagers really had been holding assemblies, and that they "among other things considered the question of expelling from their rural society their co-member Mikhail Petrov, who is the delegate of the society for land affairs and who now it seems is forcing his co-villagers into conversion and in general into going over to the new land usage." However, the township leader continued, the village leader had told him that the "assembly was gathered to collect tax arrears."[36] With his report of multiple meetings in a village possibly concerning the Land Reform, the township chief also sounded the alarm of opposition to the law.

The county chief of police sent this information to both the Kazan Provincial Gendarmes and to the governor's office on February 21.[37] He reported that he had set up "secret observations" of the Imbiurt village society to elucidate the matter, and that he would inform his superior immediately if anything "of importance" on the matter emerged. By February 27, the governor's office was in communication, by letter, with Colonel Kalinin, asking for information about the gendarmes' investigation of the matter. In the correspondence, the case took on the following worrisome label: "on the movement, arising among the peasants of Imbiurt village, Cheboksary County, directed against the implementation of the law of June 14, 1910."[38]

---

35 *Ibid.*, pp. 2–2v.

36 *Ibid.*

37 *Ibid.*, p. 1.

38 *Ibid.*, p. 3.

This series of official reports and inquiries shows that an educated peasant, Mikhail Petrov, was able to catch the attention of township, county, and provincial level authorities by making a complaint about the "political activity" of peasants who were causing him problems. Whatever had happened at the meeting of the rural assembly on February 12, 1912, had turned—in official documents—into a "movement" against the law of June 14, 1910.

Colonel Kalinin replied to the governor's office with caution. Writing back on March 1, Kalinin reported that he had received the county police chief's report, that "secret" investigations were underway, and that the police chief had asked for approval to carry out the investigation in the "ordinary" way—i.e., by the local police, not the gendarmes. The chief of the provincial gendarmes noted that if what had been reported were confirmed, he would use the procedures of the security police to look into the "political reliability" of people under suspicion. He informed the governor's office that he would write back when he had more information.[39] The governor's office agreed with the county police chief and Colonel Kalinin about conducting this investigation in the "ordinary" way. Instructions, themselves secret, were sent to both the county police chief and to Colonel Kalinin on March 5. These declared that the regular police could carry out the process.[40]

Following these instructions, the local police carried out an investigation of the villagers on the basis of the 1881 law on state security.[41] The results were fourteen separate protocols of depositions taken in the village in addition to a legal "decision" purportedly made by the village assembly. Altogether, 44 pages of evidence were bound into a volume, sealed with wax, stamped by the county police chief, and forwarded to Kalinin for his recommendation.[42] The depositions taken by the local constable, Rumiantsev, on March 13 and 14, 1912, offer a goldmine of evidence for historians on villagers and their way of life. They also reveal that the vil-

39 *Ibid.*, pp. 4–4v.

40 *Ibid.*, pp. 5–6.

41 These regulations, issued in the "Regulation on Measures for the Securing of State Order and Social Peace" (*Polozheniia o merakh k okhraneniiu Gosudarstvennogo poriadka i obshchestvennogo spokoistviia*) in 1889, have been regarded as a fundament of the Russian police state by some historians (Pipes 1974, 305–318; Daly 1998 and 2004).

42 NART, 1-4-5190, pp. 11–58.

lagers of Imbiurt were dealing with issues much more immediate and less "political" than Mikhail Petrov had led the authorities to expect.

All the villagers who testified were Chuvash.[43] At least four of them testified in Chuvash; their words were recorded in Russian on the forms, labeled "protocol for the deposition of a witness," provided by the constable.[44] The village leader (*sel'skii starosta*) was 48 years old, Orthodox by religion as were his co-villagers, a peasant by estate, employed in both agriculture and trade, and illiterate.[45] Only one witness was Russian—a peasant from another village, who was employed as the assistant to the township leader. He testified that there was indeed an issue of owed taxes for the village of Imbiurt.[46]

The protocols revealed that the village had indeed been outraged by Petrov but not over the Stolypin rules. All villagers denied speaking against the Land Reform. They were angry because Petrov had drawn up a document assigning an allotment of the village's land to a widow, Anastasia Martynova, originally from Imbiurt. This land would be held according to the new regulations "in personal property." What bothered the villagers was not this kind of land holding, but the allotment of land to Martynova from their village's common fund. They insisted that Martynova should get land from her husband's village, not her father's.[47]

Both Petrov and Martynova provided depositions to the investigator. Mikhail Petrov, 39 years old, Chuvash like the rest, had lived all his life in the village and was a peasant by occupation. His four pages of testimony corresponded to his complaint: the village leader had called him to the assembly on February 13, and there he had been beaten up for having "attached" (*ukrepil*) the land parcel in question. (This is the term for giving a peasant formal title to a parcel of land.)[48]

Anastasiia Martynova's testimony was more ambiguous. She was registered as a peasant from another village, in a different county; she was unclear about her date of birth, but indicated that she was born in the

43 The Chuvash are a Turkic ethnic group of Siberian origin who moved into the Volga region in the seventh century CE.

44 NART, 1–4-5190, pp. 30–55v.

45 *Ibid.*, pp. 41, 54.

46 *Ibid.*, pp. 29, 42.

47 *Ibid.*, pp. 30–55v.

48 *Ibid.*, pp. 30–31.

village of Opner, adjacent to Imbiurt. She, like most but not all of the testifiers, had never appeared at a court. She testified that she had begun a case for the "title to land in personal property" (again, this was a formula in the Stolypin regulations) at Cheboksary County assembly. For this purpose she had given Petrov, as the representative of the Imbiurt-Toizin rural society, who was in the city of Cheboksary at the time, a document authorizing him to act for her (*doverennost'*). She claimed that Petrov was supposed to obtain another document, the official decision of the rural assembly where she had lived with her husband, from the county assembly in Cheboksary. She testified that "Petrov did not return [...] the authorization document to her and did not bring her the decision" she had expected. "She had heard that a co-villager had taken the authorization away from him. More she did not know."[49]

In their depositions, other villagers offered more information about Petrov and Martynova. Several villagers testified that Mikhail Petrov owed taxes; some mentioned that Martynova had been living in the home of her deceased father in the village of Opner whose lands were held jointly with Imbiurt.[50] It was clear from all concerned that Petrov's actions had been a subject of controversy at the meetings of the Imbiurt village assembly in February.[51]

In the course of the investigation, the document Petrov had drawn up made its appearance. It had been the object of considerable struggle at one of the village meetings. Dated January 25, 1912, the document purported to be a "decision" of the Imbiurt village assembly.[52] But the village leader, Grigorii Fedorov, said that Petrov had made up the "decision" without his or the village society's permission, and without the society's permission, he, as village leader, could not put a stamp on the document.[53] During the constable's examinations, villagers denied having signed this document. They also denied having beaten Petrov; in the Grigorii Fedorov's words, "the society only swore at him, but no one beat him."[54] The village leader affirmed that he had asked the township leader to expel Petrov from the

49 *Ibid.*, p. 32.

50 *Ibid.*, pp. 38–41, 44v-45v, 46v-47, 48v.

51 *Ibid.*, pp. 30–56.

52 *Ibid.*, p. 53–53v.

53 *Ibid.*, pp. 54v-56.

54 *Ibid.*, pp. 30–55v; for the village leader's words, see p. 55v.

village society.[55] The signatures on the purported decision turned out to be mostly in the same hand.[56]

Confronted with this evidence, the investigating constable attached the suspicious "decision" to his dossier, made his own report on the matter, and sent these on to his superior, the county police chief. The constable's report made the following points:

All the accused in this matter deny that they are guilty of agitation against the conversion of land holding [...]. [They] never said anything about this subject [...]. [Their concern instead was] the incorrect actions with respect to the village society of Petrov himself, who with the goal of allotting land to the peasant widow Anatasiia Martynova, of Tsivil'sk County, Anish-Khiri-Bagil'dinaia village, [...] drew up a public decision about giving her a plot of land from the common area, located in the common indivisible holding of the Opner and Imbiurt rural societies, which leads clearly to losses for the societies and was completely incorrect, since Martynova should have received land not from them but from the society of her husband. Therefore, having learned of Petrov's intentions and efforts, the village leader called him to the meeting for an explanation, where he [the village leader] took back the aforementioned decision [the physical document] on the Martynova matter, and gave it later to the township leader.

This explanation [...] was confirmed by both the existence of the decision [the document] [...] and by the fact that this decision upon examination was refuted by many of the people listed in it.[57]

Upon receiving this packet of information from his constable, the county chief of police felt that the investigation could be concluded. On April 6, he wrote the following statement at the end of Constable Rumiantsev's signed report: "taking into consideration the fact that the file on the dossier on this matter has been followed up with satisfactory fullness and that this process can be concluded, [I] therefore decide: to present the dossier to the Governor of Kazan Province."[58]

After this, the whole dossier made its way rapidly back up the chain of command. The county chief of police sent his report to the governor on April 7. A week later, the governor sent it over to Colonel Kalinin, asking

55 *Ibid.*, p. 56.

56 *Ibid.*, p. 53–53v.

57 *Ibid.*, pp. 38–40, 56–57v.

58 *Ibid.*, p. 57v.

him to return the correspondence with any information the gendarmes' office might have on the accused people and for his opinion about whether it was necessary to take administrative measures according to security regulations against the people in question. Two days later, Kalinin wrote back with his concluding decision on the case.[59]

This was a detailed document that relied extensively on the investigation accomplished by Kalinin's subordinates. Kalinin cited Petrov's and other testimony that Petrov had been sworn at and beaten. The colonel also repeated the evidence that explained this behavior. His report noted that the accused peasants "had nothing against the conversion of land and therefore never said anything about this"; that the real problem was caused by "incorrect actions in relation to the society by [...] Petrov"; that Petrov's incorrect actions consisted of his having "composed a civil decision on the allotment [...] of collectively held land [...] that was clearly to the detriment of the [rural] societies and was completely incorrect because Martynova should have received land not from them, but from the society of her husband"; and that "under investigation the decision [document] itself was refuted by many of them listed in it." Concluding his observations in the village's favor, Kalinin noted that the accused peasants "had never been involved in matters in the purview of the Kazan Provincial Gendarmes and about them there is no unfavorable information of a political sort."[60]

On these grounds, Kalinin asked the Governor to end the case but to set up "secret observation" over five peasants who had been named in the investigation, including the village leader. On April 20, 1912, the governor replied to Kalinin that he agreed with his conclusions, both about dropping the case and setting up secret observation. The same day, the governor's office wrote back to the county chief of police with the results of the case and asked him to set up the observation procedures and report back on this. On May 10 the county police chief informed the Governor that his instructions had been carried out. This concluded the case against the villagers of Imbiurt.[61]

59 *Ibid.*, pp. 7–9.
60 *Ibid.*, pp. 9–10v.
61 *Ibid.*, pp. 8–10v, 59–61.

Conclusion

Although in the first case described in this article peasants tried to undermine their village leader, and in the second an educated peasant accused a whole village of going against the law, the two dossiers display many commonalities. They allow us to address and tentatively answer questions about law and sovereignty in the late Russian Empire. Did subjects (Orthodox, Muslim, Russian, Tatar, others) share a political imaginary with those who staffed the administrative and legal institutions? What assumptions about sovereignty—about the state's power and role—were extended and communicated by these civil servants as they dealt with legal issues among the people they were assigned to govern? While we should not expect to find that either subjects or officials all thought alike or consistently about the state, let us look back at the values, practices, and expectations that seem to emerge from these cases.

We might note at the outset that ethnicity or religion do not figure as decisive or even relevant for the authorities (nor do they appear to be relevant to jurists at the circuit courts, as Kirmse argues in this volume). The form used for recording testimony of witnesses in Imbiurt village asked for "descent and nationality" (*proiskhozhdenie i narodnost'*); the more detailed questionnaires for accused people also asked for "religion" (*veroispovedanie*).[62] But higher authorities did not reference these recorded qualities in these cases of ostensible disloyalty. Nothing is made of the fact that Tatars and Chuvashs inhabited the two villages.

The enemies of village leader Fazullin themselves had inserted Islam into their accusations, but somehow this element gradually dropped out of the dossier. The accusation of Fazullin as a promoter of a controversial educational method for Muslim children was mentioned in the first letter of denunciation from Constable Fatkullin in Perm. This charge was subsequently amplified, but also muddied, by testimony given in Fazullin's village. In Sergeant Shafranov's report from Aiuktergin, peasants were said to have accused Fazullin of opening a *madrassah* without permission and warning peasants not to send their children to a "Russian-Tatar school" for fear that they would be converted to Orthodoxy. Fazullin's enemies also

62 *Ibid.*, pp. 30–55v.

testified that he had said, "I am Tsar and God."[63] Perhaps the overseeing officials concluded that these accusations were so contradictory that they did not merit inclusion in the concluding decisions on the case.

Note also that some mid-level officials were not Russian. The Fazullin case involves at least two Tatar officials—Fazullin himself, the *volost'* chief, and Shafigulla Fatkullin, a constable serving in the city police of Perm—not to mention mullah Makhamed-Riza-Zamaldinov. These individuals call our attention to the Empire's practice of incorporating native intermediaries into governance, where they worked with or reported to Russian officials on a regular basis.

Both cases show the density and rapidity with which the investigative machine operated. Communications in Kazan province in 1912 functioned very fast, especially when one considers the number of different officials and offices involved. Officials sent out reports and orders or began investigations within a day or two. The governor's office logged a communication from the county police chief of Cheboksary township only a day after the document had been compiled in the county seat.[64] The interrogations in the village of Imbiurt, 95 kilometers from Kazan, began eight days after the governor wrote his message handing the investigation over to the local police.[65] These communications show the tight, crosscutting ties between the rural administration, the local police, and the provincial gendarmes, all in communication with the governor's office. If this is "red tape," it worked impressively fast.

These cases also illustrate the extensive effort expended on responses to subjects' charges of unlawful behavior—multiple reporting to police, gendarme, and civilian officials, provision of information to parties in cases, summonses, stationery, postal services, travel to villages, recording and copying of evidence and communications, translation of testimony, and instances of "secret surveillance." The Russian Empire put enormous social resources into administration, communication, and maintenance of

63 NART, 199–2-1297, pp. 38, 38v, 40–43.

64 NART, 1–4-5190, p. 61.

65 The governor wrote to the county police chief on March 5, 1912: NART, 1–4-5190, p. 5; the inquiries in the village began on March 13: NART, 1–4-5190, pp. 30–40. For the distance between Imbiurt and Kazan, see *Spisok selenii Kazanskoi gubernii* (Kazan: Izdanie Kazanskoi Gubernskoi Zemskoi Upravy, 1908), 192.

order. These efforts were expended on many kinds of cases—civil suits, family matters—not just "political" ones.[66]

What were the values communicated along these spokes of governance? Both cases show, as do many others of this type, that all along the chain of command the administration responded to charges of denouncing the law or inciting people not to obey it. The charge that someone was speaking out against the law of June 14, 1910, was sure to raise suspicions about "political reliability" and was sufficient to start an investigation into the behavior of even very modest subjects.

Defenses used by accused people against charges of opposing a law included both denial and providing evidence of law-abiding behavior. Investigating authorities added their own evidence, consisting of a person's having no prior record with the authorities for political matters and evidence of loyal service.

Administrators thus seemed to demand of imperial subjects both support of the law and abstention from "political activity." The flip side of this coin was that officials had to deal with reported opposition to the law and other forbidden "political" activities. But when disloyal behavior was reported, officials did not accept denunciations at face value. Officials took the time to find out about their subjects' behavior, and exonerated them when they found charges of political violations to be unwarranted.

What were subjects' expectations of their rulers? What kind of political imaginary did they communicate in their interactions with the state? First, it would seem that the state and the law were an ordinary part of life—a given—for people in this region. It is hard to tell what the arrival of a constable to take down evidence over two days meant to the villagers of Imbiurt. Most testified that they had never been called to a court or to give evidence before. But all were familiar with the object in question—a legal "decision"—with what made such a document legitimate, and with its consequences for property matters and taxation. On the basis of their depositions, villagers managed to get their way against their more educated deputy who for some reason was trying to help a widow obtain a parcel of land. Earlier, they had seized the falsified document from Petrov's hands and turned it over to the authorities, demonstrating their understanding of

66 See Burbank (2004, 74–77, 166–181) on the processing of civil and criminal cases at township courts.

what kind of evidence counted. Much as reform-minded jurists disdained the police and supposedly backward rural officials, these intermediaries and their investigations were important to villagers who wanted to defend their interests.

Second, subjects used the legal system for their own ends, communicating in a language they expected officials to share. The law was a field of politics where people of different ranks intersected. The Imbiurt case shows how a peasant tried to use the language of obedience to the law in his attempt to punish villagers who had uncovered his own manipulation of a land transfer. The case against village leader Fazullin arose when his enemies accused him of obstructing the implementation of the Stolypin rules. In both matters, accusers expected authorities to respond to reports of "political activity"—of trying to open a "new method" school, or of communicating with "political leaders" who "spread various sermons."[67]

My discussion of cases from the "secret" tier of investigation and from the middle-level of legal administration may seem bizarre to some students of law. But if we can escape from westernized conventions of what law "is," we can look more inclusively at the ways that law worked. From the perspective of law users in the Russian Empire—from governors to peasants—the police tier was part of the legal system. Peasants could frame charges in ways that would guarantee an investigation of an enemy. An effective charge was that a village leader had said that the law of June 14, 1910, did not exist, that it was not the Tsar's. Peasants, lower level officials, and provincial authorities all used a naturalized language of loyalty to laws that emanated from the Emperor and defined the social order. Their communications across the web of intersecting administrative institutions enacted and enforced sovereignty based on legal rule.

67 NART, 199–2-1297, p. 38, and NART 1–4-5190, p. 17.

Works Cited

Agishev, N.M. and V.D. Bushen (eds.) (1912). *Materialy po obozreniiu gorskikh i narodnykh sudov kavkazkogo kraia.* St. Petersburg: Senatskaia tipografiia.

Baberowski, Jörg (2008). Repräsentationen politischer Macht im späten Zarenreich. In Jörg Baberowski, David Feest and Christoph Gumb (eds.) *Imperiale Herrschaft in der Provinz: Repräsentationen politischer Macht im späten Zarenreich.* Frankfurt: Campus.

Babich, Irina (1999). *Evoliutsiia pravovoi kul'tury adygov (1860–1990-e gody).* Moscow: Institut etnologii i antropologii, RAN.

Bobrovnikov, V.O. (2002). *Musul'mane severnogo kavkaz: Obychai, pravo, nasilie.* Moscow: Vostochnaia literatura.

Burbank, Jane (1995). Lenin and the Law in Revolutionary Russia. *Slavic Review,* 54, 1, 23–44.

Burbank, Jane (2004). *Russian Peasants Go to Court: Legal Culture in the Countryside, 1905–1917.* Bloomington: Indiana University Press.

Burbank, Jane (2006). An Imperial Rights Regime: Law and Citizenship in the Russian Empire. *Kritika: Explorations in Russian and Eurasian History,* 7, 3, 397–431.

Burbank, Jane and Cooper, Frederick (2009). "Nouvelles colonies" et "vieux empires". *Mille neuf cent,* 27, 13–35.

Burbank, Jane and Cooper, Frederick (2010). *Empires in World History: Power and the Politics of Difference.* Princeton: Princeton University Press.

Burbank, Jane and von Hagen, Mark (2007). Coming into the Territory: Uncertainty and Empire. In Jane Burbank, Mark von Hagen and Anatolyi Remnev (eds.) *Russian Empire: Space, People, Power, 1700–1930.* Bloomington: Indiana University Press.

Daly, Jonathan (1998). *Autocracy under Siege: Security Police and Opposition in Russia, 1866–1905.* DeKalb: Northern Illinois University Press.

Daly, Jonathan (2004). *The Watchful State: Security Police and Opposition in Russia, 1906–1917*. DeKalb: Northern Illinois University Press.

Gaudin, Corinne (2007). *Ruling Peasants: Village and State in Late Imperial Russia*. DeKalb: Northern Illinois University Press.

Jersild, Austin (2002). *Orientalism and Empire: North Caucasus Mountain People and the Georgian Frontier, 1845–1917*. Montreal and Kingston: McGill-Queen's University Press.

Khalid, Adeeb (1998). *The Politics of Muslim Cultural Reform: Jadidism in Central Asia*. Berkeley: University of California Press.

Macey, David A. J. (1998). "A Wager on History": The Stolypin Agrarian Reforms as Process. In Judith Pallot (ed.) *Transforming Peasants: Society, State and the Peasantry, 1861–1930*, 149–173. New York: St. Martin's Press.

Martin, Virginia (1997). Barimta: Nomadic Custom, Imperial Crime. In Daniel R. Brower and Edward J. Lazzerini (eds.) *Russia's Orient: Imperial Borderlands and Peoples, 1700–1917*. Bloomington: Indiana University Press.

Obzor Kazanskoi gubernii za 1913 god (1915). Kazan: Tipografiia Gubernskogo pravleniia.

Pallot, Judith (1999). *Land Reform in Russia, 1906–1917: Peasant Responses to Stolypin's Project of Rural Transformation*. Oxford: Clarendon Press.

Pipes, Richard (1974). *Russia under the Old Regime*. New York: Scribner's.

Schattenberg, Susanne (2008). *Die korrupte Provinz? Russische Beamte im 19. Jahrhundert*. Frankfurt and New York: Campus.

Tissier, Michel (2007). Malaise dans la culture juridique libérale en Russie après 1905: "pédagogie des libertés" et éducation au droit. *Cahiers du Monde russe*, 48, 2–3, 185–208.

Tiutriumov, I.M. (ed.) (1916) *Svod Zakonov Rossiiskoi Imperii*. St. Petersburg: Zakonovedenie.

Velychenko, Stephen (2000). Local Officialdom and National Movements in Imperial Russia: Administrative Shortcomings and Under-government. In John

Morison (ed.) *Ethnic and National Issues in Russian and East European History*. New York: St. Martin's Press.

Williams, Stephen F. (2006). *Liberal Reform in an Illiberal Regime: The Creation of Private Property in Russia, 1906–1915*. Stanford: Hoover Institution Press.

Yemelianova, Galina M. (1999). Volga Tatars, Russians and the Russian State at the Turn of the Nineteenth Century: Relationships and Perceptions. *The Slavonic and East European Review*, 77, 3, 448–484.

When People Go to Court

Law and Courts as Negotiating Tools: Marriage and Divorce in Republican China, 1912–1949

Xiaoqun Xu

In early twentieth century China, the final decade of the Qing dynasty (1901–1911) and the ensuing Republican era (1912–1949) were a period of constant legal-judicial reform during which Western laws and judicial practices (mainly the Continental Law tradition) were followed and promoted as a guideline and universalistic model for being "modern". The reform represented the unfinished transition from a "rule of law" understood as a means of governance and state control to a rule of law underpinned by the principles of equality before the law and judicial independence that was meant to protect the rights of individuals.

The new principles stood in sharp contrast to several key elements of Chinese legal culture: the emperor's position above the law (despite his moral obligation to be benevolent given his "Mandate of Heaven"); the legal superiority of families over individuals, family seniors over juniors, men over women, and upper classes over lower classes; the judicial powers exercised by administrative officials; and the presumption of guilt in criminal cases which facilitated torture and made legal defense inconceivable. As a result, the reform had to overcome enormous political, institutional, ideological, cultural, and social resistance. The reform-minded law-makers (and by extension, the reformed laws and courts) had to try and reconcile the universalistic model with an indigenous social-cultural environment inhospitable to it. To ensure the functionality of the reformed laws and judicial institutions, they allowed some variation and deviation from the model (Xu 2008). Civil justice in matters of marriage and divorce was an important area where the reform made significant progress but had multifaceted, and sometimes paradoxical, effects due to highly particular local conditions.

Research on civil justice in imperial (pre-1912) and Republican China (1912–1949) and on dispute resolution in marriage and divorce cases, in particular, has advanced substantially in the past twenty years (Bernhardt 1999; Liang 2007; Huang 2010). The present study therefore addresses the issue from a new angle: focusing on the Republican era, it highlights the agency of the litigant and the role of local courts and county magistrates (in regions where local courts had not been established). Drawing on archival sources and print documents, it explores the ways in which ordinary men and women used the law to their own advantage. This process was both facilitated and complicated by the state's ongoing legal reform during that period. The citizens' readiness to use the law and the courts for their legitimate private agendas contextualizes the complexity of this protracted reform process.

To set the historical backdrop, I start with a brief overview of the legal framework of marriage and divorce, with attention paid to Qing law, the Draft Civil Code of 1911 and its final incarnation in the Civil Code of 1929–30. This discussion illuminates the gradual transformation of legal opinion and written codes from inequality to equality between the sexes. The main focus is on the effects of the changing criminal and civil legislation on people's legal behavior, on court decisions in cases of marriage and divorce, and on the role of women in such matters. This focus helps to shed light on the interactions and tensions between a universalistic model and particular local practices. Rather than offering a statistical summary of a large number of cases, this chapter engages in close observations and detailed analyses of several typical cases. In this manner, it illustrates the motivations and strategies of litigants, on the one hand, and the intricacies of court practice, on the other. In so doing, it seeks to achieve a greater understanding of the local and gendered effects of changing Chinese legislation on marriage and divorce.

A Changing Legal Framework: Marriage and Divorce Law under the Qing Dynasty and the Republic of China

The legal framework for matters of marriage and divorce changed significantly from the Qing dynasty (1644–1911) to the Republic of China, and within the Republican era from 1912 to 1935. Since Qing law (known as *Da Qing Lü Li*—the "Great Qing Code and Sub-Statutes") contained punishments for offenses in both criminal and civil matters, one of the fundamental tasks of the legal-judicial reform that began in 1901 was to separate civil and criminal justice. While the new Civil Code was to cover marriage, divorce, property rights of widows, etc., the new Criminal Code was to deal with issues also bearing on marriage and divorce—rape, adultery, abduction and sale of women, desertion, etc. The evolution of the legal framework for these matters suggests that the state sought to revise the law that regulated the relationship between the sexes in accordance with changing moral standards. This sets the stage for the exploration of the ways in which male and female litigants fared in marital and familial disputes in the Republican era.

In accordance with the time-honored Confucian tradition, under Qing law marriage was arranged by parents or grandparents while the prospective bride and groom had no say in the matter. As A. Viola Smith of the Joint Committee of Shanghai Women's Organizations explained in 1930, in the eyes of Western observers marriage in China was "a civil contract not between the man and woman but between the heads of the two families, reckoned according to the rule of agnatic succession." She continued:

> [It] requires no registration or celebration by any public authority civil or religious. The ordinary requirements to constitute a valid marriage are:
>
> 1. Employment of a go-between who settles verbally the contract between the two families.
> 2. Exchanging red cards giving the date of birth to each of the couple and usually drawing up a formal contract of betrothal.
> 3. Sending and receiving wedding presents.
>
> These three constitute a formal betrothal which carries legal consequences.
>
> 4. Bringing home the bride with red chair and music.
> 5. Obesiance [*sic*] by the pair to the bride-groom's parents, and kneeling to the ancestral tablets.

> Each of these steps corresponds in some measure to the requirements of Western marriage law. Go-betweens are witnesses, read cards are evidence of identity; the red chair and music give publicity; and obesiance [*sic*] is the religious ceremony.[1]

This was by and large an accurate description of Chinese marriage practice under Qing law and in Chinese tradition, and remains a good summary of this practice even if there were numerous local variations.[2] As for divorce, under Qing law the wife could not initiate one unless the husband had been missing for more than three years. The husband, by contrast, could divorce his wife for seven reasons (bearing him no son, adultery, disrespect towards his parents, loquacity, theft, jealousy, and incurable disease) unless the following conditions applied: the wife had mourned her parents-in-law for three years, the husband had turned from poor to rich during the marriage, or the wife had no relatives to return to. Although divorce by mutual consent was possible, it was legally guaranteed that a wife could not decide unilaterally to leave a "bad" marriage (for a summary, see Bernhardt 1994).[3] In short, under Qing law women had little choice in matters of marriage and divorce.

After a Draft Criminal Code had been completed in 1907 as part of the legal reform, law-makers began to focus on a Draft Civil Code. By October 1911, three books of the Civil Code were completed and two more were under revision, but neither Code was enacted before the fall of the Qing dynasty.[4] Whereas the Draft Criminal Code was quickly adopted by the newly-established Republic as the Provisional New Criminal Code (*zhanxing xin xinglü*) in March 1912, the status of the Draft Civil Code was ambiguous: while criminal and civil justice were separated in the course of the reform process, the Code was not officially enacted but rather unoffi-

1 *The North China Herald*, December 9, 1930, 359.

2 In its historical context, the comment also reflected an effort on the part of some Western women—at least those of the International Council of Women—to understand and rationalize Chinese marriage practices in terms of Western ones.

3 The relevant statutes are in the *Da Qing Lü Li*, Juan 6, "Marriage".

4 The Revolution broke out in October 1911 and the last Qing emperor abdicated in February 1912.

cially applied in court for civil litigations, often along with interpretations offered by the Supreme Court.[5]

The ambiguity of the civil law may be seen in a case as late as 1923. A nineteen-year-old Chinese woman sued for divorce at the Mixed Court of the International Settlement in Shanghai. She cited ill-treatment, non-support, and desertion as grounds for divorce. The husband's lawyer argued that "Chinese civil law has nine clauses for divorce", and the wife's complaints were not among them. In other words, the lawyer was invoking the Draft Civil Code of 1911, specifically the book on kinship that contained these nine clauses. To counter this argument, the wife's lawyer argued that the Draft Civil Code had not been promulgated by any lawful governing body in China and could not be enforced in the Mixed Court. The Chinese magistrate Yui Ying-yong ruled, however, that "the decisions of the Supreme Court hold. Though the laws have not been promulgated, the decisions of the Supreme Court are similar to them, as in this case."[6] As we shall see, while the Draft Civil Code was not applied by all legal institutions in the country on a regular basis, it is true that this Code was used at least in formal courts and even by some county magistrates performing judicial functions.

Robert T. Bryan, Jr. (1855–1936), who was a member of the American Southern Baptist Mission and the founder of Shanghai Baptist College (*Hujiang Daxue* in Chinese), explained China's divorce law in an article published in 1919:

> The Chinese [Civil] Provisional Code has never been authoritatively promulgated but nevertheless most of its sections are enforced by native courts, especially those regarding divorce. It may be correctly said that the present divorce law of China as laid down in Sections 1359–1369 is the law of the land.

Comparing it with American and British laws, Bryan found that Chinese law made divorce easy.

5 The statement in my earlier study that the "General Principles", "Debts", and "Rights to Things" of the Draft Civil Code were enacted shortly after the founding of the Republic is inaccurate if largely correct (Xu 2008, 40). In 1914 the Republican government officially applied only the sections on jurisdictions in Book I, "General Principles" (Zhang Jinfan 2004, 501–502).

6 *North China Herald*, October 27, 1923, 279.

The courts of America and England hold that marriage is a civil contract yet it cannot be dissolved by the consent of both parties; while on the other hand the Chinese law-makers have followed this theory of a marriage being a civil contract to its logical conclusion and said that because it is a civil contract entered into by the consent of both parties, it may be dissolved by the parties who made it. The reason for this, as stated in a note to Article 1359 of the Chinese Civil Provisional Code, is that when a married couple cannot live happily together they should not be compelled to go into a court of law to obtain a divorce and thereby have their family trouble published.

Even under Qing law, the dissolution of marriage by mutual consent was permitted; the Draft Civil Code differed from Qing law in that it allowed the wife to initiate divorce. It is important to bear in mind when looking at various cases later in this study that these provisions in the Draft Civil Code were intended to apply to marriage and divorce cases prior to the official promulgation of the Civil Code of 1929–1930.

After the Guomindang (Nationalist Party) had come to power in 1927, a revised Criminal Code was passed in 1928. Then the late Qing Draft Civil Code, after further revision, was promulgated in 1929–1930 (Books IV and V, on "Kinship" and "Inheritance", which covered marriage and divorce, were unveiled in 1930). For the first time, the Civil Code explicitly stated that both marriage and divorce were acts of free choice by men and women. A man of eighteen and a woman of sixteen could get married of their own accord (Articles 972 and 980), without interference from parents or anyone else. Following long-standing traditions, moreover, the law did not require any registration of marriage with a government office or court. For official marriage, it only required a public ceremony with at least two witnesses (Article 982). As for divorce, a mutual agreement between husband and wife could dissolve marriage (Article 1049). Most importantly, either the husband or the wife could sue for divorce by invoking one of the following ten clauses (instead of the nine clauses of the Draft Civil Code): 1) bigamy; 2) adultery; 3) mistreatment by the spouse; 4) mistreatment of or by parents-in-law; 5) abandonment with ill-intent; 6) attempted murder; 7) having an incurable disease; 8) having a serious incurable mental illness; 9) disappearance for more than three years; 10) imprisonment of more than three years or imprisonment for disgraceful offenses (Article 1052). Some of the causes for divorce, however, were qualified by a statute of limitation: the first and second clauses—bigamy and adultery—were valid for divorce within six months of the litigant's awareness of the fact or within two years of the act itself (Article 1053). The sixth and tenth causes—attempted murder and imprisonment—were valid within one year after the litigant's awareness of the fact or within five years of the criminal act itself (Article 1054).

The historian Philip Huang (2001) has analyzed the ideological constructions underlying Qing law and the Republican Civil Code concerning marriage, divorce, and illicit sex. Qing law offered women both protection and punishment while expecting women to be virtuous and therefore have limited or passive agency in matters of illicit sex, abduction for sale, etc (thus, they could only resist or consent to acts of men). In contrast, Republican law-makers assumed that women were of free will and autonomy, and were therefore responsible for their own actions. Accordingly, while the law gave women greater freedom in marriage and divorce, it provided neither protection nor punishment with regard to illicit sex, abduction, and sale, as Qing law had done. One important point Huang makes is that social reality often departed from the ideological constructions of both Qing and Republican law-makers and therefore the legal frameworks in both periods had paradoxical consequences in women's lives. Reinforcing this insight, this study provides further evidence of how and why the universalistic model of legal modernization necessarily had local variations.

While Republican law-makers were hesitant to do away with inequality between the sexes, the Nationalist Party's official ideology supported such equality, thus encouraging educated women to demand equality in matters of marriage and divorce (including the property rights of widows). After the enactment of Books IV and V of the Civil Code in 1930, the issue of inequality between the sexes (and an inconsistency between the Criminal and Civil Codes) moved center-stage. The Criminal Code prescribed imprisonment in cases of adultery for married women, but not for married men (Article 256). Neither the Criminal Code nor the Civil Code, moreover, mentioned concubinage, which could arguably be considered adultery by married men.

The omission of concubinage from the Civil and Criminal Codes also contributed to legal ambiguity in other respects. In 1913, for example, a Chinese man turned to the Mixed Court of the International Settlement in Shanghai to claim the return of his concubine, who had fled from him. The concubine's lawyer argued that the desertion was due to ill-treatment and that "concubine" was no longer a legal status in China. Following the advice of his Chinese colleague, the British Assessor ruled in favor of the plaintiff and ordered the return of the concubine on the grounds that the Code had not explicitly abolished this long-standing social practice. In its editorial, the *North China Herald* commented on the case in the following manner: "In giving his decision in accordance with both the old Code, which prohibits desertion, and the new Code, which makes no mention of punishment, the Assessor would appear to be fully justified by Chinese standards both of law and equity."[7]

While the debate on whether concubinage should be abolished continued in the print media, the question of adultery in the Criminal Code led to a vigorous campaign by educated Chinese women to agitate and lobby for the revision of Article 256.[8] In 1931, when the National Congress (*guomin dahui*) convened in Nanjing, women delegates put forward eleven proposals to improve the dignity of women, including the issue of Article 256. The Legislative Council (*lifa yuan*) was asked to take up the matter and, following a lengthy process of revision, adultery was criminalized for both men and women.

The road to this change, however, was difficult. The second reading of the revised Criminal Code in the Legislative Council on October 25, 1934, with female representatives in attendance, caused heated debate, and Article 256 was removed from the Code altogether: adultery was to be settled according to the Civil Code (allowing either party of a married couple to sue for divorce in cases in which the other party had committed adultery). "It is said that the presence of the women representatives during the discussion made their brothers somewhat self-conscious and it embarrassed them to insist upon the old Article 256." Yet, at the third reading of the Criminal Code on October 31, 1934, the old article, in slightly amended form and now called Article 239, was re-instated.

7 *North China Herald*, June 14, 1913, 762.

8 The following narrative about this campaign is based on Kuo (1935, 391, 409); Mu (1935, 449–450); and Cheng (2002, 74–83). For more details, also see Tran (2009, 191–223).

In response to this reversal of their precious gain, women's organizations in Nanjing, Shanghai, and Beijing held mass meetings and passed resolutions to fight for their cause to the end. Besides petitioning the Legislative Council, they resorted to what was called "feminine diplomacy"—visiting about 60 members of the Council, approaching wives of council members to influence their husbands, and recruiting some wives and daughters of council members into women's special committees on the issue. In their public campaign they invoked Article 6 of the Provisional Constitution—"The citizens of the Republic of China, irrespective of sex, race, religion and class, are all equal before the law."—and Article 12 of the "Domestic Policies of the Guomindang"—"Women shall have the right of property inheritance; laws of gender equality shall be promulgated with promptness; and marriage law shall be rooted in the principle of absolute freedom of marriage and divorce, etc." They demanded the removal of Article 239 by citing Article 84 of the Provisional Constitution: "All laws contrary to the Constitution are null and void." As a result of the campaign, the Legislative Council finally bowed to the demands of the women activists. The revised Criminal Code of 1935 recognized adultery as an offense for both men and women.

The story of this debate illustrates the importance of women's activism in cities such as Nanjing, Shanghai, and Beijing. The activism was reflected in a higher percentage of women among litigants who initiated divorce lawsuits in these and other cities (Bernhardt 1994, 195–197). This fact also puts two related points into context: first, there were complaints from Chinese men about women getting a divorce too easily;[9] and second, women from different social and geographical backgrounds (urban versus rural) faced different kinds of pressure. In cities, lower-class women fared much worse than middle-class women in their ability to make choices in marriage and divorce when they were sold or pawned by their husbands or fathers.[10] In both urban and rural areas, however, widows faced far more

9 See, for example, "Matrimonial Sanctity in China," *China Weekly Review*, December 13, 1930, 58 (originally published in the *China Critics* on November 13, 1930); Li (1935, 264–265); "Divorce Is Popular and Marriage a 'Child's Play' in Modern China," *China Weekly Review*, August 22, 1935, 463–464; Song (1935, 316–317).

10 As late as 1935 Beijing rickshaw coolie and men of similar social-economic status would pawn their wives to get loans from pawnshops. See *North China Herald*, July 31, 1935, 175.

pressure to remarry against their will in well-to-do families than in poorer families because their in-laws wanted to take over the property to which widows were entitled under the law.

Though significant in principle, the effects of the new Article 239 of the Criminal Code on marriage and divorce were limited in practice. First of all, whether having a concubine constituted adultery was not clearly settled by the law and was left to be interpreted by the court. Indeed, by 1932 the Judicial Council of the National Government issued a legal opinion, stating that "after the enactment of Book IV on Kinship of the Civil Code, taking a concubine could not be regulated by contract; if such an act occurs, it must be treated as adultery and can serve as a ground for divorce."[11] This would be used in court rulings about divorce. Yet, if a wife wanted a divorce because her husband had a concubine, she was constrained in her action by the aforementioned statute of limitation. The relevant laws—Book IV of the Civil Code, effective from May 5, 1931, and the revised Criminal Code, effective from July 1, 1935—were not retroactive, and neither was Article 9 of the Enforcement Law of the Criminal Code that explicitly forbade the application of Article 239 to men who had taken concubines before the enactment of the Criminal Code.[12] As a Western observer commented in 1945, "[i]n practice therefore, if the wife does not object, concubinage can continue in modern China. [...] In addition to the very liberal treatment concubinage received in the laws, the Supreme Court has invariably recognized concubinage as a system established by old custom and has never curtailed the concubine's rights on the ground that in principle the Criminal as well as the Civil Code condemn the institution."[13] This chapter also shows that Article 239 was rarely, if ever, invoked in court in cases in which a husband had taken a concubine.

That law-makers in Republican China took the force of social practices and customs seriously was also evident elsewhere. Following Articles 1 and 2 of the Civil Code, courts could rule in accordance with local "customs" in civil cases not covered by the Code (if these "customs" were not in violation of "public order" and "good" social mores). In fact, from

11 Wu Jingxiong and Guo Wei, *Zhonghua Minguo Liufa Liyou Panjie Huibian* (a collection of reasoning and interpretations of the six laws of the Republic of China), vol. 2, 525, quoted in Cheng (2002, 80).

12 Cheng (2002, 80).

13 Levi (1945, 272).

1918 to 1926 the Ministry of Justice sponsored ethnographic investigations of local customs in order to widen its repertoire for the resolution of civil disputes in the country. The investigations were designed to provide guidelines for courts in civil cases and to help future revisions of the Civil Code.[14] Crucially, these investigations concentrated on ethnic minority regions, for legal pluralism was a long-standing element of Chinese legal history. In the Qing dynasty and before, ethnic and religious minorities, such as Mongols, Muslims, and Manchu Bannermen, and even groups of foreign settlers in China, were, in varying degrees, allowed to use their own customs, penal practices, and legal codes (if available) in criminal and civil cases.[15] In the Republican era this legal pluralism continued, despite the efforts of the reform period to unify and standardize the legal codes and court system in the country. Certain regions with substantial shares of ethnic minorities, such as the Miao people in Guizhou Province, were not under the jurisdiction of the regular court system, especially in civil law.[16]

County Magistrates and Marriage/Divorce Cases in the 1920s

Since the Qing Draft Civil Code was not officially enacted before 1929–1930, some courts and judicial bodies applied it while others did not, especially in counties where formal courts did not exist and county magistrates performed judicial functions. These magistrates often followed Qing law and local customs in settling marriage and divorce cases, either because they were unaware of the Draft Civil Code and/or were swayed by local elites.[17] Yet this was not the only way in which a local court or magistrate could handle marriage and divorce cases in the Republican era. A few cases from the 1920s may help to illustrate the spectrum of approaches by county magistrates.

14 See Bourgon (2002) for a useful discussion of the lesser role of custom in Chinese legal practices in the Qing dynasty in comparison with European customary law.

15 Pär Cassel (2003) has argued that this legal pluralism provided the antecedent to extraterritoriality given to Westerners after the Opium War.

16 The issue deserves further study but is outside the scope of this essay.

17 See, for example, Xu (2008, 224–227).

A female missionary reported a distressing case from Jing County (Kingshien), Anhui Province. Mrs. Du had been married for three years when her husband died. She then lived with her parents-in-law, and a brother-in-law and his wife, for fourteen years. After her father-in-law died in 1922, her brother-in-law, Du Yong-hsin, fabricated a "declaration of repentance" (in which the woman confessed alleged misbehavior) and forced Mrs. Du to put her fingerprint on it. This deprived her (and her adopted son) of her share of the family estate amounting to 1,000 mu of farmland [1 mu = 1 sixth of an acre]. She was carried away from their home by force and sold to a man called Wu. When she refused to stay there, she was locked up in the house. Yet, as Mrs. Du's late husband had been a church member, the missionary learned of the event and helped to rescue Mrs. Du from Wu's home. Du Yong-hsin, however, immediately filed a lawsuit to have her returned to Wu and openly bragged that he had the money to bribe the magistrate to win the case. At the hearing of the case, the magistrate intimidated witnesses (Mrs. Du's adopted son and his brother) who testified in her favor and dismissed the issue of the fabricated document as irrelevant. The point of argument was whether Mrs. Du had willingly married Wu, which she denied. At the time of the missionary's account, the case was not over yet, but she feared that Du Yong-hsin, with his money, an opium-smoking lawyer and a corrupt magistrate, would eventually win.[18]

This case was typical in that the in-laws tried to deprive a widow of her property by forcing her to remarry. Under Qing law, a widow was protected from forced remarriage for the sake of "widow chastity," and under the Draft Civil Code, a widow's rights to her property in the family were affirmed. Du Yong-hsin had to resort to illegal means to force her out of the family by selling her and fabricating a false document about her alleged misbehavior. Yet, he still needed the judicial power of the county magistrate to legitimize his actions, and he was ready to do so because this particular magistrate could be bribed. That is to say, under the law Mrs. Du should have prevailed, but local power relations may have hindered her.

A case from Songjiang County, Jiangsu Province, in 1922 may offer a counterbalance to the above example. It shows that in some cases the late

18 *North China Herald*, August 12, 1922, 450.

Qing Draft Civil Code, along with the Supreme Court's interpretations, was still applied in the county judicial process in cases of marriage and divorce. Wang Xirong's daughter Wang Shuzhen, 21, had been engaged to marry Shen Haisheng, 19. On February 16, 1922, Wang Shuzhen was walking home from seeing her godfather and passing through a quiet area, when Shen Haisheng, who had gathered a few other men, took her by force to his home and "consummated the marriage" (*wanhun*). Wang Shuzhen had heard that Shen had a debilitating disease, and on that day Shen happened to have a swollen face due to an illness, which Wang took as proof of the rumored disease. After returning home and informing her father of what she believed to be the truth, father and daughter filed for her divorce at the county government office. While the magistrate was issuing summons for the case, Shen Haisheng filed a criminal lawsuit charging that his wife Wang Shuzhen had an adulterous affair and that his father-in-law Wang Xirong had agreed to sell his daughter as a concubine for 400 yuan. Wang Xirong counter-charged that Shen Haisheng was making false accusations. At the criminal trial, the magistrate found Shen guilty of making false accusations and punished him accordingly.[19] Notably, Shen's act of "consummating the marriage" by force was not considered criminal by either the magistrate or Wang Shuzhen and her father. The latter only wanted to dissolve the marriage.

In a separate civil lawsuit, Wang Shuzhen insisted on her request for divorce because Shen had a disease previously unknown to her and because he committed moral betrayal (*yijue*) by making a false accusation. Based on the facts and the Draft Civil Code, the magistrate argued and ruled as follows: under the law, a spouse who suffers from serious insult from the other spouse should be allowed to divorce. Falsely accusing one's wife of adultery was a serious insult, and the wife should be allowed to have a divorce. Serious insult to the wife's parents should also be a reason for divorce. Citing various Supreme Court decisions in appeals cases as precedents, the magistrate wrote: "The original reasoning that the defendant had a debilitating disease cannot be accepted as sufficient cause

19 The documents from the civil case mention this fact but do not specify the punishment. The Provisional New Criminal Law of 1912 did not contain any articles on false accusations as Qing law had done, but it included an article on "openly insulting another person by citing facts, whether they are true or not," (Article 360) and the offender was to be fined or imprisoned.

for divorce if it is not true. But the defendant's falsely accusing his wife, the plaintiff Wang Shuzhen, of adultery, and his father-in-law, the plaintiff Wang Xirong, of selling his daughter, are serious insults and moral betrayal, which meet the conditions for divorce, and the above-said precedents apply. Wang Shuzhen is therefore permitted to be divorced from Shen Haisheng, and the defendant Shen Haisheng has to pay the litigation fee."[20]

The term *yijue* that both Wang Shuzhen and the magistrate cited was taken from Qing law; yet Articles 1359–1369 of the Draft Civil Code also provided causes for divorce. One such cause was that "one of the parties [was] ill-treated or highly insulted by the other thereby making it intolerable for them to live together" (Bryan 1919, 515–517).[21] In the aforementioned case, the Wang family and the magistrate relied on both Qing legal tradition and Republican civil law to pursue and decide on a lawsuit for divorce.[22] And Shen Haisheng's "defense by offense," that is, his filing of a criminal lawsuit to counter Wang's civil lawsuit, was a familiar litigation strategy in local society (see also below). In this instance, however, the strategy backfired—the false accusation became the cause for the magistrate to grant divorce to Shen's wife.

Application of the Criminal Code in Adultery Cases, 1930s–1940s

The legal framework created by the Civil Code in 1929–30 and the revised Criminal Code in 1935 was more favorable to women in matters of marriage and divorce than any predecessor. Yet, age-old legal traditions could still cast a spell over the judicial officers who handled such cases. The following criminal case from Chuansha County, Jiangsu Province, in

20 Jiangsu High Court Archives, file number 1047–41 (Statistics)–547. Jiangsu Provincial Archives, Nanjing.

21 See also *Min Fa* (Civil Code), in *Zhanghua Minguo Xianxing Fagui Daquan* (A complete collection of the laws and ordinances of the Republic of China). Section L, 60–61.

22 Jennifer Neighbors (2009) has shown that in criminal cases the Qing legal tradition also had strong influences on the Republican Criminal Code and court decisions.

1936 shows the continued influence of Qing law on the county magistrate even though he consciously applied the new Criminal Code.

Cai Wenqin, 29, was a single woman who lived with her mother and made a living by weaving towels for sale. She began a sexual affair with a married man, Cai Maosheng, in August 1935. On the night of March 17, 1936, Maosheng, upon returning from selling towels in Shanghai, sneaked into Wenqin's home to have sex with her and died of a heart attack during intercourse. Frightened by the man's sudden death, Wenqin ran away and told her mother about the incident. After failing to revive Maosheng, the mother and the daughter disposed of the man's body beside a public toilet in a nearby street, hoping they would not be connected with his death. Learning of her husband's death, however, Maosheng's wife accused Cai Wenqin, Cai's mother, and their relatives of murdering Maosheng for money and then hiding his corpse (this seems to suggest that she was aware or suspicious of her husband's affair with Cai Wenqin). The county magistrate sent Maosheng's body to the Ministry of Justice's Forensic Research Institute for an autopsy. The accused escaped but were caught in July.

The trial established that Maosheng had died of an accidental death caused by a heart attack, rather than being murdered, and that Cai Wenqin and her mother had committed the offence of abandoning a corpse, for which Cai was sentenced to imprisonment for eighteen months and her mother to twelve months. The court documents suggest that the magistrate strongly disapproved of Cai Wenqin's behavior on moral grounds. While confirming that Cai Maosheng's death was not to be blamed on anyone, he explained in flowery language: "Cai Wenqin is as loose as a peach flower, with licentious behavior, leaving disgrace in her bed and stains on her family, ruining her own personal standing and reputation, which is really shameless to the extreme." The dead man was not spared, either: "Cai Maosheng seeks sexual affairs like a wild butterfly chasing flowers, greedy with indecent desires, entering a woman's chamber in the quietness of the night and going unrestrained for a fleeting moment, which results in sudden death during sexual intercourse and brings sin and misfortune on himself." In spite of such strong opinions, the magistrate adhered to the law and did not try to punish Cai Wenqin outside the law for having sexual affairs with a married man. In fact, if Cai Maosheng had still been alive and his wife had sued him for adultery, both he and his lover could have been sentenced to imprisonment under Article 239 of the Criminal Code. Yet, since Maosheng was dead, the wife could only sue Cai Wenqin and her mother for murder, and when the latter were acquitted, there was no other lawful way to punish Cai Wenqin. Evidently, when the Criminal Code of 1935 was applied in court, women fared better than under imperial law.

Another case also shows how the new Republican Codes helped women in an unprecedented way. Jin Yafeng, who was 19 in 1940, was engaged to Xu Tianxiong, 26, but did not get to marry him because her family became refugees (the area had been under Japanese occupation since 1937). Later her father arranged to marry her to Bao Ziyuan, but Jin left her husband in December 1939 to move in with her previous fiancé, Xu Tianxiong. Unable to find his wife, Bao Ziyuan requested assistance from the Self-Defense Corp (SDC) (*ziweituan*). On July 23, 1940, two SDC officers named Gu Linsheng and Wang He found Xu in a teahouse and handcuffed him, and soon arrested Jin Yafeng as well. The officers took the couple to the county police station and reported the case to the procurator at the Songjiang District Court. Here, the procurator charged the officers with "interfering with personal liberty," while accusing Xu and Jin of adultery.

The court found one officer guilty as charged and sentenced him to pay a fine of 40 yuan, exchangeable for labor (one yuan per day), with the sentence suspended for two years, while the other officer was still at large. The charge of adultery against Xu Tianxiong and Jin Yafeng was dropped. The court explained this decision as follows: as a member of the SDC, Gu Linsheng had no authority to conduct a criminal investigation and carry out an arrest in a common criminal case, and therefore the arrest of the couple qualified as "interference with personal liberty". In view of the fact that Gu had no record of prior offenses and that his parents, wife, and children relied on him for support, the sentence was suspended. As for the charge of adultery, the court could not prosecute this unless the husband, Bao Ziyuan, filed a criminal lawsuit. Bao, however, had stated that he would withdraw all charges against his wife. Thus, the court did not proceed with the case.[23] Bao Ziyuan only wanted to have his wife back and

23 Songjiang County Archives, file number: 4–2–231.

did not intend to sue her, even if he probably would have liked to punish Xu Tianxiong. Under Republican law, Xu could not be punished for an extra-marital affair with a married woman unless the woman had been convicted after being sued by her husband. The case ended up in court simply because Gu Linsheng and Wang He carried out an arrest for which they had no authority. The court was able to set things straight according to the law.

Legal Games by Litigants in Marriage and Divorce Cases, the 1940s

So far, this chapter has explored the ways in which the courts and county magistrates handled cases of adultery, marriage, and divorce. In order to understand the implications of the Republican reforms, however, we also need to examine the litigants' use of the courts. As the Republican Codes were more favorable to women than imperial law, litigants may have seen new opportunities to advance their personal interests, regardless of the legal merit of their lawsuits.

A typical strategy in such legal games in the Republican era, especially after the revised Criminal Code and Civil Codes were passed, was to confuse civil disputes with criminal lawsuits. In December 1940, Wang Yingxiu, 33, brought a criminal charge to the procurator of the Songjiang District Court, accusing her husband of bigamy and his illegal wife of harassing her. According to Wang, she and her husband, Lu Gensheng, had been embroiled in an ongoing divorce suit for more than ten years, and she had been living with her natal family all these years. When her husband suddenly died in the home of another woman, Qian Yuebao, Wang also discovered that Lu had been living with this woman. As seen elsewhere, an unhappy or mistreated wife would often leave her husband for her natal family because this was the only legal recourse available to wives in the Qing era (Huang 2001). Under the Republican Civil Code, husband and wife had the joint obligation to live together. As a result, one of them could sue the other for not doing so. This, however, was not what

Wang Yingxiu wanted. She wanted to establish through legal action that she was the deceased man's legitimate wife.

Yet, the procurator dismissed the case. He argued that according to various witnesses, Lu Gensheng had formally married Qian Yuebao after his divorce from Wang Yingxiu. The witnesses all noted that the divorce case had dragged on for more than ten years, echoing Wang's words that she and Lu had lived separately for more than ten years because of the divorce case, even though she seems to have refused to accept the divorce. The procurator concluded that the question of whether Lu had committed bigamy depended on whether Lu and Wang were still considered married by the law. This had to be decided by the civil chamber, and therefore the criminal chamber could not take up the case.[24] Lu was dead; but even if he had still been alive, Wang Yingxiu could not have sued him because of the Criminal Code's statute of limitation—in other words, there was no case anyhow. The reason why it was launched at all was probably Wang Yingxiu's intention to share Lu Gensheng's property, which was why she refused to accept a formal divorce in the first place. At the same time, she wanted to pre-empt Qian Yuebao's claim to this property by having her marriage declared illegal. She chose to launch a criminal lawsuit instead of a civil one, for if the criminal chamber had taken up this lawsuit, it would have established the fact that she and Lu were considered married. Yet, the procurator stopped Wang Yinxiu in her legal maneuvering.

A case from Baoshan County, Jiangsu Province, in 1947 illustrates the ways in which litigants used the law and the court system as negotiating tools to settle their family problems. Gu Huilan, a woman of 31 (in 1947), was married to Sun Guanyi, 30 (in 1939). Her sister-in-law had served as the go-between. This marriage was between relatively well-to-do families—Sun Guanyi worked in a seafood store that was probably owned by the family, and Gu Huilan provided a long list of her personal property in her lawsuit documents, including over sixty pieces of fine clothing, eight pieces of jewelry, and nine pieces of furniture. According to Gu Huilan, who filed a criminal complaint on December 6, 1947, she gave birth to a boy who died early and a girl who was eight years of age in 1947. However, as her father-in-law, Sun Daokui, a powerful man in the local area, wanted a grandson, her husband decided to marry another woman, Wu

24 Songjiang County Archives, file number: 4–2–236.

Fenfang. On the evening of July 21, Sun Daokui led a group of three men who forced their way into the house, found Gu Huilan accompanied by Huang Xiangnuan, a cattle herder, and accused them of committing adultery in order to make her sign an agreement to accept a divorce from Sun Guanyi. When she refused, she and Huang were taken to the police station. Lu Jiaqing, a police officer, tried to persuade her to agree to the divorce but again she refused. After Shi Zhengqing, a neighbor, posted her bail she continued to be pressured to sign the agreement. On July 28 she escaped to her natal family, who lived on an island across the Yangzi River mouth from Baoshan County. In her complaint Gu Huilan accused Sun Guangyi, Sun Daokui, and Wu Fenfang of committing bigamy and interfering with her personal liberty. She also demanded her personal property and her share of the income from the family's farmland. She named Shi Zhengqin and Lu Jiaqing as witnesses.

Within two days, Sun Guanyi filed a civil lawsuit for divorce, claiming that Gu Huilan had committed adultery. He referred to the same event that Gu Huilan described, but in terms of capturing adultery in the act. According to Sun, he had been aware of his wife's affairs with Huang for some time. On July 21, a family helper, Zhou Heshang (Monk Zhou), saw that Huang was in Gu Huilan's room and informed Sun Guanyi. Sun then went to the police station to ask for help. Sun and the police captured Huang and Gu in the room. In his civil complaint, Sun Guanyi named Zhou Heshang and Cai Wangqing, a neighbor, as witnesses to the act of adultery. Thus, hearings for the criminal case filed by Gu Huilan and the civil case filed by Sun Guanyi proceeded in parallel from December 1947 to January 1948.

The hearings, at which Sun Daokui, Wu Fenfang, and Huang Xiangnuan never appeared, established two facts: first, Sun Guanyi had been co-habiting (*tongju*) with Wu Fenfang since 1945. According to Sun, his wife had known about this all along. As Sun had not formally married Wu, however, he was not guilty of bigamy. Second, the police officer Lu Jiaqing testified in writing that Sun Guanyi had reported his wife's adultery on the night of July 21; his visit to the house, however, did not confirm whether Gu and Huang had committed adultery. Lu Jiaqing and two other policemen did not actually capture Gu and Huang in the act but were led into a room where Sun's people already held the two. The question remained whether Gu Huilan was having an affair with Huang Xiangnuan or whether they had been framed. Yet, a revealing fact came to light during the hearings, to which Gu Huilan, Sun Guanyi, and Yang Hongxun, another witness, all attested. After the confrontation on July 21, Sun Guanyi offered a monetary settlement to Gu Huilan: if she agreed to the divorce, she would receive money as compensation. The negotiations on the exact amount, however, broke down before Gu Huilan left for her natal family. It seems reasonable to suggest that if the woman had indeed committed adultery, Sun would not have felt compelled to make such an offer since he would have been likely to win the divorce case in court.

Thus both the criminal and civil cases looked weak for the respective plaintiffs, and inconclusive to the court. In the civil case, in January 1948 Gu Huilan requested to have the trial moved to the District Court of Chongming County where she and her natal family were based. Invoking the principle of equality between the sexes, she argued that the current venue imposed too much financial cost on her that she could not afford since she was no longer supported by her husband. The court rejected the request. In addition, on January 26, 1948, the procurator concluded that there was insufficient evidence to prosecute Sun Guanyi, Sun Daokui, and Wu Fenfang, and dismissed the criminal case filed by Gu.

In any case, the two sides had already begun to negotiate out of court more intensively than before. The trial, in fact, had to be postponed twice before the case was put on hold because the litigants had not shown up in court. Finally, on January 30, Gu Huilan officially withdrew her criminal complaint that had already been dismissed, saying that the two parties had agreed to resolve all misunderstandings through mediation by relatives. On January 31, Sun Guanyi withdrew his civil suit for divorce, citing the same reason (in almost the same words).[25]

The case illustrates the litigants' use of law and the court system to deal with marital and family disputes. The strategies used by Sun Guanyi and Gu Huilan were nothing new. They simply responded to the development of civil law in the Republican era. Legal experts were well aware of such behavior from the early 1920s. In the ethnographic studies of local customs sponsored by the Ministry of Justice and mentioned earlier, one

25 Baoshan County Archives, file number: 43–1–410.

set of publications was about the Miao ethnic group in Guizhou Province. According to Miao customs, one spouse of a married couple could divorce the other by offering eight *taels* of silver. Yet:

> Under the current provisions of the law, if husband and wife are not in harmony and both parties are willing to divorce, they can do so without committing an offence. The requirement is very clear that such free divorces must be based on a mutual agreement between husband and wife. In recent times Han people all understand this requirement, so it often happens that when one party wants a divorce but the other party disagrees, one would fabricate conditions that meet the grounds for divorce in order to reach a court decision. Miao people do not understand this legal requirement and think that if one party wants to divorce and offers eight *taels* of silver, it is necessarily binding for both parties. That is why although there are many divorces [among Miao people], few involved lawsuits.[26]

What Sun Guanyi did was exactly to fabricate a cause for divorce under the civil law, namely his wife's alleged adultery. However, he did so in response to Gu's filing of a criminal lawsuit against him. Gu's legal action, in turn, was probably due to the fact that she had been forced to leave without compensation while she had tolerated Sun's informal, second wife. Sun Daokui and Sun Guanyi apparently knew that co-habitation had no legal consequences. It seems that Sun wanted to have an official divorce, either through mutual agreement after a financial settlement or, failing that, by court decision, so that he could officially marry Wu Fenfang. Yet, he only used the lawsuit as a negotiating tool; after all, he did not have any real reason to sue for divorce. In so doing, however, he demonstrated that he could mobilize resources (for example, people willing to testify in his favor), which was enough to make Gu accept his offer of a financial settlement. Gu Huilan did not have a real case, either, but used the criminal lawsuit to exert pressure on Sun to make more concessions. All these maneuverings were possible, of course, because in comparison with imperial law, the Republican Civil Code had advanced the rights of women.

A similar strategy can be seen in another case. In 1948, the peddler Chen Dongshan of Chuansha County went to the county police station and accused Yu Suozhi, who was staying in Chen's home, of having sexual affairs with his wife Wang and inciting his wife to flee with him. The investigation then revealed that Yu was the woman's relative and was staying

26 *Falü Pinglun* (Law Review), no.116 (Sept. 20, 1925), 19.

in Chen's home because of an injured foot. Yu, however, also admitted to having an affair with Wang who confirmed this, citing economic reasons (which presumably meant that Yu had paid her). Both claimed that Chen Dongshan was aware of their affair. When Chen Dongshan was then asked how to proceed, he said that he wanted Yu to leave his home and leave his wife alone. Both Yu and Wang promised that they would not resume their affair. Yu was asked to produce a guarantor for his promise, as a result of which a certain Yin Baosheng came forward and signed a written guarantee saying that he would have Yu detained by the County Judicial Section if the man ever had sexual contact with Wang again. In the meantime, Chen Dongshan officially withdrew his charges, upon which the magistrate closed the case.[27] Again, as in the previous case, the litigant did not really want to pursue a criminal lawsuit; he only wanted to make sure that his wife would be left alone once and for all. By bringing the case to the county and letting the magistrate tell Yu to give a binding promise with a guarantor, Chen achieved his objective at minimal cost.

Let me turn to a final case. He Lianjun, 24, the husband, and Shao Yahua, 20, the wife, married in a group wedding on December 9, 1948. On the night of the wedding, however, Shao refused to sleep with her husband and ran away the next morning. After learning that she had gone back to her natal family, He Lianjun ordered a dinner banquet to be delivered there. The presence of Shao's relatives and friends at the banquet helped to persuade Shao to return to her husband. Yet Shao still refused to sleep with him and left once again in the morning. In the following weeks, the go-between and relatives failed to persuade Shao to return, with Shao threatening to commit suicide. By mid-February 1949, He Lianjun filed a criminal lawsuit at the Songjiang District Court, accusing his wife of adultery with He Liben, an accountant at the Peasant Bank in Songjiang. The circumstantial evidence given by the litigant was that a friend of his had seen Shao Yahua and He Liben eating in a restaurant and going to the movies in Shanghai. After He Lianjun's lawyer sent a warning letter to He Liben, Shao Yahua returned to He Lianjun's home the next day,

27 Chuansha County Archives, file number: 4–1–908. The County Judicial Section was a mid-way institution between a county district court and a county magistrate performing judicial functions.

which seemed to confirm the suspicion that she was indeed involved with He Liben.

In the hearings, however, the case became increasingly inconclusive. Asked whether she had married He Lianjun willingly, Shao Yahua said that it had been her mother's decision and that she had gone along initially. She admitted that she had refused to sleep with He Lianjun and left him, explaining that He Lianjun had lied to her about his wealth and had not bought her an overcoat as he had promised. It appears that Shao Yahua was disappointed to find that He Lianjun was not as rich as she was led to believe before the marriage.[28] But Shao Yahua denied having an affair with He Liben or even knowing the man. There was another intriguing development: when He Liben was summoned to court, he said his name was Wu Liben, not He Liben, and therefore the case had nothing to do with him and he did not know Shao Yahua. He did receive the lawyer's letter, but since it was not addressed to him, he did not pay any attention to it. The testimony given by Lianjun's friend, the key witness, did not help He's case, either. The witness stated that he had known the married couple because he had been at the wedding banquet and that he had known He Lianjun before his marriage. He added that he had seen Shao Yahua in a red overcoat with a man in a department store in Shanghai, but that was all he had seen; he had not seen where she was going, to a restaurant or a cinema or some other place. Shao Yahua testified that she owned a red overcoat before adding that she had never been to Shanghai, alone or with anyone else. The case file ends with these hearings and no conclusion. Very likely, the procurator dismissed the case for lack of evidence.

An important clue for us to understand this case is that during the hearings He Lianjun unequivocally stated twice that he did not want to have his wife back because he could not trust her anymore.[29] In other words, this criminal complaint, regardless of whether it went to trial or not, was a step toward a civil lawsuit, as the Civil Code recognized adultery as a cause for divorce. Admittedly, since Shao Yahua did not want to be married to him anyway, such a lawsuit was probably unnecessary. Yet, taking the initiative and rejecting Shao Yahua helped He Lianjun save face and

28 According to the case file, He Lianjun lived on the upper floor of a barbershop and his occupation was listed as "business" (*shang*). It is not clear whether he was a barber.

29 Songjiang County Archives, file number: 4–2–427.

was preferable to being rejected by the woman for a lack of money. In this light, the confusion about the name of He Liben or Wu Liben appears to make sense. Since "He" and "Wu" were pronounced almost the same in the local dialect, it was very easy to mistake one for the other. It is possible that either He Lianjun mistook Wu Liben's family name for "He," or more likely that he deliberately made the mistake because the so-called affair was made up. In other words, he made sure that in case the complaint backfired, Wu Liben would have no cause to sue him for damage. This shows that the litigant, no doubt aided by his lawyer, knew how to manipulate the law and use the court system.

Concluding Remarks

The evolution of marriage and divorce law in China must be understood in the context of the country's "modernization", a transformation underpinned by the universalization of Western norms in legal as well as economic, social, and political spheres. The late Qing and Republican legal-judicial reform was part of modern state-building and wider social-cultural transformations. This process involved continuous interactions between state and society. The "state" was not an abstract entity but a set of concrete institutions and the large number of individuals who manned them. The reform-minded officials at the national and provincial levels were crucial to the reform of the law and the judicial system; but equally important was the way in which agents of the state such as judges and county magistrates carried out reform measures, or failed to do so, at the lower levels.

On the other hand, the reforms must also be understood in terms of how ordinary citizens used the law and court system, and their adaptation to the changing legal framework and its impact on their lives. In matters of marriage and divorce, the state made gradual progress in reforming the legal codes to level the playing field for men and women, while struggling to reconcile the universalistic legal model and existing cultural practices (e.g., the issue of concubinage). In response, both men and women learned to use and manipulate the law and judicial procedures as additional tools in their cultural repertoire of daily struggle for better life chances, along with informal, customary, and extralegal mechanisms rooted in the power structure of local society. As we have seen, a pattern emerges of increasing instances in which women, who had often been victims of marriage practices in the past, also learned, especially in the 1930s and 1940s, to use the courts to fight for their own well-being. Both men and women used lawsuits about marital disputes as a negotiating tool in settling marital and family matters. Under Qing law, these strategies had already been used in other categories of civil disputes (Huang 1996). In the Republican era, the same strategies were then extended to marriage and divorce cases after women's rights had expanded substantially. In many ways, people's readiness to use and manipulate the law for their own purposes was natural and logical—it was their right to do so. At the same time, this use of state resources undoubtedly increased the cost of maintaining and operating the court system (and the state as a whole) and decreased its efficiency, which in turn slowed down the pace of the reform. This study has only presented a small window through which to view that complex process in early-twentieth-century China.

Works Cited

Bernhardt, Kathryn (1994). Women and the Law: Divorce in the Republican Period. In Kathryn Bernhardt and Philip Huang (eds.) *Civil Law in Qing and Republican China*. Stanford, CA: Stanford University Press.

Bernhardt, Kathryn (1999). *Women and Property in China: 960–1949*. Stanford, CA: Stanford University Press.

Bourgon, Jerome (2002). Uncivil Dialogue: Custom and Law Did Not Merge into Civil Law under Qing. *Late Imperial China*, 23, 1, 50–90.

Bryan, Robert T. Jr. (1919). The Divorce Law of China. *Millard's China National Review*, May 31, 515–518.

Cassel, Pär (2003). Excavating Extraterritoriality: The "Judicial Sub-Perfect" as a Prototype for the Mixed Court in Shanghai. *Late Imperial China*, 24, 2, 156–182.

Cheng, Yu (2002). Minguo Shiqi Qie De Falü Diwei Jiqi Bianqian [The Legal Status of a Concubine and Its Change in the Republican Era]. *Shi Lin* [Historical Review], 2, 74–83.

Huang, Philip (2010). *Chinese Civil Justice, Past and Present*. Lanham, MD: Rowman and Littlefield Publishers.

Huang, Philip (2001). Women's Choice under the Law: Marriage, Divorce, and Illicit Sex under the Qing and the Republic. *Modern China*, 27, 1, 3–58.

Kuo, Wei-Hung (1935). Chinese Women and Men Argue about the New Adultery Code. *China Weekly Review*, February 16.

Levi, Werner (1945). The Family in Modern Chinese Law. *The Far Eastern Quarterly*, 4, 3.

Li, Bingvu (B. Y. Lee) (1935). Modern Education and Divorce in China. *China Weekly Review*, January 19, 264–265.

Liang, Linxia (2007). *Delivering Justice in Qing China*. Oxford: Oxford University Press.

Mu, Sah-Men (1935). Marriage Morality in China Today: Women's Fight for Single Standard under the New Regime of the Republic. *North China Herald*, June 12.

Neighbors, Jennifer (2009). The Long Arm of the Qing Law? Qing Dynasty Homicide Rulings in Republican Courts. *Modern China*, 35, 3, 3–37

Song, Ziming (Hubert T. Mi. Soong) (1935). The Marriage Problem in China. *China Weekly Review*, November 2.

Tran, Lisa (2009). Sex and Equality in Republican China: The Debate over the Adultery Law. *Modern China*, 35, 2, 191–223.

Xu, Xiaoqun (2008). *Trial of Modernity: Judicial Reform in Early Twentieth-Century China, 1901–1937*. Stanford, CA: Stanford University Press.

Zhang, Jinfan (2004). *Zhongguo Sifa Zhidu Shi* (A History of the Chinese Judicial System). Beijing: Renmin fayuan chubanshe.

Dealing with Crime in Late Tsarist Russia: Muslim Tatars and the Imperial Legal System

Stefan B. Kirmse

On May 19, 1871, at 4 am, the Tatar peasant Kurtpedin Mengli Amet oglu entered the police station of the small Crimean town of Karasubazary, all covered in blood.[1] Kurtpedin, who had come into town to buy various goods, had been attacked, stabbed and robbed by four young Tatars earlier that night. Initially, he had dragged himself back to his night's lodging at a Tatar-owned coffee house (*kofeinia*), but after his wound had stopped bleeding, he went out again to find the police.

The previous night the peasant had met the four Tatars in a tavern and spent several hours drinking vodka with them. When the assistant police captain Timofeev called in on his rounds and asked the customers to finish up, Kurtpedin paid for the whole group with a large banknote, which caught the attention of his drinking companions. Thus, instead of taking him back to his lodgings, the young men led him into a deserted part of the town. Here they attacked him, thrust a knife into his side and fled with his wallet.

Soon after Kurtpedin's report of the crime in the early hours of the morning, Timofeev set off with the peasant to search the local taverns, and by the afternoon all four robbers had been detained.[2] The city doctor was summoned to the police station on the same day and examined the victim as well as the suspects. His report contained a detailed description of Kurtpedin's various wounds and, in addition, documented numerous fresh scratches, cuts and bloodstains on the suspects' bodies—signs of a recent fight. The police then informed the public prosecutor (*prokuror*) of

1 GAARK (State Archive in the Autonomous Republic of Crimea), file 376–6-36 (1871), pp. 3, 23.

2 *Ibid.*, pp. 23v., 24.

the newly established circuit court in the nearby city of Simferopol who decided to try the four Tatars for robbery (*razboi*).

Four months later, the case was brought before a jury. The chairman proposed a legal trainee called Menirov as interpreter between Russian and Tatar for the duration of the trial. All parties then approved this selection, as was the usual procedure in the Empire's multilingual courtrooms.[3] The public trial, with its cross-examinations, pleadings and the jurors' retirement for deliberations, took about five hours. While the jury—composed of townspeople, civil servants, merchants and peasants from the city and district of Simferopol—rejected the prosecutor's suggestion that the men had attempted to kill Kurtpedin, they confirmed the charge of premeditated robbery. In the end, the judges sentenced the young men to between six and eight years of hard labor in a fortress.

This chapter examines numerous court cases such as this in order to combine an investigation of law and law-enforcement in late tsarist Russia with an analysis of imperial rule. By discussing ordinary people's contact with state courts in the second half of the nineteenth century, it offers a point of entry into the study of state-society relations. Crucially, I explore the legal sphere "from below": that is, as an interactive space in which jurists, policemen and ordinary subjects of the Empire shaped and experienced imperial policy. By concentrating on two regions that were home to significant Muslim populations, Crimea and Kazan, the chapter shows that imperial courts created arenas of encounter for ethnic and religious minorities and the wider society around them. Focusing on a variety of "crimes" and the ways in which Muslim communities dealt with these, it argues that peasants did not just reject state courts but actively turned to them for help. At the same time, the Russian state made significant, if sometimes unintended, strides towards the legal integration of its diverse population. This study draws mainly on court records from Kazan and Simferopol (Crimea), and on the local press coverage of court cases.

3 *Ibid.*, p. 15.

New Courts for the Empire

In the 1860s and 1870s, Tsar Alexander II enacted a series of reforms that significantly changed the nature of autocratic rule in Russia. The Judicial Reform was but one piece in the mosaic of measures aimed at transforming the Empire, defeated in the Crimean War (1853–56), into a "modern", centralized, and competitive international actor. Yet the transformation of the legal system was a radical step. Baberowski goes so far as to call the Judicial Reform "Russia's first constitution" (2006, 344). In particular, the introduction of an independent judiciary helped to establish a legal system oriented towards the rule of law in which the courts no longer functioned as the long arm of the state. Trials were now held in public, and in the courtroom lawyers could attack the regime without censorship. In the last three decades of the nineteenth century, Russia was perhaps closer to the ideal of the rule of law than ever before, or after.

The Judicial Reform of 1864 affected the everyday lives of ordinary people in several ways. Most importantly, it established a range of new institutions. This chapter looks at the most important of these, the so-called circuit courts (*okruzhnye sudy*), which were designed to address serious crimes and major civil disputes. The jurisdiction of these new courts extended over large territories, usually covering whole provinces. For some civil and most criminal cases (as the aforementioned trial of the four Tatar robbers illustrates), the circuit courts relied on trial by jury.

The new court system was not immediately introduced in all parts of Russia.[4] The government was hesitant to launch the new courts in borderland regions where Russian authority was tenuous or embattled, such as Poland, the Steppe region or Turkestan. The reforms were quickly implemented, however, in more central parts of the Empire, including the Crimean peninsula (1869) and Kazan on the Volga river (1870). The early inclusion of these two regions was striking insofar as Muslims formed about 30 percent of the population in Kazan Province while their share in Crimea was just under 50 percent.[5] Both regions had formed indepen-

4 For an account of its gradual expansion, see Baberowski (1996, 339–427).

5 In Kazan, this share remained stable over the decades that followed. In Crimea, by 1917 it had decreased to 12 percent in the towns and 42 percent in the surrounding districts. See Bodarskii et al. (2003, 131).

dent Muslim khanates before they were annexed by the Russian Empire in 1552 (Kazan) and 1783 (Crimea).

Studies of the Russian legal system (Kucherov 1953; Atwell 1975; Wortman 1976; Bhat 1996) have largely neglected ethnic and religious minorities, with the exception of Jews (Baberowski 1990, 68–70).[6] At the same time, over the last ten years, scholars have produced numerous studies of law and legal practice in Russia's imperial borderlands including the North Caucasus and Central Asia, where distinctive legal regimes were allowed to continue, modified or even put in place by the Russian authorities (Bobrovnikov 1999; Martin 2001; Jersild 2002, 89–109; Auch 2004; Kemper 2005; Kemper and Reinkowski 2005). These peripheral regions, however, present rather specific cases. They were only annexed in the course of the nineteenth century and not fully integrated into the civil-administrative structure of the Empire. Non-Russians had few of the legal rights and opportunities in these regions that they enjoyed in many parts of European Russia. It is only in the more central regions, therefore, that the full extent and implications of the use of state courts by non-Russians can be examined. Yet, historians focusing on these regions have so far paid little attention to legal practice. Most works on Crimea (Fisher 1878; O'Neill 2006; Jobst 2007; Kozelsky 2008) and the Volga-Kama region (Kappeler 1982; Frank 2001; Geraci 2001; Werth 2002) hardly mention the legal system. Part of the reason for this omission may be the fact that generations of Russian ethnographers presented non-Russians as followers of "customary law". What interest would these people have in state courts?

Crews's recent study of Muslim interaction with state institutions (2006) in the Russian Empire admittedly focuses on questions of legal authority (and is thus repeatedly referred to in this chapter for comparative purposes). Analyzing the legal responses to petitions sent by Muslims to religious and secular administrative bodies, it points to the cooperation and interpenetration of Islamic law and state law (*ibid.*, 159, 166). Crews's discussion of the Tatar regions, however, mainly addresses the pre-Reform period and (perhaps for that reason) touches on the ways

6 While Baberowski (1996) offers a discussion of state law among non-Russian populations, he limits this discussion to borderland regions such as the South Caucasus, the Steppe region and Central Asia.

in which Muslim individuals and communities turned to state courts only in passing. After 1864, they certainly did so in considerable numbers, and for a variety of reasons discussed below.

The introduction of the reformed court system in Crimea and Kazan was a significant step. First, it promoted the legal integration of Muslim Tatars, but in so doing also contributed to an increasing differentiation of Muslims in the Empire (as Muslim groups in borderlands remained outside the system). The new courts, which were a blend of French, Prussian and Anglo-Saxon models, reflected the concerns of their creators: a new class of liberal jurists and bureaucrats who increasingly advanced positions contrary to those of the old elites (Baberowski 2008, 17–37; Schattenberg 2008, 212–230). From 1839, the recently founded Imperial Law School in St. Petersburg supplied the state with a steady flow of graduates. Over the following decades, the number of law faculties and students at Russian universities grew continually, so that by the early twentieth century, with law now being the most popular course of study, over 20,000 civil servants, lawyers, prosecutors and judges were working in the Empire (Kassow 1989, 58–59). These jurists were keen to promote a *Rechtsstaat* based on European models. Seeking to introduce, in the words of Alexander II, a "quick, just, merciful and equal law for all our subjects (*sud skoryi, pravyi, milostivyi, ravnyi dlia vsekh poddannykh nashikh*)" (quoted in Dzhanshiev 1900, 388), the reforms established a system of state courts that were, with some caveats, open to all.

For Muslim Tatars, this was a significant break with the past. In Crimea, legal institutions had discriminated against them since the Russian conquest (Fisher 1987, 357). In the cities of Kazan and Orenburg, until the mid-1850s the Tatar populations had been governed by separate administrations that employed Muslim judges for handling cases between Tatars (Khäyrutdinov 2001). Far from seeking legal unification, then, the Russian authorities had encouraged the use of particular, local judicial practices. And indeed, for some minorities, this construction and perpetuation of difference was maintained until the end of imperial rule. Most non-Christian inhabitants of Siberia, Central Asia and the Caucasus were put into the legal category of *inorodtsy* ("aliens"), who stood outside the general laws of the Empire. The settled Tatars of the Volga-Kama region and Crimea, by contrast, were integrated with the estate system as state peasants, townspeople or merchants (Slocum 1998, 179). In these two regions, the new courts thus ended up being responsible for large groups of Muslims.

Second, the establishment of the circuit courts heralded new forms of legal pluralism. Like other mid-nineteenth century imperial powers, the Russian Empire imposed a state-centered form of legal pluralism onto an already complex plural legal order.[7] All parts of the Empire were home to specific and changeable forms of legal pluralism. This complexity is not captured by the dual model of colonial law (courts for the "colonizers" vs. courts for the "colonized") that has been widely applied in the context of expanding empires. Not only did the post-reform legal system include specific military, ecclesiastical, peasant and other courts, but the ways in which "local" (religious or "customary") jurisprudence was integrated into the legal system differed from region to region. In more peripheral parts such as Central Asia, Siberia and Dagestan, the Russian authorities had various "customary laws" codified and incorporated into the state legal system, often by promoting specific local courts. Such all-purpose "native" courts, however, were considered archaic for the South Caucasus and the Volga region where the authorities employed Islamic judges for many cases concerning family and inheritance law. In most central regions of the Empire, moreover, rural *volost'* courts were allowed to draw on "customs" in (some) civil disputes among peasants.

Cultural differences played a more modest role in the newly-established circuit courts. Only in the mountain region west of Dagestan were these courts formally allowed to rule "in consideration of traditional law" (*adat* and *shari'a*). Elsewhere, the new courts relied on the Civil and Criminal Codes. Dating back to the pre-Reform period, these codes contained a number of religious specifications.[8] The analysis of the reformed courts, however, must look beyond the codes. As I suggest in what follows, jurists

7 See the introduction to this volume for a discussion of the term "legal pluralism".

8 See Burbank (2006) for a discussion of such specifications in the Civil Code. Examples of special provisions in the Criminal Code included the definition of crimes and punishments. Thus, blasphemy, sacrilege, apostasy and proselytism were criminal offenses only when they were carried out at the expense of Russian Orthodoxy. Secular courts not only imposed punishments on criminal offenders but also required them to do penance in accordance with their faiths. Many of these rules officially remained in force until 1905.

not only felt free to circumvent these specifications in practice, but the new courts also served as widely accessible interactive spaces that were used by many, regardless of ethnic or religious affiliation.

That said, the multiplicity of legal institutions in Russia did not provide litigants with endless choice. The opportunity to choose between different legal forums—religious, administrative, customary, or other—has often been discussed as a key feature of colonial and post-colonial legal systems.[9] Benda-Beckmann (1981) suggested the notion of "forum shopping" for this kind of behavior. Yet, not all forums are willing to take on any case. In imperial Russia, most courts had clearly defined areas of jurisdiction. After 1864, serious criminal cases would usually be heard in circuit courts. In civil cases, the Muslims of Crimea and Kazan could turn to Islamic judges only in intra-Muslim cases of family and inheritance law, and provided there was no disagreement between the two parties.[10] In all other cases, the appropriate forum (that is, circuit court or lower-level courts) was determined by the severity of the case. In short, Russia's legal pluralism was clearly demarcated, and few exceptions were made for religious minorities, at least in central parts of the Empire.

Third, the introduction of the reformed courts to Crimea and Kazan is striking when seen against the background of dominant views of non-Russians and wider trends in nationality policy in the second half of the nineteenth century. While Russian attitudes towards the Tatars varied over time and between institutions and individuals (see Kappeler 1982, 479–506; Becker 1986; Yemelianova 1999), there was considerable agreement that most Tatars, like other Muslims, were not well-integrated in imperial society. From the mid-nineteenth century, Russian writers began to produce ethnographic studies, ranging from sympathetic to openly hostile accounts, which helped to folklorise and exoticise the Tatars as alien

9 For the case of post-colonial India, for example, various scholars have observed that people use state courts instead of community legal forums mainly in cases in which they want to delay the resolution of a dispute, harass or punish their opponents, or demonstrate their influence outside the local community (Cohn 1965, 105; Randeria 2006, 237).

10 According to Article 1399 of the Statutes of Spiritual Matters of Foreign Faiths (Vol. XI, Part 1 of the Collection of Laws of the Russian Empire, 1900 edition) inheritance cases between Muslims could be decided by Islamic judges only if there was no disagreement between the litigants. Otherwise, the cases had to be heard by imperial courts.

"others".[11] As part of this process, numerous studies of "customary law" in the Russian and non-Russian village appeared.[12] Yet, this did little to change the fact that Russia's new generation of jurists, the designers and driving forces of the new courts, had little interest in culture. What they wanted was a simple and efficient legal system.

This drive for uniformity and efficiency fit in well with increasing calls for integrating the Empire. From the 1880s, in particular, the government made attempts to further unification by promoting Great Russian culture. As Russia was seen as having to fulfill a civilizing mission towards its various internal "others", the spread of the rule of law (*zakonnost'*) could be seen as one aspect of this mission.

Legal unification, however, was not a realistic scenario for imperial borderlands. In the Steppe region, for example, a member of a special committee concluded that the Kirgiz[13] could not be judged by Russian laws: "Constituting another tribal organism and living under different elementary and environmental conditions, the Kirgiz cannot be expected to have the same understanding and view of crimes and offenses as Russians and other Europeans" (Valikhanov 1904 [1864], 170). While the Russian government sought to introduce a new ethos of citizenship in its Eastern borderlands from the 1860s, local resistance revealed the state's inability to reach people beyond local elite networks (Yaroshevski 1997). In Crimea and Kazan, the integration of Muslims into the new legal system was more successful. Jurists no longer even discussed the option of special rules or institutions for Tatars when they submitted their report on the possibility of introducing the reformed courts.[14] Beyond generic statements that the two regions were culturally heterogeneous, ethnic and religious consider-

11 See, for example, Fuks (1844); Shino (1860); Laptev (1861, 214–232); Rittikh (1870); and Lavrskii (1884).

12 For a comprehensive bibliography, see E.I. Iakushkin (1899). See also the two special issues of the Journal *Zapiski Imperatorskago Russkago Geograficheskago Obshchestva (po otdeleniiu etnografii)* that focus on customary law among non-Russians: vol. VIII (1878) and vol. XVIII (1900). Most writings on Tatars, however, examined wedding and other lifecycle rituals. For a study of legal practice among Tatars, see N-ch (1869).

13 In the Russian Empire, the nomads of the Central Eurasian Steppe were referred to as "Kirgiz". Under Soviet rule, these groups then became known as "Kazakhs".

14 See the chapters on Kazan and Taurida in *Sudebno-statisticheskie svedeniia i soobrazheniia o vvedenii v deistvie sudebnykh ustavov 20-noiabria 1864g.* (St. Petersburg, 1866).

ations were completely absent in this report, and the introduction of the circuit courts was thoroughly recommended.

This chapter focuses on the use of the new courts "on the ground". It argues that imperial courts helped to deal with crime and thus regulate the lives of ordinary subjects, including Muslim Tatars. In the towns and villages of the Empire, people did not simply reject and resist the Russian courts, as some have suggested for the Caucasus (Jersild 2002, 97; Auch 2004, 314–316) and as contemporary Russian jurists routinely complained. Like other imperial subjects, Tatars acted pragmatically. This confirms recent suggestions about the readiness of Muslims to turn to civil authorities in cases in which they were dissatisfied with the rulings of Islamic judges (Crews 2006, 155). While accommodation is now recognized as the dominant mode of interaction between imperial powers and local populations in the general literature on empires (Aguirre and Salvatore 2001; Benton 2002, 27; Burbank and Cooper 2010, 14), the scholarly focus still tends to be on resistance in the Russian context. Crews already documented a general "openness to incorporating tsarist institutions" among Muslim Tatars (2006, 167), and this chapter shows that Tatar peasants turned to, and cooperated with, imperial courts and police when it was in their interests to do so. Moreover, because legal practice in the new circuit courts took few ethnic and religious distinctions into account, it contributed to the development of a hesitatingly unified legal space.

A Question of Access

The hearings and investigations of imperial courts were not limited to the central court buildings but also took place in external sessions (*vyezdy*). In the cities of Kazan and Simferopol, the circuit court met on a regular basis: every month, it held eight to twelve-day sessions in which about 30 criminal and civil cases were decided. Most of these cases involved people from the city and its surrounding districts. In addition, to expand access to the reformed justice system, the circuit court also travelled to more remote districts several times a year. In 1884, the head of the Kazan Circuit

Court, for example, informed the Ministry of Justice that in the course of the previous two years, the city of Kazan had seen 20 jury court sessions dealing with criminal cases whereas the smaller district towns of the province had hosted 65 such sessions.[15]

The records of the Simferopol Circuit Court suggest even closer contact between legal representatives and Muslim peasants. In Crimea, the external sessions of the court were not limited to the administrative centers of the peninsula's districts. In the district of Simferopol, which surrounded the capital city, external sessions were regularly held in the merchant towns of Bakhchisaray and Karasubazary.[16] In various districts, regular travel to villages was recorded, sometimes to several villages on the same day.[17] In villages and districts predominantly inhabited by Tatars, entire sessions of the Circuit Court could be devoted to Tatar cases.[18] In some of these, such as burglary and theft, the imperial courts ended up defending Tatar interests. For example, in the village of Chongurchy, in the Crimean district of Evpatoriia, a travelling judge recorded the case of the brothers Alexei, Maksim and Mikhail Litvinenko accused of breaking into the mill and stealing the property of Matbet Abdulrashid oglu.[19] At another session in the nearby village of Ak-Mechet, the same judge then heard the case of Fedot Iushchenko, accused of stealing the sheep of Abdul Annan Mambet oglu.[20] In these cases, then, Tatar homes and livelihoods were protected against Russian or Ukrainian thieves and burglars. In other cases, the Circuit Court defended Muslims against crimes committed by other Muslims. For example, at the court session in Ak-Mechet, Seliadin Djeliakoi

15 RGIA (Russian State Historical Archive, St. Petersburg), 1405–73–3656b (1884), p. 351.

16 GAARK, 376–1-195 (1901).

17 GAARK, 376–1-229 (1902), p. 51.

18 For an example of a Tatar-dominated court session in Yalta, see "List of cases to be heard in the city of Yalta, with and without the participation of jurors, from March 20 to 24, 1891," *Tavricheskie Gubernskie Vedomosti* 10, March 7, 1891.

19 GAARK, 376–1-195, pp. 5, 5v. The Turkic suffix "oglu" means "son of" and was still used among Crimean Tatars at this time whereas the surnames of Kazan-based Tatars, who had already been part of the Empire for over 300 years, tended to end in the Russian "-ov".

20 GAARK, 376–1-229, p. 39.

oglu and Emir-Suin Abii-Bulla oglu were tried before the circuit court for stealing the property of Abduraim Menumer oglu.[21]

These cases offer a first hint that circuit courts were more than alien state institutions rejected at the village level (for further details on Tatar access to courts, see Kirmse 2012). They helped to regulate the everyday lives of Tatars and other subjects of the Empire. What were the reasons for Tatar interaction with these courts?

Crime and the Search for "Outside" Help

As the court case at the outset of this chapter suggests, state institutions could be a useful resource for peasants who came to the cities to trade or seek work. Whether the Crimean peasant Kurtpedin got his money back or not is not mentioned in the court records, but he certainly managed to get his assailants "off the street".

Tatars, like other subjects of the Empire, had several options when they fell victim to serious crime, at least in theory. They could try to enlist the support of their local communities to catch and punish the criminals themselves. Such cases of *samosud* (self-administered justice) were widely reported in the Russian Empire (Frierson 1987). Alternatively, they could turn to the state, an appealing option for those who were stranded in the city or on the road without their usual support networks. Yet the state was more than an "emergency hotline" for travelers.

On January 4, 1896, the peasant woman Bibi Fatyma Sabitova, from the Tatar village of Aziiak, about 60 miles east of Kazan, was held at gunpoint and robbed by the 25-year old Tatar peasant Sibegatulla Saifullin who had earlier seen her wearing a precious necklace.[22] The robbery took place on the road between two Tatar villages—the village of the accused (where the woman had visited friends), and the village of the victim. Although it has been claimed (Frank 1999, 34–35) that Russian peasants generally distrusted policemen and had the least respect for the notoriously corrupt local police constables (*uriadniki*), it is to an *uriadnik* that

21 *Ibid.*, p. 45.
22 NART (National Archive of the Republic of Tatarstan, Kazan), 390–1-38 (1896).

Sabitova turned for help.[23] The day after the robbery the woman thus made for the town of Arsk (a six-mile walk from the scene of the crime), where the closest police station was located. The constable immediately rode into the village to detain the suspect, after which he sent a report of Sabitova's account of the robbery to the investigator (*sudebnyi sledovatel'*) and the local police captain (*pristav*). Within two weeks, both of these had forwarded reports of the case to the assistant prosecutor of Kazan Circuit Court. Saifullin was seized, charged, and tried in April.

Peasant communities in the Russian Empire are sometimes portrayed as rather closed-off social spaces that strongly resisted external influence, and law-enforcement by the state, in particular (Worobec 1995). In this case, however, the *uriadnik* found the peasants co-operative. The suspect's fellow villager Khusain Khasanov, for one, testified that Saifullin had asked him to tell the police that he had seen the suspect shooting hares with his gun at the time of the crime. Instead of giving his neighbor an alibi, however, Khasanov told the police of this attempt at manipulation.[24] Peasants, then, did not necessarily act collectively, but used state officials in their local disputes and power struggles, for example by incriminating their neighbors. Three other peasants came to Saifullin's aid and paid the significant amount of 150 rubles to have the accused released on bail. In the end, the man was acquitted by the Circuit Court, largely because of a lack of "hard" evidence against him (crucially, the stolen items were never found).

Let us briefly consider the similarities and differences between the cases of the peasant woman Sabitova and the Crimean peasant Kurtpedin. Both were attacked "on the road", outside their usual village environments, and decided to report the crimes to which they had fallen victim to the police, which brought the two cases before imperial courts. While Kurtpedin may have had few other options, Sabitova could have turned back to her village (which was closer than the police station) and mobilized family and friends to punish the criminal and get her property back. The attack on Sabitova had taken place in an area overwhelmingly inhabited by Tatars.[25]

23 See Burbank (2008) for a discussion of how peasants used these constables.

24 NART, 390–1-38 (1896), pp. 7–8.

25 In 1894, the records of the small administrative unit in which the villages of the accused and the victim were located showed 1,153 Russians and 9,809 Tatars (Liustritskii 1894, 82).

Why would she seek outside support? Perhaps her kinship networks were weak, and as Hoebel's study of court use in Pakistan (1965) suggested, people turn to state courts "to equalize a relationship of opposition that has become uncontrollably out of balance" (p. 46). Or, perhaps Sabitova considered the Russian authorities to be more likely to help her dispose of the criminal (for the court practice of exiling offenders to Siberia was well-known). It seems most likely, in any case, that she and her kin preferred external mediation to a confrontation with Saifullin and his relatives and neighbors (those who posted his bail). Studies from elsewhere in the imperial world have also pointed to two important qualities of state representatives: first, they are considered to be outside local networks and therefore neutral, and second, they are often perceived in terms of power and distance.[26]

Tatars, like other peasants, also turned to the Russian system of law-enforcement and justice when they needed support against decisions made by village assemblies. On March 12, 1896, the Kazan Judicial Chamber (a court of appeal for circuit court decisions) examined the case of six Tatar peasants who had been convicted for beating their fellow villager Valeeva Kameliutdinova on allegations of adultery so badly that the woman had almost died. The case was as follows.[27] One day the Tatar peasant Gubaidullin told his fellow villagers that he was secretly meeting Valeeva, a married woman. In response, a village assembly was called at which the elders decided that in accordance with Islamic law, Kameliutdinov had to divorce his unfaithful wife. The peasant, however, refused, insisting that the slanderer was telling lies out of spite. Yet the assembly did not listen to him. Several peasants then broke into Kameliutdinov's house, dragged his wife out into the street, smeared the woman's face with dirt and started beating her until she fell unconscious. The husband, in the meantime, ran off to get help and returned the next morning with the local *uriadnik*. Six of the villagers were put on trial. While the accused pleaded

26 A classic study of law-enforcement in the Australian colonies, for example, explains the authority of colonial policemen in terms of their appearance of power and distance. Post-colonial police, who are often staffed with "locals" and not perceived as neutral, have lost much of this authority (Gordon and Meggitt 1985). For the argument that the threatening power of the distant state increased the appeal of courts at all levels, see also Macauley (1998, 5).

27 *Kazanskii Telegraf*, March 15, 1896, No. 966.

not-guilty, they were faced with incriminating statements from witnesses, and thus the Chamber passed jail sentences of eight to twelve months.

As in the aforementioned cases, a Tatar peasant needed external support; this time, however, it was not support against unknown assailants, but against his own village authorities, which had decided to take justice into their own hands. Such *samosud* was not only unnecessary but also illegal, as there were formal rules for dealing with adultery and other "crimes against religion": Muslims could ask Islamic scholars to assess the degree of guilt and then have a state court determine and administer the punishment (Crews 2006, 165). In the given case, however, the village assembly chose not to do this, and as a result, the police and courts, like the peasant himself, focused on another crime, namely the mob beating that almost led to the death of the woman.

Two further points may be added. First, the Russian authorities were not faced with monolithic rural communities. Peasants acted as individuals, not as collectivities (see also Burbank 2004, 13). In this case, instead of claiming not to have seen anything, several villagers confirmed in court that the accused had beaten the woman. This was hardly just ignorance of the consequences, for many testimonies in late imperial court cases show that peasants were fully aware of the possibility of exile and imprisonment. Second, in their commitment to the ideal of a rule of law, imperial courts attached great importance to formal rules. This precluded undifferentiated mass convictions. In Kameliudinova's case, the accused were found guilty and punished because they were six identifiable individuals. In other cases, crowds of peasants were acquitted by circuit courts because the prosecution failed to prove who exactly had violated which law.[28]

These acquittals, in part, reflected the fact that the Judicial Reform had introduced a number of novelties into the Russian legal system, including: the separation of justice from the Empire's administrative and law-enforcement organs, the promotion of and increasing reliance on professional jurists, and the presumption of innocence. Not only was the burden of proof now on the prosecution; but the courts could no longer

28 For examples of trials resulting in such acquittals of peasant "crowds", see "Armed Resistance against authorities," *Volzhskii Vestnik*, May 15, 1884, No. 56, and "Serious Mutilation Inflicted," *Kazanskii Telegraf*, June 1, 1896, No. 1021.

be employed as instruments of autocratic rule.[29] In the late 1820s, the head of the Russian security police could still publicly claim that "laws are written for subordinates, not for the authorities" (quoted in Pipes 1995, 290). The Reform, however, created a legal infrastructure that allowed peasants and townspeople alike to take officials (even governors!) to court and thus hold them accountable for their actions. As the following case from Crimea illustrates, the police could no longer get away with arbitrary orders.[30]

On August 9, 1871, the police captain (*pristav*) of Simferopol's first police district, Maryshev, submitted a complaint to the prosecution of the Circuit Court about the following incident. The policeman had been instructed by the city administration to clean the city fountain. Yet when he demanded a bucket from the water-carrier Ramazan Memet oglu, the latter not only refused but insulted Maryshev by pointing at his genitals and shouting, "You can stick your police captain right here!" (*Vot tebe pristav*!). The captain then hit Ramazan and took the bucket by force; in addition, he had the insolent water-carrier arrested by auxiliary policemen (*desiatskie*), who also beat him. Maryshev may have wanted to get official praise for his resolute move against local "resistance"; but the Circuit Court thought differently. The prosecution argued that since the cleaning of fountains was not among the service obligations of police captains, the insults inflicted on him at this time did not count as offences against the administrative order. Moreover, the court reprimanded the policeman for transgressing his powers, reminding him that he had no right to demand a bucket, let alone hit or arrest the Tatar, who had done nothing illegal. Thus, the matter was dismissed and the Tatar cleared of all accusations.

Some Tatars used their new powers vis-à-vis the police force by bringing these to trial. In the town of Yalta, an external session of the Simferopol Circuit Court heard one such case in March 1891: the Russian nobleman and *uriadnik* Sol'ntsevich was tried for using violence on duty.[31] The *uriadnik* had walked past a teahouse in the village of Alushta while doing his rounds. There he got into an argument with a Tatar, took out his saber

29 For a discussion of criminal procedure in central and local courts before the Reform, see LeDonne (1991, 181–199); Baberowski (1996, 11–37); and Schmidt (1996, 338–380).

30 GAARK, 376-6-70 (1872).

31 For detailed coverage, see "Iz zala suda," *Krymskii Vestnik* 74, April 3, 1891.

and hit the Tatar on the arm who cried out and ran back into the teahouse. Shortly afterwards, the Tatar filed a complaint against the *uriadnik* who was eventually sentenced by the Circuit Court to a two-week arrest. The journalist reporting from the courtroom admittedly criticized that the Russian court system now allowed people to be tried "for nothing" (*za pustiaki*). Yet crucially, the Tatar did not just accept being hit by the policeman; he went to court and made sure the *uriadnik* got his penalty.

Another case from Crimea, however, suggests that the new commitment to the rule of law could be boon and bane for victims of "crime". In June 1871, the Tatar landowner Esaul Sultan Shagan Girey, who lived in a village outside Simferopol, approached the local justice of the peace (an office also created by the Judicial Reform), accusing a man called Konstantin Samodurov, whom the landowner had hired as a wage laborer, of having insulted his Muslim faith.[32] Insults and other minor crimes usually fell outside the jurisdiction of circuit courts, so the Muslim landowner had correctly turned to the justice of the peace. The latter, however, forwarded the matter to the investigator, arguing that Samodurov had violated article 178 of the Criminal Code and was thus subject to prosecution by the circuit court. The investigator objected, pointing out that the said article explicitly referred to insults against "the Christian faith or the Orthodox Church" and that Samodurov had therefore committed no crime. Yet this objection was not shared by the jurists at the Simferopol Circuit Court. They ruled that while insults against the Muslim faith were not mentioned as such in the Criminal Code, by their nature (*po priznakam svoim*) they should be treated like insults against Orthodoxy. Yet, while they recognized the insult as a "crime", they refused to prosecute it for formal reasons: apparently, none of the documents the court had received contained any information on "how exactly the insult was expressed" (*ne vidno v chem imenno vyrazilos' eto poritsanie*); hence, there was no direct evidence of a criminal act.[33]

The case illustrates a number of important issues. It shows that Muslims turned to state legal institutions even to have their faith protected—which is consistent with Crews's claim that Muslims viewed the Russian state as guardian of the *shari'a* (2006, 148, 191). Furthermore,

32 GAARK, 376–6-49 (1871).

33 *Ibid.*, p.2.

and in addition to highlighting the commitment to formal rules once again, it suggests that the jurists who worked in the new courts could choose to rule by analogy and thus circumvent the relics of religious discrimination in the Criminal Code. In fact, the initiative of Tatars like Shagan Girey even spurred the jurists to rule by analogy. The implications are twofold. First, as Merry (1994) argued in a different context, the decisions of courts do not necessarily reflect a dominant ideology but rather the views of those who staff these courts (p. 38); yet more importantly for the case of post-Reform Russia, legal integration partly resulted from the ongoing interaction between jurists and ordinary subjects.

For the new generation of jurists, it seemed irrelevant whether the parties in court were Russians, Tatars or members of other minorities. The following case offers another example of the fact that Muslims were subjected to many of the same rules and procedures as their Christian counterparts. As Gautam's chapter in this volume shows, towards the late nineteenth century, Russian jurists became fascinated with new medical theories which they then applied in the courtroom. The "luxury" of a thorough medical examination, however, was not reserved for the Russians. On February 19, 1870, the 24-year-old Tatar peasant Aduraim Veli Akai oglu stabbed his wife to death, whom he suspected of unfaithfulness.[34] While Aduraim confessed the murder to the investigator, his father explained that the young man was ill, for he suffered from strange sounds in his ears and frequent hallucinations. Shortly after the murder, the young Tatar was therefore taken to a hospital in Simferopol on the suspicion of insanity, where he spent four months "for tests" (*na ispytanie*). As Tatars had been excluded by law from some city and district courts as a cost-cutting measure only a few decades earlier (Khäyrutdinov 2001, 36)[35], it is striking that the Russian state was now willing to pay for hospital expenses and transportation costs. In fact, the court investigator explicitly told the police to transfer Abduraim from his village to Simferopol (a journey of

34 GAARK, 376–6-35 (1871).

35 In 1834, all Tatars living in the city of Kazan were banned from using Russian city and district courts and transferred to the jurisdiction of the local Tatar self-administration (*Tatarskaia ratusha*) which employed Islamic judges. The aim of this decision was to reduce costs for the Russian state; the Tatar community of Kazan paid for the maintenance of the *ratusha* and its staff.

about 75 miles) "as a patient (*bol'noi*) on a cart, not on foot".[36] At the hospital, the doctor conducted numerous interviews with him, all of which had to be translated. Abduraim, moreover, was hardly an exception at this institution: as the doctor later informed the court, the young man "[had] talked with pleasure with the other Tatars in the hospital".[37] The doctor, and subsequently the prosecution, came to the conclusion that Abduraim was only pretending to be ill. The jurors at his trial, however, followed the argumentation of the defense that he had committed the murder "in a fit of illness that led him to madness".[38] Thus, they acquitted the accused and returned him to the custody of his father. The parallels between the cases of this young Tatar and the Russian nobleman Skadovskii (see Gautam) are anything but coincidental. By the late nineteenth century, cultural differences played only a minor role in criminal law where "one law for all" was becoming more and more common.

The imperial court archives are full of cases in which Tatars appeared as injured parties, witnesses, defendants, and plaintiffs. Unlike civil cases, which involved litigation fees, the report of a crime did not cost the victims anything. And thus, peasants also used the imperial court system as a tool in their local struggles over power and resources. The next case offers an illustration.

In the village of Ungut near the town of Feodosiia on the Eastern shore of the Crimean peninsula, a straw stack was set on fire one night in late June 1871.[39] The next day, the village and *volost'* administrations informed the local investigator who soon arrived in the village to make his preliminary enquiries. The injured party, a 29-year-old Tatar peasant by the name of Kara-Kamii oglu told the investigator that he suspected the 50-year-old peasant Mengli-Issa-Suin-oglu to be the culprit: not only had the man threatened him that his straw would go up in flames ten days before the incident, but he had also seen the suspect running away from the burning straw.[40]

The case was heard in an external session of the Simferopol Circuit Court in the town of Feodosiia the following spring. On trial, the accused

36 *Ibid.*, p. 29.
37 *Ibid.*, pp. 4–5.
38 *Ibid.*, p. 13.
39 GAARK, 376–6-55 (1871).
40 *Ibid.*, pp. 1, 20.

admitted his argument with the injured party but denied having made any threats, let alone setting his neighbor's straw on fire. In his final statement he only asked the court "to be judged in accordance with the law" (*sudit' ego po zakonu*).[41]

Found guilty by the court and sentenced to three months' imprisonment (in addition to having to bear the costs for the trial), the alleged arsonist, however, soon filed a protest against the verdict. Four months after the trial, the court of appeal (the Odessa Judicial Chamber) discovered numerous problems with the testimony given at the Feodosiia trial. Not only was the injured person the only one who had seen the accused running away from the straw, but the statements of various witnesses also contradicted each other. In addition, the Judicial Chamber began to explore the relationship between the two protagonists of the trial, discovering that the 50-year-old defendant had served as the village elder and steward of the land adjacent to the barn of the 29-year-old victim. The two had repeatedly quarreled over land issues. Yet, since the steward was widely respected in the village and only defended the landowner's interests, the court concluded that no personal motives and lust for revenge could be attributed to him.[42] Arguing that there was insufficient evidence against the accused, the Chamber decided to repeal the verdict.

While it is possible that the steward committed this arson at the order of the landowner, as an experienced local functionary he is unlikely to have gone to such risks. Arson was considered a serious crime, and there was little to gain for him. He was more influential and respected than his young opponent. Thus, it is more likely—and the contradictory and changing statements of the witnesses confirm this—that the injured person set the fire himself in order to incriminate the steward. The circuit courts, in other words, could be manipulated and utilized as tools in local power struggles.

In some cases, Tatar peasants did not just turn to the police and let the state take it from there, but approached the courts directly with written complaints or requests. In contrast to the simple report of a crime, such complaints implied expenses for having these prepared (for most peasants were illiterate). Yet there were clearly cases in which peasants were willing to incur these.

41 *Ibid.*, p. 11.

42 *Ibid.*, p. 16.

In May 1873, the prosecutor of the Simferopol Circuit Court received a letter from four Tatars. The letter stated that Fat'ma Khanym A., the bride of one of them and close relative of the others, had been married by her parents to another man. The four asked the prosecution, supposedly at the request of Fat'ma Khanym A., to investigate and rescue her. And indeed, the prosecution decided to hear the bride and sent various officials into the village. Capitalizing on his religious difference, however, the husband refused to have any stranger see his wife, and certainly not a Christian. But the prosecution insisted that the woman be heard and soon returned to the village with more officials. In the end, realizing that the husband would not yield to the law, the prosecution had him arrested and the lock to the woman's quarters forced. This time, the prosecution had also brought along some of the wife's relatives. Fat'ma Khanym exclaimed that she no longer wanted to stay with her dreaded husband. Upon leaving the premises, however, Fat'ma Khanym's uncle said to the prosecutor:

> You have rescued an unlucky girl, but you have also ruined her. What sort of future can she have now? Who will marry her? According to our customs, she is a lost person (*propashchii chelovek*).

The prosecutor curtly replied: "I've done my job (*Ia sdelal svoe delo*). Everything else is not my concern." At this point, however, the person who had informed the prosecutor in the first place intervened and claimed his bride.[43]

This case is hardly striking because of its "fairytale" ending, even though it is probably this ending that accounts for the coverage of the story in several local and national newspapers. It matters for other reasons. As in the case of Kameliutdinov and his allegedly unfaithful wife, a Muslim Tatar turned to the Russian authorities for help. In this case, he even wrote a letter to the prosecutor of the Circuit Court. Not unlike Kameliutdinov, he probably did so because local institutions would not have been much use. In theory, he could have turned to an Islamic judge. These judges, who were elected by Muslim communities and then appointed by the Russian authorities, oversaw the majority of family

43 For full coverage, see *Kamsko-Volzhskaia Gazeta*, July 8, 1873, No. 78. For a more explicitly "Orientalist" presentation of the case, in which the outcome is extolled as a victory over Tatar "backwardness", see *Sankt Peterburgskie Vedomosti*, July 2, 1873, No. 179.

disputes among Muslims. Yet an Islamic judge might have confirmed the arranged marriage: some religious judges admittedly insisted on the bride's consent for marriage, yet others prioritized parental authority. The public prosecutor of the Circuit Court, by contrast, was only concerned about whether a "crime" as defined by the Criminal Code had been committed, and bride kidnapping could be prosecuted as a form of "violent abduction" (*nasil'stvennoe pokhishchenie*). Thus he concluded, "I've done my job."

That, however, points to another implication of the case, namely, the fact that while Muslim Tatars had the chance to use Russian institutions as external arbiters, this appeal to "outside" help may have had negative local repercussions. We do not know the reaction of Fat'ma Khanym's parents to the case, or the response by the village communities. Seeking outside support could have caused uproar in the village.

Another case of bride abduction that did not make it into the newspapers illustrates that Tatars who turned to imperial courts for help may have ended up with more problems than solutions.[44] Two years before Fat'ma Khanym's case, on May 19 1871, the Simferopol Circuit Court heard the case of Iag'ia Dzhelial' oglu, accused of the "violent abduction" of Fat'ma Abdurazak kyzy, and also of burglary. In early January, the father of the abducted girl, a man by the name of Seit Veli Seit Mustafa oglu, had informed the local court investigator that his window had been broken and his daughter taken along with 25 silver rubles. He told the police that he suspected Iag'ia Dzhelial' oglu to be behind the abduction. During the later part of the investigation, however, the father suddenly changed his mind. He now explained that Fat'ma had left the house voluntarily. Moreover, he now claimed that no window had been broken and that no money had been stolen, and thus he asked for the investigation to be terminated. There is little doubt, then, that the father had come to an arrangement with the supposed "criminal" out of court.

The legal system, however, could not accommodate such extra-legal arrangements. While the investigator had complied with the victim's request and stopped his enquiries, the Circuit Court did not accept the Tatar's explanation. It argued that the sudden renunciation of previously reported crimes could not serve as grounds for the termination of a criminal in-

44 GAARK, 376-6-39, (1871).

vestigation. Thus, it ruled that the investigator had acted incorrectly and returned the case to him in late June.[45]

In short, as Crews (2006) has shown for earlier periods, the records of post-1864 circuit courts suggest that Tatars turned to the Russian authorities even in intra-Muslim family affairs, including the abduction of brides. Yet the last case also indicates that once you went to an imperial court, there was no way back. Governed by formal rules, the new courts were not places where you could easily come to informal deals with the jurists, unlike the pre-Reform courts in which the presumption of guilt, along with low degrees of professionalization, provided the accused with incentives to seek such deals.[46]

Regardless of such risks, however, Tatars went to court. In the summer of 1884, according to a local newspaper, a Tatar peasant quite literally entered the Circuit Court building in central Kazan.[47] He held a written complaint in his hands in which he explained that his daughter had been raped. The newspaper does not dwell on the crime or on its perpetrators, for it is mainly concerned with uncovering corruption among junior staff at the Court. The article describes how the porters and junior clerks in the building had set up a lucrative business whereby all peasants who turned up at the Court were told that their written statements were faulty and that they had to pay someone on the second floor to get a proper statement and file a lawsuit. The Tatar peasant then went upstairs and started haggling with the clerks, but when it became clear that he was not prepared to pay the money they demanded, they dragged him out of the building. The case, however, did not stop here because the Tatar had another letter written. This time, he addressed it to the chairman of the Circuit Court, denouncing the money-extorting practices among his clerks, and attached his original complaint. As a result of his letter, or so the newspaper claims, several court cases began: both the original rape case, and another case against the clerks.

45 *Ibid.*, pp. 1–2. The continuation of the case has not been preserved in the records.

46 While comprehensive "bottom-up" studies of pre-Reform courts are not yet available, several scholars point to the importance of informal deals in the pre-Reform justice system (LeDonne 1991, 181–199; Pipes 1995; Hartley 2000; Schattenberg 2008, 199–230).

47 *Volzhskii Vestnik*, August 23, 1884, No. 99.

As in several previous cases, this brief episode shows a Tatar peasant who approached a Russian court in a case in which local forms of conflict resolution may not have helped him punish the wrongdoer. Moreover, having the rape of his daughter discussed by the local community would have done neither him nor his daughter any favors. A victim of rape, just like victims of forced marriage or mob beatings, was more likely to be helped by imperial courts. At the same time, the case also reveals problems of access. This particular Tatar was persistent. Others who were thrown out of the building may not have had the determination or the resources to have a second letter written.

These cases are not meant to reinforce images of the Russian Empire as a society divided into state law and village norms. As ideas of law were multiple, dynamic, and involved constant border-crossing, binary models fail to capture the complexity "on the ground". Acting as individuals (whether as litigants, witnesses or other), locals strayed from communal expectations. Moreover, just as villages were not monolithic, Russian courts were made up of individuals who advanced different views. Some of these could be very similar to those expressed by rural actors, not least because peasants participated in the courtroom as jurors. One final case may help to illustrate this.

In October 1885, the *Tarjuman* (Translator), the only secular Tatar-language periodical in the Russian Empire before 1905, published a report of a case heard by the Kazan Circuit Court.[48] A young Tatar peasant woman was tried for the murder of her husband, the 60-year-old Ibetulla Gizetullin. The body of the man, covered in stab wounds, had been found in the river running through her village. The police were called, and during the ensuing inquiry, Gizetullin's wife confessed the murder. However, the investigation also exposed doubts about the character of the victim, which became the subject of heated debate in court. The accused and a large number of witnesses described the dead husband as a coarse man. In front of the jury, the wife also described her husband's sexual insatiability. After she had killed him during a fight, she told her oldest son about the killing and the two of them disposed of the body in the river. In court, all the witnesses denounced the husband, but said that his wife, the confessed murderer, was a modest and humble woman. While the prose-

48 *Tarjuman*, October 28, 1885, No. 12.

cution insisted that an unfortunate life was no excuse for murder, which the woman had clearly committed, the jury's deliberation took only a few minutes, after which they announced: "No, not guilty".

The case not only offers yet another example of Tatar peasants turning to the authorities to deal with a serious crime (after all, the body of the unpopular man could have simply been buried), but also highlights the lack of a clear boundary between state and local understandings of law. In imperial courts, a variety of opinions coexisted. While the prosecution was guided by an abstract "rule of law" which was mainly interested in whether the accused had committed the crime[49], the defense and witnesses dwelt on the fact that Gizetullin, the victim, was an unpleasant character, while his wife, the murderer, was a respected member of the community. To all appearances, the jurors accepted the second line of argument. Imperial circuit courts, then, did not necessarily enforce abstract laws. The Judicial Reforms had led to the emergence of a genuinely adversarial courtroom in Russia in which jurists presented competing views, and jurors had to choose sides (McReynolds 2010, 622). As a result, the verdicts could also coincide with the views held by a majority of people from a particular village.

Conclusion

Any study of court cases—be they criminal or civil—poses a twofold methodological challenge. First, since the number of cases under discussion is bound to be limited, the study must limit itself to suggestions and descriptions of legal process; it cannot make broad generalizations about legal behavior. More importantly, court cases are unusual situations. Scholars working on areas as diverse as American civil law and African "customary" law agree that most "injurious experiences" are not taken to court (Holleman 1973, 592; Felstiner et al. 1980–81, 651). But while the report of a crime and the launch of a criminal case may not have been

49 In other cases, this commitment to the rule of law was embodied by the chairman and judges while the prosecution defended the interests of the state. See Pipes on the famous Vera Zasulich trial (2010, esp. 40–61).

part of daily life (and thankfully, in most countries, they are not!), these forms of legal behavior are striking in the context of the Russian Empire where the attitude of peasants towards state institutions has often been discussed in terms of indifference or resistance.

By the late nineteenth century, using the courts was clearly considered an option. The Kazan Circuit Court processed cases at remarkable speed in certain years. For example, of all criminal cases closed for lack of evidence in introductory meetings in 1881 (a total of 1,099 cases), 95.5 percent were heard and closed within one month. Of the cases that were brought to trial in that year (952), 82.7 percent were decided by the court within six months.[50] The Judicial Reform had introduced relatively quick, transparent and accessible courts that provided a substantial degree of reliability. It seems that people expected to benefit from going to court in one way or another (even if this did not always happen). They not only launched civil lawsuits (as other studies have shown), but also reported criminals to have them prosecuted and punished.

The new circuit courts took little interest in ethnic and religious distinctions and thus contributed, in some ways, to the integration of imperial society. While the cases discussed in this chapter were about Kurtpedin Mengli Amet oglu, Bibi Fatyma Sabitova, or Ibetulla Gizetullin, most of them could just as well have featured people called Ivan Petrov. In the reports of pre-trial investigations or the minutes of the trials themselves, a short note usually mentioned the fact that Tatar witnesses or defendants required translators and had their oaths administered by mullahs. Other than that, their cultural or religious distinctiveness was rarely mentioned or taken into account. Behind this there was no liberal policy of integrating minorities; rather, the apparent neutrality of courts concerning ethnicity and religion was the result of a court system designed to strengthen the Empire and run by jurists who had little interest in culture. In the clearly demarcated, state-centered form of legal pluralism that followed the Great Reforms, cultural differences mattered mainly in lower-level courts and specific civil cases (usually of minor monetary value). The circuit courts, on the other hand, formed part of an increasingly unified legal space—thanks to both their design and the ways in which they were used.

50 See Ministry of Justice, *Svod statisticheskikh svedenii po delam ugolovnym, proizvodivshimsia v 1881 godu*, Part I, p. 23.

The fact that ordinary people became active participants in the legal system is not to suggest the disappearance of inequalities. As Starr and Collier noted (1989, 3, 7), the law is never neutral and impartial, but always constructed by human agency in a way that is advantageous to some at the expense of others. In imperial Russia, there is little doubt that linguistic, financial, geographical and other barriers put Tatar peasants at a disadvantage regarding the use of imperial courts. And yet, individuals and groups of Tatars actively turned to the circuit courts for help. Unfortunately, there are no reliable data on the numbers that went to court. The reports prepared by the circuit courts, on the one hand, and the Ministry of Justice, on the other, only give details, such as religion or ethnicity, of those who were *convicted* in court, not of those who turned to court. As far as convictions were concerned, the share of Muslims was lower than their share of the population. In Kazan, the share of "Muhammadans" (*magometane*) among the convicts oscillated between 29% (in 1880) and 15.4% (in 1900).[51] At the Simferopol Circuit Court, the share of Muslim convicts ranged from 20.3% (in 1879) to 16.2% (in 1900).[52] Muslims, then, probably interacted with the imperial courts less frequently than other groups. And yet, these figures also show that they were a more important part of the system than their virtual absence from the literature suggests.

Why did Tatars go to court then? In criminal cases in which they happened to be the victims, they may have seen the imperial courts as outside support in an unequal struggle with their neighbors and as reliable, external arbiters. Perceived reliability, in fact, may have persuaded Tatars as much as other imperial subjects to work with the courts. The system imprisoned criminals, at least for a while, and provided assistance in cases in which the community would have done little to help, such as rape or forced marriage. The Russian bureaucrats got the job done with-

51 See the following annual reports by the Ministry of Justice: *Svod statisticheskikh svedenii po delam ugolovnym, proizvodivshimsia v 1880 godu*, Part II, p. 135; and *Svod statisticheskikh svedenii po delam ugolovnym, proizvodivshimsia v 1900 godu*, Part II, p. 194.

52 For the percentage of Muslim convicts, see the Ministry of Justice: *Svod statisticheskikh svedenii po delam ugolovnym, proizvodivshimsia v 1879 godu*, Part II, p. 137; and *Svod statisticheskikh svedenii po delam ugolovnym, proizvodivshimsia v 1900 godu*, Part II, p. 193.

out thinking about local consequences. Peasants, admittedly, may have favored communal solutions, and surely there were many cases in which they ignored or resisted the Russian law-enforcement agents. But where local forms of conflict resolution were not available, or where alternative legal institutions such as Islamic judges or village courts were likely to rule against them, they pragmatically turned to those who could offer help.

Works Cited

Aguirre, Carlos and Salvatore, Ricardo D. (2001). Introduction: Writing the History of Law, Crime, and Punishment in Latin America. In Ricardo D. Salvatore, Carlos Aguirre and Gilbert M. Joseph (eds.) *Crime and Punishment in Latin America. Law and Society since Late Colonial Times*, 1–32. Durham, NC: Duke University Press.

Atwell, John W. (1975). The Russian Jury. *Slavonic and East European Review* , 53, 130, 44–61.

Auch, Eva-Maria (2004). Adat, Shari'a, Zakon: Zur Implementierung russischen Rechts in Kaukasien. *Rechtstheorie*, 35, 289–321.

Baberowski, Jörg (1990). Geschworenengerichte und Anwaltschaft. Ein Beitrag zur Erforschung der Rechtswirklichkeit im ausgehenden Zarenreich. *Jahrbücher für Geschichte Osteuropas*, 38, 25–72.

Baberowski, Jörg (1996). *Autokratie und Justiz. Zum Verhältnis von Rechtsstaatlichkeit und Rückständigkeit im ausgehenden Zarenreich, 1864–1914*. Frankfurt am Main: Klostermann.

Baberowski, Jörg (2006). Law, the Judicial System and the Legal Profession. In Dominic Lieven (ed.) *The Cambridge History of Russia. Imperial Russia, 1689–1917*, Vol. II, 344–368. Cambridge, UK: Cambridge University Press.

Baberowski, Jörg (2008). Vertrauen durch Anwesenheit. Vormoderne Herrschaft im späten Zarenreich. In Jörg Baberowski, David Feest and Christoph Gumb (eds.) *Imperiale Herrschaft in der Provinz*, 17–37. Frankfurt and New York: Campus.

Becker, Seymour (1986). The Muslim East in Nineteenth-Century Russian Popular Historiography. *Central Asian Survey*, 5, 3–4, 25–47.

Benda-Beckmann, Keebet von (1981). Forum Shopping and Shopping Forums. Dispute Settlement in a Minangkabau Village in West Sumatra. *Journal of Legal Pluralism*, 19, 117–159.

Benton, Lauren (2002). *Law and Colonial Cultures. Legal Regimes in World History, 1400–1900.* Cambridge, UK, and New York: Cambridge University Press.

Bhat, Girish N. (1994). *Trial by Jury in the Reign of Alexander II: A Study in the Legal Culture of Late Imperial Russia, 1864–1881.* Ph.D. Diss., University of California, Berkeley.

Bobrovnikov, Vladimir (1999). Sud po adatu v dorevoliutsionnom Dagestane (1860–1917). *Etnograficheskoe obozrenie*, 2, 31–45.

Bodarskii, Ia. E., Eliseeva, O.I. and Kabuzan, V.M. (2003). *Naselenie Kryma v kontse XVIII-kontse XX vekov*. Moscow: Rossiiskaia akademiia nauk.

Burbank, Jane (2004). *Russian Peasants Go to Court: Legal Culture in the Countryside, 1905–1917.* Indianapolis: Indiana University Press.

Burbank, Jane (2006). An Imperial Rights Regime: Law and Citizenship in the Russian Empire. *Kritika*, 7, 3, 397–431.

Burbank, Jane (2008). The Well-Ordered Peasant Village: Law and Sanitation at Russian Local Courts. In Belinda Davis, Thomas Lindenberger and Michael Wildt (eds.) *Alltag, Erfahrung, Eigensinn,* 218–231. Frankfurt and New York: Campus.

Burbank, Jane and Cooper, Frederick (2010). *Empires in World History. Power and the Politics of Difference.* Princeton: Princeton University Press.

Cohn, Bernard S. (1965). Anthropological Notes on Disputes and Law in India. *American Anthropologist*, 67, 6, 82–122.

Crews, Robert D. (2006). *For Prophet and Tsar. Islam and Empire in Russia and Central Asia.* Cambridge, MA, and London: Harvard University Press.

Dzhanshiev, Grigoriy A. (1900). *Epokha velikikh reform: istoricheskie spravki.* Moscow: Kushnerev.

Felstiner, William L. F., Abel, Richard L. and Sarat, Austin (1980–81). The Emergence and Transformation of Disputes. Naming, Blaming, Claiming...*Law & Society Review*, 15, 3/4, 631–654.

Fisher, Alan W. (1978). *The Crimean Tatars.* Stanford, CA: Hoover Institution Press.

Fisher, Alan W. (1987). Emigration of Muslims from the Russian Empire in the Years after the Crimean War. *Jahrbücher für Geschichte Osteuropas*, 35, 3, 356–371.

Frank, Allen J. (2001). *Muslim Religious Institutions in Imperial Russia. The Islamic World of Novouzensk District and the Kazakh Inner Horde, 1780–1910.* Leiden: Brill.

Frank, Stephen P. (1999). *Crime, Cultural Conflict, and Justice in Rural Russia, 1856–1914.* Berkeley, CA: University of California Press.

Frierson, Cathy A. (1987). Crime and Punishment in the Russian Village: Rural Concepts of Criminality at the End of the Nineteenth Century. *Slavic Review*, 46, 1, 55–69.

Fuks, Karl (1844). *Kazanskie Tatary v statisticheskom i etnograficheskom otnosheniiakh.* Kazan: Universitetskaia Tipografiia.

Geraci, Robert (2001). *Window on the East. National and Imperial Identities in Late Tsarist Russia.* Ithaca and London: Cornell University Press.

Gordon, Robert J. and Meggitt, Mervyn J. (1985). *Law and Order in the New Guinea Highlands: Encounters with Enga.* Hanover, NH: Vermont.

Hartley, Janet (2000). Bribery and Justice in the Provinces in the Reign of Catherine II. In Stephen Lovell, Alena Ledenova and Andrei Rogachevskii (eds.) *Bribery and* Blat *in Russia*, 48–64. Basingstoke and London: Macmillan.

Hoebel, E. Adamson (1965). Fundamental Cultural Postulates and Judicial Lawmaking in Pakistan. *American Anthropologist*, 67, 6, 43–56.

Holleman, J. F. (1973). Trouble-cases and Trouble-less Cases in the Study of Customary Law and Legal Reform. *Law & Society Review*, 7, 4, 585–610.

Iakushkin, E.I. (1899). *Obychnoe Pravo Russkikh Inorodtsev* (Customary Law of the Russian *Inorodtsy*). Moscow: Universitetskaia tipografiia.

Jersild, Austin (2002). *Orientalism and Empire. North Caucasus Mountain Peoples and the Georgian Frontier, 1845–1917*. Montreal: McGill-Queen's University Press.

Jobst, Kerstin S. (2007). *Die Perle des Imperiums. Der russische Krim-Diskurs im Zarenreich*. Constance: UVK.

Kappeler, Andreas (1982). *Rußlands erste Nationalitäten. Das Zarenreich und die Völker der Mittleren Wolga vom 16. bis 19. Jahrhundert*. Cologne and Vienna: Böhlau.

Kassow, Samuel D. (1989). *Students, Professors, and the State in Tsarist Russia*. Berkeley, CA: University of California Press.

Kemper, Michael (2005). Adat against Shari'a: Russian Approaches towards Daghestani "Customary Law" in the 19th Century. *Ab Imperio*, 3, 147–174.

Kemper, Michael and Reinkowski, Maurus (eds.) (2005). *Rechtspluralismus in der Islamischen Welt*. Berlin: Walter de Gruyter.

Khäyrutdinov, Rämil (2001). The Tatar Ratusha of Kazan: National Self-Administration in Autocratic Russia, 1781–1855. In Stéphane A. Dudoignon and Hisao Komatsu (eds.) *Islam in Politics in Russia and Central Asia*, 27–42. London: Kegan Paul.

Kirmse, Stefan B. (2012). New Courts in Late Tsarist Russia. Of Imperial Representation and Muslim Participation. *Journal of Modern European History*, forthcoming.

Kozelsky, Mara (2008). Casualties of Conflict: Crimean Tatars during the Crimean War. *Slavic Review*, 67, 4, 866–891.

Kucherov, Samuel (1953). *Courts, Lawyers and Trials under the Last Three Tsars*. New York: Praeger.

Laptev, M. (1861). *Materialy dlia geografii i statistiki Rossii: Kazanskaia Guberniia*. St. Petersburg: Voennaia Tipografiia.

Lavrskii, K. (1884). *Tatarskaia Bednota.* Kazan: Tipografiia Gubernskago Pravleniia.

Lazarus-Black, Mindie and Hirsch, Susan F. (eds.) (1994). *Contested States: Law, Hegemony, and Resistance.* New York and London: Routledge.

Lazzarini, Edward J. (1981). Tatarovedenie and the "New Historiography" in the Soviet Union. Revising the Interpretation of the Tatar-Russian Relationship. *Slavic Review*, 40, 4, 625–635.

LeDonne, John P. (1991). *Absolutism and Ruling Class. The Formation of the Russian Political Order, 1700–1825.* New York and Oxford: Oxford University Press.

Liustritskii, V. (1894). *Pamiatnaia Knizhka Kazanskoi Gubernii za 1893–94 gody.* Kazan: Tipografiia Gubernskogo Pravleniia.

Macauley, Melissa Ann (1998). *Social Power and Legal Culture. Litigation Masters in Late Imperial China.* Stanford, CA: Stanford University Press.

Martin, Virginia (2001). *Law and Custom in the Steppe. The Kazakhs of the Middle Horde and Russian Colonialism in the Nineteenth Century.* Richmond: Curzon.

McReynolds, Louise (2010). Witnessing for the Defense: The Adversarial Court and Narratives of Criminal Behavior in Nineteenth-Century Russia. *Slavic Review*, 69, 3, 620–644.

Merry, Sally E. (1994). Courts as Performances. Domestic Violence Hearings in a Hawai'i Family Court. In Mindie Lazarus-Black and Susan F. Hirsch (eds.) *Contested States: Law, Hegemony, and Resistance*, 35–58. New York and London. Routledge.

Mukhametshin, Rafik (2010). Islamic Discourse in the Volga-Urals Region. In Galina Yemelianova (ed.) *Radical Islam in the Former Soviet Union*, 31–61. London and New York: Routledge.

N-ch, N. (1869). Narodnye iuridicheskie obychai u Tatar Kazanskoi gubernii. In N.N. Vecheslav (ed.) *Trudy Kazanskago Gubernskago Statisticheskago Komiteta.* Vol. 3, 21–42. Kazan: Gubernskaia tipografiia.

O'Neill, Kelly (2006). *Between Subversion and Submission: The Integration of the Crimean Khanate in the Russian Empire, 1783–1853.* PhD diss., Harvard University.

Pipes, Richard (1995 [1974]). *Russia under the Old Regime*. London and New York: Penguin.

Pipes, Richard (2010). The Vera Zasulich Trial. *Russian History*, 37.

Randeria, Shalini (2006). Entangled Histories: Civil Society, Caste Solidarities and Legal Pluralism in Post-Colonial India. In John Keane (ed.) *Civil Society: Berlin Perspectives*, 213–242. New York and Oxford: Berghahn.

Rittikh, A.F. (1870). *Materialy dlia etnografii Rossii: Kazanskaia guberniia*. Kazan: Tipografiia Imperatorskogo Kazanskogo Universiteta.

Schattenberg, Susanne (2008). *Die korrupte Provinz? Russische Beamte im 19. Jahrhundert*. Frankfurt and New York: Campus.

Schmidt, Christoph (1996). *Sozialkontrolle in Moskau. Justiz, Kriminalität und Leibeigenschaft, 1649–1785*. Stuttgart: Franz Steiner Verlag.

Shino, P.A. (1860). Volzhskie Tatary. *Sovremennik* 81 and 82, May-June and July-August, 255–290 and 121–142.

Slocum, John W. (1998). Who, and When, Were the *Inorodtsy*? The Evolution of the Category of "Aliens" in Imperial Russia. *The Russian Review*, 57, 170–193.

Starr, June and Collier, Jane F. (eds.) (1989). *History and Power in the Study of Law. New Directions in Legal Anthropology*. Ithaca, NY, and London: Cornell University Press.

Valikhanov, Chokan. Ch. (1904 [1864]). Zapiska o sudebnoi reforme. *Zapiski Imperatorskago Russkago Geograficheskago Obshchestva po otdeleniiu etnografii*, 29, 151–178.

Werth, Paul W. (2002). *At the Margins of Orthodoxy. Mission, Governance, and Confessional Politics in Russia's Volga-Kama Region, 1827–1905*. Ithaca, NY: Cornell University Press.

Worobec, Christine D. (1995). *Peasant Russia. Family and Community in the Post-Emancipation Period*. DeKalb: Northern Illinois University Press.

Wortman, Richard S. (1976). *The Development of a Russian Legal Consciousness*. Chicago: University of Chicago Press.

Yaroshevski, Dov (1997). Empire and Citizenship. In Daniel R. Brower and Edward J. Lazzerini (eds.) *Russia's Orient. Imperial Borderlands and Peoples, 1700–1917*, 58–79. Bloomington: Indiana University Press.

Yemelianova, Galina M. (1999). Volga Tatars, Russians and the Russian State at the Turn of the Nineteenth Century: Relationships and Perceptions. *The Slavonic and East European Review*, 77, 3, 448–484.

Entanglements and Interactions within a Plural Legal Order: The Case of the German Colony Cameroon, 1884–1916

Ulrike Schaper

Introduction

By approving treaties between German trading companies and local authorities of the coastal population in 1884, the German Empire began its colonization of the territory that more or less equals present-day Cameroon. This political act stirred debate among German elites about the legal relation of the two political entities and the legal status of the African population. Since the colonies were not included as part of the territory of Germany as defined by the German constitution of 1871, German law did not automatically apply within the German colonies. Legal relations in all German colonies were uniformly regulated for the first time in 1886. The "Law concerning legal relationships in the German colonies" (Gesetz betreffend die Rechtsverhältnisse der deutschen Schutzgebiete)—after several amendments referred to as the "Law concerning the colonies" (*Schutzgebietsgesetz*)—introduced a plural legal order.[1]

German law was introduced in the colonies, including Cameroon, in the form of consular jurisdiction, which allowed consuls to preside over (some) legal cases involving German citizens. Yet, German law was im-

1 Current research in law and the social sciences has stressed that gradations of "legal pluralism" can be found in every society (see Merry 1988, 873, or Rehbinder 2000). Different social contexts show regulations and sanctioning mechanisms that can be relatively independent of the state. In contexts of colonial domination, distinctive forms of "legal pluralism" developed in which different legal orders were more or less formally integrated into a common legal system, sometimes competing for authority in the same contexts. Even if the colonial state raised the claim to dominate the legal system—which according to Benton (2002) did not happen before the end of the nineteenth century—it often failed to enforce it.

plemented only for German citizens or citizens of other states recognized by international law. All other inhabitants of the colonies were assigned to the legal status of "natives". "Natives" were not subject to German law, and their legal cases fell outside the jurisdiction of German imperial courts. The legal order thus established two distinct legal categories: native and non-native. These categories were built on a racialized distinction between colonized and colonizers and largely corresponded to the distinction between "black" and "white".[2] The division between colonizers and colonized was thus affirmed and granted legal and political power. Law became an instrument of colonial power politics aimed at rule and control through "racial" segregation.

Research on law in the German colonies has, thus far, emphasized the importance of law for the institutionalization of colonial difference and the exclusion of the African population from the German legal order (Essner 1992; Sippel 1997; Joeden-Forgey 2004). Such a perspective is undoubtedly useful, as this order indeed played a key role in the colonial policy of "racial" segregation. However, the focus on segregation has been accompanied by a concentration on criminal law and a disregard for legal practice and court proceedings (see, for example, Walz 1981; Fischer 2001; Wagner 2002; Schlottau 2007). German colonial historiography also continues to neglect several important issues, including the ways in which German legal policies served to establish and maintain colonial power, the effects of the interaction between litigants and colonial officials on legal reality, and the actual running of the day-to-day trial business.[3]

This chapter attempts to contribute to some of these questions. Focusing on the legal reality "on the ground" rather than institutional and normative designs from "above", and including disputes then understood as civil disputes under German law, I demonstrate that in spite of legal segregation, legal relations and conflicts between Africans and Europeans

2 Throughout German colonial rule, the exact legal definition of the status "native" remained controversial. For the legal debate on the "natives" and the different decrees concerning their definition, see e.g. Aitken (2007, 101–108); Nagl (2007, 56–61). To avoid the racist implications of the original terms, the two groups of "natives" and "non-natives" are referred to as "Europeans" and "Africans" in the following.

3 For some inspiring work on French and British colonies that includes legal practice, see Chanock (2001) and Roberts (2005).

were inextricably linked. Colonial and local institutions frequently interacted.

To make matters more complicated, in addition to the dual structure that established different laws for Africans and Europeans, the colonial legal order also created a plural legal structure for the African population, according to which legal conflicts between "natives" were to be decided on the grounds of the so-called "native law" (*Eingeborenenrecht*). The *Eingeborenenrecht* drew on two legal traditions: first, colonial law consisting of decrees and administrative directions enacted by the German or colonial governments, which applied to all Africans in the colony; and second, various "customary laws" for the different groups of Africans. In accordance with the *Eingeborenenrecht*, legal cases, especially those which the Germans saw as criminal law, were to be decided by local officials based on both African and colonial law. In addition, the Germans authorized African chiefs to preside over petty crime and over cases which the German colonizers considered to be "civil law". The right to judge was linked to the official rank of chiefs (*Häuptlingswürde*) and implied influence over the political community. By appointing local leaders as judges, the colonial government sought to create a loyal elite (Stockhausen 1911, 312–313). The Germans understood these courts as a continuation of pre-colonial practices in which decisions were made in accordance with an allegedly "customary" law.[4] This customary law was thus incorporated in the *Eingeborenenrecht*. Colonial politicians called for the preservation of local customs as a means to prevent resistance, which immediate intervention in local social structures might otherwise provoke.[5] By establishing continuity, the Germans hoped to ensure peaceful "development" and promote the acceptance of the German government. The confirmation or appointment of chiefs, however, often changed the local power structure and concentrated all legal functions in one person. In addition to the courts of the chief, the Germans introduced courts of arbitration, col-

4 The question of how far "customary law" was a pre-colonial institution or how it was constructed and "invented" as part of colonialism has been discussed elsewhere at length. See e.g. Snyder (1981), Fitzpatrick (1984) and Chanock (1985).

5 See e.g. Bundesarchiv Berlin-Lichterfelde (BArch) R 1001/5004, Gouvernement to Secretary of the Colonial Office, September 21, 1907, p. 2; Archives Nationales, Yaoundé, (ANY) FA 1/622, Attachment to the report of the Station Akoloniga, August 21, 1912, p. 106; Schreiber (1904, 768).

lective decision-making bodies staffed with several chiefs of a particular region, in certain areas along the coast.[6] The inclusion of such local courts was meant to diminish the workload of the colonial administration.[7] The integration of local authorities in the legal system was intended to provide the colony with an efficient and economical administration of justice. Beyond the courts that were formally included in the colonial legal order, disputes continued to be settled by families and in other social or religious contexts. Colonial officials often did not know about these mechanisms of conflict resolution or could not influence them. In fact, they tried to prohibit such activities whenever they heard about them.

In order to analyze the entanglements and interactions within this plural legal order, I adopt Merry's term "legal spheres" (1982, 71) that can serve to systematize the different courts and bodies of law. Merry uses the term to capture alternative sets of rules, procedures and forums involved in the settlement of disputes by socially legitimate third parties. According to Merry, each legal sphere possesses 1) a set of rules, 2) a set of procedures for handling disputes, 3) a political and economic context within which the third party acts and 4) specified requirements (such as ethnicity, economic status, and sex) for access to the legal sphere. The term allows us to include structural, rule-related aspects as well as the litigants' behavior and perception of the different ways in which disputes can be resolved. In the German colony Cameroon, a number of legal spheres can be identified: first, a European legal sphere in which German law was applied by judges in formal courts, access to which was restricted to citizens of internationally recognized states; second, a colonial legal sphere for Africans in which colonial officials judged and were instructed to apply colonial law and modified customary law; third, a customary legal sphere with native courts authorized by the colonial government; and finally, legal spheres that were largely independent of colonial institutions. As I show later, such unofficial arenas for dispute resolution could impinge on the authority of formal courts.

6 Verordnung des Gouverneurs, betreffend Einführung eines Eingeborenen-Schiedsgerichts für den Duala-Stamm. In Ruppel (1912), no. 434, fn. 3.

7 See ANY FA 1/614, Gouvernement to District Office Edea, January 31, 1906, p. 28; BArch R1001/5003, Governor to Imperial Chancellor, September 16, 1893, p. 60; BArch 1001/5003 Governor to Foreign Office, Colonial Department, April 23, 1904, p. 168.

In what follows, I first discuss cases that did not fit into the existing system of legal segregation and were taken to court as so-called "mixed cases" between Africans and Europeans. I explore the ways in which these cases transgressed established legal boundaries and stirred legal and political debate. Using the example of the "mixed cases" I show that the European and the colonial legal spheres for Africans could not be separated as easily as their legal distinction would suggest. Second, I demonstrate that the colonial and the customary legal spheres did not merely coexist. Using the examples of imprisonment, summons, searches for persons accused of crimes, and appeals, I highlight the interaction between institutions from different legal spheres. Third, I argue that the African population perceived one single space in which legal matters could be handled, and used different courts within that environment.

Thus I argue that beyond the duality of courts for Europeans and courts for Africans and the distinction between colonial law and customary law, the laws and legal institutions that sometimes competed for the same cases constituted, and were experienced as, one legal system. In this sense, there existed only one legal reality in the German colony Cameroon.

"Mixed Cases"

Colonial law did not define the legal relations between Europeans and Africans. At the same time, social and economic relations transgressed the legal boundaries that had been constructed between "natives" and "non-natives". The legal spheres, separate only in theory, became as intertwined as the lives of Europeans and Africans themselves. Naturally, these social and economic relationships sometimes caused conflicts which the opponents then tried to resolve with judicial help. Yet such an undertaking, simple only at first sight, raised numerous questions. As the parties were subject to different laws, no regulation determined how "mixed cases" should be handled. It was unclear which court had jurisdiction in "mixed cases", and no conflict-of-law rules determined which law was to be applied. Existing scholarship has discussed the legal relations between Africans and Europeans in the German colonies mainly in the context of "mixed marriages" (Essner 2005, 29; for examples, see Schulte-Althoff 1985, Sippel 1995, Wildenthal 1997). Marriages, however, were only one and not even the most common example of legal relations between Africans and Europeans following colonial expansion. Since the German colony Cameroon was not a settler colony and colonial officials, tradesmen and explorers often stayed there only for a short period of time, conflicts concerning marriage law formed only a small part of the "mixed cases".

More often, these "mixed cases" resulted from trade between European merchants and African traders or contractual relations between European employers and African employees. A considerable number of Africans, for example, filed cases against their employers, usually in order to claim their wages. In 1913, local merchants even complained about the district court in Lomie, accusing a judge of too eagerly supporting lawsuits by African claimants against their European employers. In his response, the judge in question stressed the legitimacy of these lawsuits. He argued that some European firms did not meet their obligation to pay wages to their African employees or often reduced these wages arbitrarily in order to punish the employees for alleged misbehavior.[8]

The conflicts that were taken to court as "mixed cases" were the result of intensifying relations between Europeans and Africans in the German colonies. Colonial administrators considered "mixed" legal relations to be an inevitable and welcome consequence of the colonial encounter:

> The separation of the legal systems by law does of course not prevent —and considering the intention of the legislator should not prevent—legal relations between black and white people, especially business of all kinds. It is not the case that business (*commercium*) is legally forbidden; on the contrary, it is the basis of trade and welfare in the colony.[9]

While there were no definite rules that defined the jurisdiction in "mixed cases", these cases had to be decided somewhere. In practice, this jurisdiction was determined by the legal status of the defendant. If an African worker wanted to sue his European employer to claim his wages, he had to turn to the court for Europeans. A European merchant who

8 ANY FA 1/299, Copy of the report of the district Judge Schuhmacher in Lomie, August 9, 1913, pp. 20–21.

9 BArch R 1001/5517, internal statement, January 26, 1909, p. 141.

had claims against an African trader had to make his case before a colonial official. European tradesmen also had to apply to colonial officials if they sued African traders for large sums of money. There were, however, exceptions to this unwritten rule. Sometimes a judge from a court for Europeans simply asserted his own authority over cases in which the defendant was "native" in the legal sense.[10]

Since the responsibility for criminal cases that involved both Africans and Europeans was also determined by the legal status of the defendant, Africans and Europeans who were involved in the same criminal offence had to be sent to different courts.

In order to understand why "mixed cases" caused such difficulties in the colonial system, we must take into account the context of the jurisdiction exercised by colonial officials and the role of law and legal policy as part of colonial domination. One of the main purposes of the legal powers of officials was the maintenance of public order. The Germans saw public order as vital to the continuation of colonial power. German authority had to be maintained and the safety of Germans in the colony protected. According to most colonial politicians, legal regulations had to be kept to a minimum to secure the officials' freedom of action.[11] As a consequence, colonial law concerning Africans included few procedural regulations. Substantive law that defined statutory rules for Africans was not enforced until the end of German rule. Colonial officials who presided over civil lawsuits by African litigants were instructed to base their decisions on local customs, provided these customs were not "repugnant to Western civilization" and did not endanger German domination. In criminal law cases, the officials had to consider both German criminal law and the local "sense of justice".[12]

These vague instructions meant that colonial officials had great discretion and could make decisions more or less arbitrarily. In addition, most officials had a military background and no legal training whatsoever. This contributed considerably to the legal insecurity of the African population.

10 BArch R1001/5517, copy, p. 23; BArch R1001/5517, Prange to Imperial Chancellor, January 6, 1908, p. 26.

11 For the discussion of the attempts to codify the colonial criminal law, see Schaper (2009, 25–26).

12 See e.g. ANY FA 1/292, District Office Victoria to Gouvernement, April 29, 1906, p. 177.

After the turn of the century, the Colonial Office in Berlin attempted to bring the decisions of colonial officials more closely in line with German criminal law (Walz 1981, 97–104 and 174–185). In 1907, the Colonial Office replaced the Colonial Department of the Foreign Office and was directly subordinated to the Imperial Chancellor. It was responsible for the administration of the colonies, including the selection of officials who were to be sent to the colonies.

These attempts to strengthen the enforcement of German criminal law, however, had little success. Insecurity and arbitrariness continued to characterize the legal work of colonial officials in the German colony Cameroon. More than legal and political actors in Germany, these officials saw the central function of the law as the creation and perpetuation of the colonial hierarchy.[13] They saw the law as an instrument to punish a lack of respect for colonial authorities and used their legal powers as a means of control and repression vis-à-vis the African population. The strength of the law as a means of subjection resulted from the lack of legal security for the colonized. When "mixed cases" were brought before a colonial official, this legal uncertainty, usually to the disadvantage of the local population, also affected Europeans.

It was in reaction to this disadvantage that after the turn of the century, the Colonial Office in Berlin made efforts to produce legal regulations and conflict of law rules for "mixed cases". These efforts were, among other things, triggered by a petition submitted by the Cameroon-based lawyer Kurt Prange in 1908. The court for Europeans in Lome, the capital of the German colony of Togo, had dismissed a case in which a German tradesman had sued two African merchants for 125,000 marks. The joint court of appeal for Togo and Cameroon then refused to handle the case because it fell outside its jurisdiction. The gist of the petition was that Prange wanted his client to be allowed to make his case before a court of justice rather than before a colonial official.[14] While the German merchant eventually hired a different lawyer, Prange continued to pursue the matter of "mixed cases". For example, he chaired the Chamber of Trade in

13 See e.g. ANY FA 1/292, Zimmerer to Imperial Chancellor Caprivi, May 4, 1894, p. 3; ANY FA 1/292, District Office Duala to Gouvernement, p. 110; ANY FA 1/292, Military Station Ebolova October 13, 1902, p. 108; ANY FA 1/292, Military Station Bango to Gouvernement December 10, 1902, p. 117.

14 BArch R 1001/5517, Prange to the Imperial Chancellor, January 6, 1908, pp. 25–27.

South Cameroon and had the Chamber submit a petition to the Imperial Chancellor, the parliament and the Federal Assembly of Germany and to the Governor of Togo and Cameroon. The petition demanded that jurisdiction be given to ordinary courts of justice in non-wage-related cases in which the value of the claim exceeded 300 marks.[15]

This incident indicates one key motivation behind the Germans' attempts to regulate "mixed cases". They aimed at increasing the predictability of legal decisions for the European party. Critics of the existing practice found it unacceptable that Europeans had to make their legal claims before colonial officials:

> That non-natives should be allowed to seek their right in an ordinary court where important cases against natives are concerned, appears very desirable to me. We have to consider that colonial officials who are now appointed to decide in most of the cases lack legal training and that there are few guarantees in this kind of proceedings.[16]

Critics of the existing practice argued that for the sake of the European litigants it was necessary to allow the ordinary courts to rule over "mixed cases".[17] Ultimately they voiced their concern in explicitly racist terms of a feared "niggerization" (*Verniggerung*)[18] of the jurisdiction that would come about if Europeans were placed legally on par with Africans.

The proposal to transfer the jurisdiction for "mixed cases" to ordinary courts was sometimes also supported with reference to the African party. It was pointed out that the assumption of African impecuniousness could no longer be sustained. Therefore, it was also necessary to protect the financial interests of Africans by law.[19] In cases that involved large amounts of money, legal security had to be increased, first and foremost to protect the property rights of Europeans, but also—even if this was stressed less frequently—to protect the property rights of Africans.

---

15 BArch R 1001/5517, Chamber of Trade in South Cameroon to the Imperial Chancellor, April 1, 1908, pp. 32–34.

16 BArch R 1001/5517, Governor Seitz to Colonial Office, December 1, 1908, p. 122.

17 BArch R1001/5518, Judge (*Oberrichter*) Authenrieth to Governor of Cameroon, May 11, 1912, Attachment to report no. 796, p. 26.

18 BArch R 1001/5517, copy of the judgment, Deputy Judge (*stellv. Oberrichter*) Lämmermann, June 16, 1908, p. 135.

19 BArch R 1001/5517, internal statement, January 26, 1909, p. 141.

This proposal, however, ran counter to the political ideal of segregation and thus potentially undermined the foundations of colonial rule. The colonial order was constructed around the segregation of Germans from the local population. As I have argued above, legal policy was a means to stabilize this order through the establishment and maintenance of the difference between the colonizers and the colonized. Law was one sphere in and with which the authorities sought to uphold a clear division.

Yet, if laws and legal institutions for Africans and Europeans were to be kept separate as much as possible, "mixed cases" could not be decided in the courts for Europeans. From a racist point of view, "mixed cases" had to be treated with caution. In this line of argumentation, the question of the regulation of "mixed cases" could not be decided independently of the question of legal (in)equality. The unconditional superiority of Europeans had to be secured by legal privileges, segregation and by the possibility to use trials against Africans as a means of control and suppression. In this view, the transfer of "mixed cases" to the courts for Europeans was a dangerous step towards legal equality. Opponents of this proposal even stated that the possibility to appear before ordinary courts would be too much of an "honor" for Africans.[20] Clearly, the question of access to courts could not be separated from the perceived need to keep the colonized population in a subordinate position.

In February 1912, the Colonial Office in Berlin proposed a first solution to the issue of "mixed cases". It sent a draft decree to the governors of all German colonies, according to which the ordinary courts for Europeans were to receive jurisdiction over land disputes, in compulsory auctions of land and in all cases that involved a minimum amount of 5,000 marks, even if Africans had taken action. All other "mixed cases" were to be handled by colonial officials.[21]

The governor and supreme judge (*Oberrichter*) of Cameroon opposed this decree. Considering the local circumstances, they viewed the decree as inappropriate because in theory it allowed intra-African lawsuits to be

20 BArch R 1001/5517, copy of the judgment, Deputy Judge (*stellv. Oberrichter*) Lämmermann, June 16, 1908, p. 134. The judgment, however, declares this point obsolete since the "mixed cases" could be relegated to the ordinary courts already within the existing situation. This happened, for example, in the case of counter-claim or if the European party was convicted to pay the legal expenses.

21 BArch R1001/5517, draft decree, pp. 259–260.

negotiated before the ordinary courts for Europeans. They feared that the decree would lead towards greater equality, which eroded racial domination: "In my opinion we cannot warn strongly enough against taking this first step on a course that descends steeply. Once we decide to take this course, we cannot go back again," the judge wrote in his report.[22]

The governors of the other German colonies also opposed the draft decree. Above all, they insisted that the differences within and between the German colonies militated against a uniform regulation in all the colonies. Accepting these concerns, the Colonial Office abandoned its plan to enforce an all-encompassing solution to "mixed cases" for all colonies. It decided that the matter was to be dealt with at the local level and called for each Governor to present a draft decree for the colony over which he governed.[23] The Colonial Office requested these decrees in June 1914, that is, just before the outbreak of World War I, and the issue of "mixed cases" in the German colony Cameroon remained unresolved until the Germans lost this territory in 1916.

The attempts to regulate the issue of "mixed cases" reveal the tensions between the different aims of colonial policy. The regulation of "mixed cases" was a matter of conflicting interests. On the one hand, trade and the colonial economy were to be protected and developed, as the entire colonial enterprise existed in part for economic reasons. The claim to introduce the rule of law in the colonies allegedly suffering from despotic, irrational and arbitrary local legal orders served to justify colonial expansion. On the other hand, the colonized population was not to be granted too many rights since their subordinate legal status was an important means of colonial rule. The segregation between colonizers and colonized formed the basis of the German domination in the colony Cameroon. Any regulation of "mixed cases" had to be consistent with this ideology. The segregation was not to be diluted by admitting Africans to take legal action before ordinary courts, for this could be interpreted as a first step towards legal equality. To deny Africans access to the courts of Europeans, however, also meant that Europeans sometimes had to claim their rights before colonial

22 BArch R1001/5518, expert assessment of the Judge (*Oberrichter*) Authenrieth, May 11, 1912, p. 24.

23 BArch R 1001/5518, Gleim to the Governors of all Colonies, June 18, 1914, p. 59.

officials. The strict segregation thus eroded the legal protection and property rights of Europeans.

The issue of "mixed cases" illustrates not only the problems of forming a legal framework for colonial domination that would reconcile the different aims of colonial policy. The debates surrounding the issue further suggest that legal reality in the German colony Cameroon was shaped by far more entanglements and exchanges than the dual structure of the legal order had arranged for. The debates reveal numerous points of contact between the colonizers and the colonized. The different legal systems did not coexist in isolation from one another, and cases often transgressed the walls of legal segregation. The two legal spheres, separate only in theory, merged and overlapped in practice as much as the everyday lives of Europeans and Africans. Strict legal segregation must therefore be seen as a utopian vision of the colonizers rather than as an adequate description of legal reality in Cameroon.

Cooperation between Local Courts and the Colonial Administration

The colonial and the constructed customary legal spheres interacted in many ways. The prison system, for example, was deeply entangled and remained so until the early twentieth century. At the beginning of colonial rule, prison sentences passed by the native courts had to be served in the prisons of the colonial government. Only after 1905 did the colonial government try to increase the autonomy of the native courts in this respect.[24] It then pushed for the institutional separation of penal institutions within the plural legal order. By establishing separate prisons, the German authorities sought to increase the African awareness of the "different meaning of a judgment pronounced by a white or a black judge."[25] In August 1906, the governor reported the completion of this process.

24 BArch R 1001/5003, Foreign Office, Colonial Department to Gouvernement, September 16, 1905, p. 171.

25 BArch R 1001/5003, Foreign Office, Colonial Department to Gouvernement, September 16, 1905, p. 171.

All African criminals convicted by a native court were henceforth to be imprisoned separately from those convicted by a colonial official.[26]

Colonial officials and native courts also cooperated in searches for suspects and wanted criminals. Officials were often forced to fall back on local power structures because their own resources were limited. Thus, they turned to the native courts for support in finding wanted persons.[27] In many cases, however, the African party did not cooperate voluntarily. In certain situations, colonial officials secured local support for the state legal system by force. Villages or local chiefs who did not cooperate were faced with severe punishments. These collective punishments, which the local population strongly denounced, can be seen as indications that the colonial state did not have the capacity to carry out searches for suspected criminals without local support.

Yet, cooperation was sometimes initiated by African chiefs. They requested help from the colonial administration, for example, when people refused to appear in the native court.[28] They also relied on the assistance of the colonial administration for the arrest and transfer of people who had left the geographical area of their jurisdiction.[29] The colonial government, in turn, sometimes issued a threat of punishment in order to support the native courts in their work.[30] Within the colonial legal system, the native courts had the function of securing the efficient processing of legal cases on the basis of the local law. That said, the chiefs were appointed as judges by the governorate; similarly, the courts of arbitration were established by

26 BArch R 1001/5003, Governor of Cameroon to Foreign Office, Colonial Department, August, 13, 1906, p. 185. Only few Europeans were sentenced to imprisonment in Cameroon and often the prisons in which sentences were to be carried out did not exist. In order to spare Europeans from serving time in prison together with Africans, they were sent to prisons in Germany if the period of imprisonment was longer than six months. Very little is known about those few Europeans imprisoned in the colony Cameroon (Walz 1981, 335–336).

27 ANY FA 4/434, Wuri court of arbitration to District Office Duala, July 2, 1913, without page number.

28 ANY FA 1/37, report, June 2, 1894, p. 261.

29 ANY FA 4/434, Wuri court of arbitration to District Office Duala, November 28, 1913, without page number.

30 A case in which the colonial government threatened a local authority with punishment in case he would not provide for the appearance of the defendant and a litigious child before the court of arbitration can be found in ANY FA 4/434, note, March 22, 1913, without page number.

the colonial administration, and the staff chosen by African chiefs had to be acknowledged by the colonial administration. As institutions integrated in the colonial legal system, they sometimes faced protest or boycott from the African population.[31] The colonial administration also regarded them, in some ways, as part of the colonial court system whose functioning was important for the authority of the colonial administration. Thus, colonial officials sometimes supported the native courts by using the power of the state. Their hybrid character made the native courts worthy of this protection.

Moreover, decrees enacted from 1890 onward linked native courts and colonial courts as different stages of the appeal process. The governor was installed as the court of appeals for decisions by the native courts. He monitored the verdicts and could ultimately decide the cases. Thus, the same legal conflicts could be decided by institutions of the colonial state as well as by local institutions. Colonial officials who dealt with appeals on behalf of the governor drew on the decisions of the native courts. These decisions had to be submitted to the colonial administration.[32] Even with regard to the structure of the court system, the native courts and the jurisdiction by colonial officials functioned as different parts of the same court system. Yet, the system of different stages of appeal was a model derived from colonial law. The actual relations between native and state courts did not always fit into that scheme. Initially, and later on because of infrastructure problems at least in the interior regions of the colony, the colonial officials did not always follow the rules. Thus, they did not take into account in whose jurisdiction the cases fell but took them on regardless of jurisdiction. When colonial officials ruled over civil law cases on the basis of what they understood as customary law, they related to the same set of rules as the native courts, although native courts and colonial officials functioned as third parties in different legal spheres. Again, the colonial and the customary spheres became blurred.

31 ANY FA 1/100, Ekobo und Njanga, Kings of Dibombadito to the Governor, July 3, 1893, p. 45.

32 The colonial officials relied on material from the courts of arbitration for the resolution of appeals. This is indicated, for example, by a case in which the president of the court of arbitration in the Abo-area was fined 50 marks because he had failed to submit a report to the colonial administration. See ANY FA 4/292, C54/11, p. 2.

The Germans only reluctantly institutionalized legal structures and procedures in Cameroon. In the first years of German rule, which were characterized by an atmosphere of improvisation, the colonial officials who acted as judges were forced to cooperate with local authorities because of unstable power relations and a chronic lack of resources. Yet, even later the two legal spheres interacted in various contexts, including summons and appeals. When trying to catch suspects or enforcing court summons, the colonial administration and African chiefs used each other's authority and power resources to ensure the functioning of their respective jurisdictions. From the perspective of colonial officials this was crucial because the native courts and the courts of arbitration were part of a colonial system which ultimately drew its legitimacy and authority from the state.

Forum Shopping

In the judiciary in the colony Cameroon, governmental and non-governmental institutions cooperated closely and strongly influenced each other's functionality. Their systematic cooperation, in fact, suggests that it is not helpful to see the colonial legal system as a number of separate legal spheres. The cooperation between different legal institutions and across the boundaries of legal spheres formed a constituent part of the legal system in the colony Cameroon. In order to examine the functioning of different courts in the colonial power structure, we must therefore focus on the interrelations and mutual influences of the different legal spheres. The research of legal anthropologists on the behavior of litigants under conditions of legal pluralism gives further indications of why such a perspective might be productive. This research suggests that litigants perceive different rules and courts as one legal space, even if the rules, in theory, belong to different bodies of law and the courts to different legal spheres. Moreover, it shows that people routinely use both native and state courts (Keebet von Benda-Beckmann 1981; Merry 1988, 873; Franz von Benda-Beckmann 1992). In plural legal orders, behavior is not only determined by rules. Even where litigants selectively draw on specific rules or institutions, the normative and institutional world as a whole influences their behavior (Franz von Benda-Beckmann 1992, 314). If two parties can see different ways to pursue their aims, they will choose the alternative which they consider to be most beneficial to them (Merry 1982, 71). Keebet von Benda-Beckmann (1981, 117) has used the term "forum shopping" for such browsing through different legal choices under conditions of legal pluralism: "disputants have a choice between different institutions and they base their choice on what they hope the outcome of the dispute will be, however vague or ill-founded their expectations may be."

In the German colony Cameroon, Africans sometimes took their cases to courts that had no jurisdiction under the institutional order. For some, this might suggest that they did not or did not always understand the court system that the Germans had introduced. Using the concept of "forum shopping", however, we see that Africans deliberately used courts that belonged to different legal spheres. They used the totality of institutions at their disposal, which, for them, constituted only one legal space. Depending on the situation, the litigants referred to different bodies of law. Sometimes they even invoked African and German law at the same time.[33] They did not strictly adhere to special bodies of law, but used those laws that supported their claims.

There is another point to be made about "forum shopping". Many lawsuits before colonial officials ended without a decision because after the first hearing, the parties no longer appeared in court. Presumably, they had resolved their conflicts by using other forums for dispute resolution.[34] This behavior also illustrates the selective and parallel use of different forums. A lawsuit before a colonial official did not necessarily put an end to other types of conflict resolution.[35] The frequent absence of parties may also indicate that other forums were used at the same time. Moreover, the litigants not only used different institutions as alternatives but also employed them against each other. Research on law in colonial situations has shown that, especially in the early phases of colonialism, the colo-

33 ANY FA 4/981, Bille Mbule to deputy district officer Schroeder, May 5, 1914, without pages.

34 See, for example, ANY FA 4/319, C 600/12, February 18, 1913; FA 4/292, C 62/11, March 28, 1911; ANY FA 4/333, C 509/13, February 3, 1914, p. 2; ANY FA 4/333, C 521/13, September 19, 1914.

35 This is, however, not specific to colonial legal systems (Dinges 1993, 205).

nized instrumentalized their knowledge of jurisdictional tensions in the legal system and developed strategies to exploit these tensions (Serulnikov 1996; Benton 2002, 13–14). Thus, I argue that in the case of the German colony Cameroon, "forum shopping" greatly influenced the development of the colonial state and its legal system.

To understand how Africans used different courts against each other, we need to recall that colonial institutions not only served as courts of appeal, but also applied different criteria to reach their decisions. Even when colonial officials tried to take African law into account, they judged the facts of the case against a different background. Their knowledge of "customs" was limited; they were socialized in a different culture and applied legal concepts that differed from those used in native courts. For all these reasons, their decisions could differ from those made by native courts. That said, most often the litigants probably did not follow a clear strategy to exploit the latent rivalry between legal institutions. Rather, they used different courts in a parallel fashion to increase the chance of success. Yet, while they may not have pursued proper "strategies", the simple fact that they used a variety of courts undermined the significance of each individual court.

"Forum shopping" thus affected the authority and functioning of every institution, as each was but one among several options. The greater variety of courts that followed colonial expansion limited the significance and power of African institutions. At the same time, however, the persistence of these institutions, of which only some were considered legal by the colonial government, also limited the significance and power of state institutions. The supposedly final decisions of state institutions did not always resolve the conflicts in question. Frequently, the colonial officials lacked the power to enforce their decisions. Their judgment was often only one factor in continuing disputes. In short, then, the plurality of the colonial legal system had effects on all of its constituent elements.

Conclusion

Actual legal relations in the German colony Cameroon did not fit into the boundaries defined by the dual legal order. In "mixed cases", the authority of different laws and courts overlapped despite the fact that the normative order attempted to establish and maintain separate legal spheres for Africans and Europeans. The colonial and the customary legal spheres were closely entangled. The colonial administration and the native courts interacted in various contexts. This plural legal order could not but affect all legal spheres. Both customary and colonial forms of conflict resolution were shaped by the availability of "forum shopping." The litigants' decision in favor of or against a particular court could strengthen the authority of the chosen court. By making a choice, the parties decided who gained control over the resolution of a certain dispute.

These insights have implications for the analysis and assessment of the colonial legal situation. As far as the issue of agency is concerned, they suggest that the decisions and actions of the colonized population helped to shape the legal reality in the German colony Cameroon. The selective use of the legal system enabled the litigant parties to influence legal practice, determining the authority of different courts and the scope of their decisions.

These conclusions are also important for the methodology of analyzing legal practice in imperial contexts. The integration of different courts and bodies of law into the analysis has allowed me to identify many entanglements and interactions between different legal spheres in Cameroon. My findings suggest that for the analysis of courts under colonialism, the whole range of rules, authorities and options must be taken into account. The case of the German colony Cameroon shows that, from the perspective of the African population, the different institutions for conflict resolution were perceived as options within a unitary space. Locals utilized this variety by taking their case to the forum from which they expected the most favorable judgment. When they suspected that their expectations would not be met, however, they withdrew their cases, usually by no longer appearing in court. The customary and the colonial legal spheres were thus greatly affected by each other's existence. An isolated discussion of the colonial or the customary spheres therefore does little to explain the functionality of these spheres, precisely because interaction was an inherent element of the colonial legal system.

Within the broader context of civilizing discourses, claims were articulated that African law should be slowly transformed towards the ideal of European values, legal principles, and practices. These demands often were only legitimizing and programmatic and in no way represented an attempt to lay the ground for the creation of a uniform law or legal equality within the colonies. The German colonial administration at no point sought to implement "one law for all." On the contrary, as my discussion of the "mixed cases" has shown, colonial administrators tried to prevent Africans from being judged according to the same laws as Europeans. Separating the legal spheres of the colonizers and colonized and maintaining distinct bodies of law for different social—or, as they were viewed at the time—racial groups, formed an important basis for German colonial politics. Such practices were justified by reference to the different states of "development" which allegedly forbade confronting Africans with a complex and "civilized" law.

However, to stress my point, one could say that there was but "one colonial legal system for all", if we understand this system as one that included multiple legal spheres as well as different mechanisms to regulate access to and exclusion from its various laws and institutions. It included different colonial and "native" courts, as well as sanctions against mechanisms of conflict resolution not approved by the state. Legal segregation between Africans and Europeans was as much a part of this colonial legal system as were arrangements for handling "mixed cases". Within this one legal system, however, different groups faced different exclusions and restrictions. The legal reality could look very different depending above all on the legal status of the actor utilizing, or being subjected to, the colonial legal system.

Works Cited

Aitken, Robbie (2007). *Exclusion and Inclusion. Gradations of Whiteness and Socio-Economic Engineering in German Southwest Africa, 1884–1914.* Oxford et. al.: Peter Lang.

Benton, Lauren (2002). *Law and Colonial Cultures. Legal Regimes in World History, 1400–1900.* Cambridge: Cambridge University Press.

Chanock, Martin (1985). *Law, Custom, and Social Order: Colonial Experience in Malawi and Zambia.* Cambridge: Cambridge University Press.

Chanock, Martin (2001). *The Making of South African legal culture, 1902–1936: Fear Favour and Prejudice.* Cambridge: Cambridge University Press.

Dinges, Martin (1993). Michel Foucault, Justizphantasien und die Macht. In Andreas Blauert (ed.) *Mit den Waffen der Justiz. Zur Kriminalitätsgeschichte des späten Mittelalters und der frühen Neuzeit*, 189–212. Frankfurt am Main: Fischer-Taschenbuch-Verlag.

Essner, Cornelia (1992). "Wo Rauch ist, da ist auch Feuer.": Zu den Ansätzen eines Rassenrechts für die Deutschen Kolonien. In Wilfried Wagner and Ulrich van der Heyden (eds.) *Rassendiskriminierung, Kolonialpolitik und ethnisch-nationale Identität*, 145–160. Münster.

Essner, Cornelia (2005). "Borderline" im Menschenblut und Struktur rassistischer Rechtsspaltung: Koloniales Kaiserreich und "Drittes Reich". In Micha Brumlik et al. (eds.) *Gesetzliches Unrecht. Rassistisches Recht im 20. Jahrhundert*, 27–64. Frankfurt am Main: Campus-Verlag.

Fischer, Hans-Jörg (2001). *Die deutschen Kolonien. Die koloniale Rechtsordnung und ihre Entwicklung nach dem ersten Weltkrieg.* Berlin: Duncker & Humblot.

Fitzpatrick, Peter (1984). Traditionalism and Traditional Law. *Journal of African Law*, 28, 1/2 ("The Construction of African Customary Law"), 20–27.

Joeden-Forgey, Elisa (2004). *Nobody's people: Colonial Subjects, Race Power and the German State, 1884–1945.* Diss. Pennsylvania.

Merry, Sally Engle (1982). The Articulation of Legal Spheres. In Margaret Jean Hay and Marcia Wright (eds.) *African Women and the Law: Historical Perspectives*, 68–89. Boston: Boston University Press.

Merry, Sally Engle (1988). Legal Pluralism. *Law and Society Review*, 22, 5, 869–896.

Nagl, Dominik (2007). *Grenzfälle. Staatsangehörigkeit, Rassismus und nationale Identität unter deutscher Kolonialherrschaft*. Frankfurt am Main: Peter Lang.

Rehbinder, Manfred (2000). *Rechtssoziologie*. München: C.H. Beck.

Roberts, Richard L. (2005). *Litigants and Households. African Disputes and Colonial Courts in the French Soudan, 1895–1912*. Portsmouth, NH: Heinemann.

Ruppel, Julius (ed.) (1912). *Die Landesgesetzgebung für das Schutzgebiet Kamerun. Sammlung der in Kamerun zur Zeit geltenden völkerrechtlichen Verträge, Gesetze, Verordnungen und Dienstvorschriften mit Anmerkungen und Registern*. Berlin: Mittler.

Schaper, Ulrike (2009). Law and Colonial Order: Legal Policy in German Cameroon between Civilizing and Public Peace. *Comparativ*, 19, 17–33.

Schlottau, Ralf et al. (2007). *Deutsche Kolonialrechtspflege. Strafrecht und Strafmacht in den deutschen Schutzgebieten, 1884 bis 1914*. Frankfurt am Main: Peter Lang.

Schreiber (1904). Die rechtliche Stellung der Bewohner der deutschen Schutzgebiete. *Zeitschrift für Kolonialpolitik, Kolonialwirtschaft und Kolonialrecht*, 6, 760–775.

Schulte-Althoff, Franz-Josef (1985). Rassenmischung im kolonialen System: Zur deutschen Kolonialpolitik im letzten Jahrzehnt vor dem Ersten Weltkrieg. *Historisches Jahrbuch*, 105, 52–94.

Serulnikov, Sergio (1996). Disputed Images of Colonialism: Spanish Rule and Indian Subversion in Northern Potosí, 1777–1780. *The Hispanic American Historical Review*, 76, 2, 189–226.

Sippel, Harald (1995). "Im Interesse des Deutschtums und der weißen Rasse": Behandlung und Rechtswirkung von 'Rassenmischehen' in den Kolonien

Deutsch-Ostafrika und Deutsch-Südwestafrika. *Jahrbuch für afrikanisches Recht*, 9, 123–159.

Sippel, Harald (1997). Die Klassifizierung des "Afrikaners" und des "Europäers" im Rahmen der dualen kolonialen Rechtsordnung am Beispiel von Deutsch-Südwestafrika. In Andreas Eckert, Andreas and Jürgen Müller (eds.) *Transformationen der europäischen Expansion vom 16. bis zum 20. Jahrhundert*, 154–170. Rehburg-Loccum: Evangelische Akademie Loccum.

Snyder, Francis G. (1981). Colonialism and Legal Form: The Creation of "Customary Law" in Senegal. *Journal of Legal Pluralism*, 19, 49–90.

Stockhausen (1911). Verwertung der Eingeborenen-Organisationen Tropisch-West-Afrikas zum Zwecke Europäischer Verwaltung. *Koloniale Rundschau*, 5, 306–317.

Wagner, Norbert Berthold (2002). *Die deutschen Schutzgebiete. Erwerb, Organisation und Verlust aus juristischer Sicht*. Baden-Baden: Nomos.

von Benda-Beckmann, Franz (1992). Symbiosis of Indigenous and Western Law in Africa and Asia: An Essay in Legal Pluralism. In Wolfgang J. Mommsen and J. A. De Moor (eds.) *European Expansion and Law. The Encounter of European and Indigenous Law in 19th- and 20th-century Africa and Asia*, 307–325. Oxford: Berg.

von Benda-Beckmann, Keebet (1981). Forum Shopping and Shopping Forums: Dispute Processing in a Minangkabau Village in West Sumatra. *Journal of Legal Pluralism*, 19, 117–159.

Walz, Gotthilf (1981). *Die Entwicklung der Strafrechtspflege in Kamerun unter deutscher Herrschaft. 1884–1914*. Freiburg im Breisgau: Klaus Schwarz Verlag.

Wildenthal, Lora (1997). Race, Gender, and Citizenship in the German Colonial Empire. In Frederick Cooper and Ann Laura Stoler (eds.) *Tensions of Empire. Colonial Cultures in a Bourgeois World*, 263–283. Berkeley, CA: University of California Press.

De jure and *de facto*: The Penal Code of 1871 and Juridical Culture in Mexico City

Manuel de los Reyes García Márkina

Introduction

In order to understand a society, we must take into account the gap between the written and unwritten rules structuring life within it. This allows us to distinguish the "national project" of the ruling classes from the social reality that they seek to influence, while also identifying the ideas and values prevailing among the population. This article examines these differences in Mexico around 1870, when jury trials and the first legal code[1] after Mexican independence from the Spanish Empire (1821) were introduced. It explores the emerging legal sphere in the Mexican capital, arguing that the proclaimed introduction and institutionalization of legal monism were not attained in practice. I suggest this resulted from the existence of alternative principles and values held by the common urban population and ruling classes. These reflected underlying racial and class-based considerations that hindered the development of a unified legal culture.

The first section deals with the distinction between types of juridical cultures. Without elaboration, the term "culture" could be too all-encompassing to be analytically useful. The second section is a brief exposition of the liberal ideas behind the central legal reforms of the period: the Constitution of 1857, which proclaimed universal equality before the law as a fundamental principle; and the introduction of the jury trial and the Legal Code in 1869/1871. The third section explores the alternative commonly held principles, ideas, and attitudes towards the law that coexisted and interacted with the Legal Code. In the final

1 After independence, the inherited colonial legal system with its multiple sources of law remained in force. I discuss this later in greater detail.

section I present conclusions and summarize findings that may point to and guide further research.

Internal Juridical Culture, External Juridical Culture

I use the concept of "juridical culture" (*cultura jurídica*) to refer to both the "set of expository and interpretative techniques of the legal professionals" (Tarello 1995, 24) and to the common citizens' opinions and attitudes towards the law and the notion of justice. Following Tarello, I trace a distinction between the "internal juridical culture", that of the practitioners and theorists of the law (judges, lawyers, officials, law specialists and professors) and the "external juridical culture" characteristic of the common citizenry or, more specifically, the non-legal professionals (*ibid.*, 24).

Tarello further distinguishes between several dimensions of the concept of internal legal culture. First, it refers to "the set of doctrines and conceptual systems" elaborated by jurists and legal theoreticians in a unified normative text that incorporates provisions and norms from many textual sources. When understood in this sense, the internal legal culture may temporarily match the "conceptual representations" of the dominant legal dogma. Second, it incorporates the ways in which legal practitioners apply and interpret the text. Third, it points to the "models of reasoning" that jurists use to reach legal conclusions that could be considered valid and legally well-grounded, in terms of both doctrine and jurisprudence. Finally, in a different and broader sense, the term implies the interests of legal professionals as a specific class or corporation and the manifestations of these corporate interests in their professional practice (*ibid.*, 24–25). The case of the capital Mexico City around 1870 demonstrates the tensions and divergences not only between internal and external juridical cultures, but also *within* internal juridical culture. This internal culture exhibits such conflicts among its first three dimensions—as the source of legal codes and systems, as arbiter of normative legal interpretation and application, and as discursive structure facilitating effective implementation of the law.

Tarello's distinction helps to clarify the concept of "culture" in the legal sphere. It also highlights how this concept may reflect legal principles and concepts as well as social attitudes, opinions and ideas. One might assume the internal juridical culture of legal professionals would focus mainly on the former, whereas the latter would primarily comprise the external juridical culture. However, legal professionals and lawmakers also acted under the influence of the attitudes and ideas supposedly inherent to the external juridical culture. Additionally, some practices and principles associated with the internal legal culture also influenced the common people's attitudes and perceptions, even if not replacing them altogether.

The "distance between law and other norms", or the gulf between the internal and external juridical cultures, may connote "former foreign domination" or "the imposition of foreign models of law" among other things (Nelken 2004, 117). This general observation is perfectly applicable to the Mexican case. After independence there were many more continuities than there were ruptures or "new beginnings", and the legal sphere is no exception. It is true that Mexican legislators appropriated and refashioned European models in the Penal Code of 1871, partly in an effort to establish Mexico among the "civilized nations", as Antonio Martínez de Castro, chairman of the Code's drafting commission, put it (1968 [1876], 185). The stress on legal import, however, downplays the continuities between the legal system developed and used during Mexico's colonial period (1521–1821) and the one adopted by the Mexican Republic. Though independence, the adoption of jury courts in 1869, and the first national Penal Code in 1871 appear as ruptures, reality is more nuanced. The shaping of the external legal culture by the population's contact and contrast with the written law and the legal institutions in Mexico City did not begin with the adoption of the Penal Code, nor did it change dramatically; it shows a remarkable continuity with earlier legal culture. Public consciousness of the inequality and unfairness of the legal experience was already widespread among the Mexican population as a product of colonialism and its lingering vestiges.

Nevertheless, people went to court in Mexico City in large numbers. In light of this fact, we could suppose, following Aguirre and Salvatore, that "people valorize(d) the legal component of their social and civic identity and exercise of rights", and thus conclude that we are analyzing a regime that has achieved the "hegemony of the law" (2001, 14). However, the stark contrast between the law's ideals and the crude experiences of the majority of the population with the law and its institutions—particularly the police—could hardly have helped to establish a "hegemony of law" in Mexico. Why, then, did ordinary Mexicans continue to file complaints with the police, and engage in lawsuits? The potentially uncomfortable answer is that people continued, and still continue, to go to court in Mexico simply because they have the opportunity to do so, and not because they have internalized the idea and legal category of "citizens".

The Liberal Spirit of the Mexican Penal Code of 1871

The adoption of jury trials in Mexico City in 1869 and the enactment of the first Penal Code for the capital in 1871[2] resulted from the Liberal triumph in the civil war known as the Reform War (1857–1861). The war was a clash between the eventually Conservatives, whose motto was "religion and legal privileges" (*religión y fueros*), and the Liberals who advocated a secular state grounded in universalistic principles and legal monism. The Penal Code reflected the spirit of the 1857 Constitution, written under the Liberal government of President Benito Juárez. The constitution's approval led to the Reform War, and indirectly to the French intervention in Mexico (1862–1867), and to Maximilian of Hapsburg's short-lived Second Mexican Empire (1864–1867).

After the declaration of independence Mexico was governed by Agustín de Iturbide, an officer of the Spanish colonial army in New Spain during the War of Independence (1811–1821). He initially fought against the insurgents but switched sides following his appointment as commander of the royalist army. He then saw himself in the advantageous position to proclaim independence and maneuver his election first as the head of the *junta provisional gubernativa* (provisional governing board), and later to be proclaimed Agustín I, Emperor of Mexico in 1822. The first Mexican Empire, however, soon came to an end when de Iturbide was overthrown

2 The Penal Code of 1871, also known as "Code Martínez de Castro", was valid until 1929.

in 1823, just eight months after his coronation. After a provisional government that lasted 18 months, Guadalupe Victoria was elected the first President of Mexico, holding the office from 1824 to 1829. He was to be the only Mexican president to finish his presidential term for nearly twenty years. Only José Joaquín de Herrera, who was elected in 1848 in the aftermath of two years of war and invasion by the United States, was next able to complete his term. Finally, the aforementioned Benito Juárez, following a decade of general civil war between 1857 and 1867, could run for re-election in 1868 and 1871. In the time span between 1829 and 1868 there were 48 different governments in Mexico, foreign armies occupied its capital twice and in the last occasion established the second, Hapsburg Mexican Empire.

The first Mexican Empire (1822–1823) was an ill-fated attempt of the upper classes (the rich *criollos*[3], the military and the clergy) to preserve their privileges and thwart the liberal ideas that motivated a large portion of the rebels. The Plan of Iguala (1821) was a 24-point peace treaty offered by Iturbide to the rebels to win their support. It held these main guarantees: the preservation of the Roman Catholic faith as the state church without tolerance for any other, the preservation of all the rights and property of the secular and regular clergy, the proclamation of independence from Spain (crucial for the rebels), the offer of the Mexican crown to the Spanish King Ferdinand VII or to another Bourbon royal head, the social equality of all the inhabitants of the new country and the protection of both their person and property, and the conservation of all branches of the state and public employees with the removal of only those opposed to the plan (Moreno Bonett 1997, 207). The Plan of Iguala led to the Cordoba Treaty (1821) proclaiming the establishment of the new regime. It created the provisional governing board[4] with Iturbide as President, and which in turn designated a provisional regency whose six members were Iturbide, Juan O'Donojú (the last Spanish viceroy), the last viceroyalty secretary, a judge of the Royal Audience of Mexico (the highest tribunal of the Spanish crown in the colony), and the Archbishop of Puebla and

3 American-born children of Spaniards could not aspire to the highest ranks in the colony as they were reserved for the *peninsulares*, Spanish-born Spaniards.

4 This institution consisted of thirty-eight members, in their great part conservatives: fourteen former colonial officials, nine noblemen, seven clergymen, five military officers, two merchants and one great landowner.

an archdeacon.[5] The regency thus held the highest representatives of the military (Iturbide), of the colonial administration (the viceroyalty and the Royal Audience of Mexico), and of the Catholic Church (the Archbishop of Puebla), but not a single insurgent leader. Agustin I was later overthrown by former rebel leaders, regrouped around the Liberal members of the first elected Congress. After the Republic and its first constitution (1824) were proclaimed, the former insurgent leader Guadalupe Victoria was elected President.

This early confrontation between monarchists and conservatives against liberals would become one of the main causes of the uprisings, coups, riots and unrest that marked the first half-century of Mexican independence. This created a situation in which it was almost impossible to undertake the task of redacting a penal code. But when the conservative dictatorship of Antonio López de Santa Anna (1853–1855) was overthrown by the liberal Ayutla Revolution (1854–1855), a new generation of liberal politicians came to power, opening the door to the promulgation of the 1857 constitution. This was complemented by the Reform Laws[6], especially by the *Ley Juárez* (Juarez's Law), which abolished special rights for the army and clergy members. Keeping in mind the motto of the conservatives in the Reform War—*religión y fueros*—we return to our starting point in this section: the liberal principles of the 1871 Penal Code.

Delayed by civil war and foreign invasions, the Penal Code was completed in 1871, fourteen years the promulgation of the Constitution. Nevertheless, the same liberal spirit permeates both documents. Universal equality before the law was a cornerstone of liberal thought and a guiding principle for the documents' authors. The drafters of the Penal Code believed all adults enjoyed agency and understanding of their actions, and were therefore equally responsible for them. Following from this belief, the main criterion to define the penalty was by the crime committed itself, along with "a meticulous and thorough enumeration of all mitigating and aggravating circumstances" (Martínez de Castro 1968 [1876], 138).

5 Universidad Nacional Autónoma de México-Instituto de Investigaciones Jurídicas, Senado de la República, *Actas constitucionales mexicanas (1821–1824),* Vol. I (Mexico city: UNAM-IIJ 1980).

6 These were enacted between 1855 and 1857 and—in the midst of the civil war—between 1859 and 1860. They were aimed at the separation of state and Church.

The liberal conception of the law viewed offences as violations of the social contract and injurious to the whole society. The legal bodies of the state, considered to be the embodiment and depositary of the popular sovereignty and will, therefore had the right to prosecute offenders. The liberal perspective also viewed suspects, defendants, and convicts as having inalienable rights that the state must nevertheless respect and guard.

This view of the state as the sole representative of the will of the sovereign people leads directly to a third pillar of the liberal legal system: the state monopoly on lawmaking. The state had to standardize the rights and obligations of its citizens. Those subject to the law were therefore stripped of particular individual privileges and group rights, as these were also incompatible with universal legal equality. This argument was employed in favor of the drafting of a unified penal code, applicable to the whole population without exception. In short, the Penal Code of 1871 mirrored the liberal spirit of the Constitution.

The creation of the Code offers a prime example of the import (but also adaptation) of Western legal models. The draft commission studied and compared more than twenty foreign civil and criminal codes and drafted codes (Martínez de Castro 1968 [1876], 183), including those of France, Great Britain, Spain, Portugal, Belgium, Italy, Austria, Bavaria, Saxony, and the US state of Louisiana. By contrast, it used no blueprints from other Latin American countries, as these might face similar problems with Mexico. By studying and emulating societies where issues of class and race were not bound up together, as they were in Mexico, the Liberals could only achieve superficial positive effects through their reforms.

Contested Legal Culture in Mexico around 1871

Although liberal in principle, the 1824 Constitution, like the 1812 Spanish Constitution[7] upon which it was based, preserved Catholicism as the

7 Also known as the Cádiz constitution, this had been drafted by the *cortes* (the legislative body), during the Napoleonic occupation of Spain as an attempt to fill the power vacuum created by the absence of King Ferdinand VII, held prisoner in France. It established the principles of national sovereignty, freedom of the press, and indirect universal male suffrage. See *Constitución política de la monarquía española, promulgada*

state religion and, crucially for this essay, the special courts for the clergy and military personnel. As the Liberals desired equality before the law, judicial uniformity would be necessary to ensure its equal application on all citizens. This objective was achieved neither with the Reform Laws nor with the 1857 Constitution. Due to the inability to create a new legal system prior to the 1871 Penal Code, the pluralist colonial legal system remained in place for fifty years after independence.

Yet by 1871, when the liberal ideal of legal monism was finally reached and the conservatives were defeated, new ideas and concepts about the law were circulating amongst groups of young politicians, journalists and lawyers. These differed from the ideals of the authors of the Reform Laws and the Constitution of 1857. During the time span between the 1857 Constitution and the 1871 Penal Code, a new generation of lawyers and journalists had emerged and slowly began to make its way into national political and administrative bodies.

Speaking in terms of Tarello's dimensions of internal legal culture, one might say that while the Penal Code reflected the legal dogma dominant at the start of its drafting in 1862, it was confronted with new ideas by the time it was completed in 1871. The liberal ideas embodied in the Penal Code not only interacted with the remnants of the legal system it was meant to replace, but also with new conceptions about how the state and society ought to be organized. These new conceptions considered the ideals of the Constitution and Penal Code to be largely outdated or false. In the remainder of the chapter, I further explore these alternative ideas, values, and attitudes that the Penal Code had to contend with.

As in most post-colonial states, the legal sphere in the Mexican Republic was heavily influenced by Spanish colonial law. This body of law was highly heterogeneous. Privileges and special courts existed for different collective bodies, including groups of the population, unions and corporations. To illustrate the point: in New Spain—the region of the Spanish Empire to which Mexico belonged—there were ecclesiastical, military, university, and commercial courts, the mining charter, the jurisdiction of artisans, and the Indian Law.

---

en Cádiz a 19 de marzo de 1812. Valladolid: Ed. Maxtor, 2001, facs. ed. of the 1820 Madrid edition.

Before the liberal reforms in the mid-nineteenth century, judges could not only apply the law differently to different parts of the population, but they could also draw on different legal sources: thus, they could enforce laws issued by the Cortes of Cádiz, or laws contained in the *Novísima recoplicación de leyes* (Newest Collection of Laws, 1805), *Real Ordenanza de Intendentes* (Royal Ordinance of Intendants, 1786), *Recopilación de Leyes de los Reynos de las Indias* (Collection of Laws of the Kingdoms of the Indies, 1681) and even the *Siete Partidas* (the Seven-Part Code, a statutory code redacted in the middle of thirteenth century, during the reign of Alfonso X of Castile). For example, in the trial against Agustín Foro for the murder of Martín Suárez held between November 1870 and March 1871, just months before the new Penal Code's introduction, the Judge Jesús María Gaxiola turned to two different legal bodies to support the release of a co-defendant acquitted by the jury. These were the Law no. 2, title 16, book 16 of the *Novísima recopliación de leyes*—enacted during the Spanish colonial regime—and article 49 of the *Ley de jurados en materia criminal para el distrito federal* (Juries Act in criminal cases to federal district), enacted as recently as 1869.[8]

The role of the judges also differed from that envisioned by the lawmakers who had drafted the Penal Code since these had tried to minimize the judges' discretion and maximize legal uniformity. Spanish law was highly casuistic, as the role of the judge was subdued to the principle *ius est ars boni et aequi* (The law is the art of what is good and fair). Consequently, judges tried to find the appropriate solution for each particular case; it was even possible for them to modify a sentence after the fact in order to correct possible errors (Dougnac Rodriguez 1994, 12).

This characteristic of the Spanish legal system was very useful for the colonization of the conquered American territories. It was well-equipped to deal with the cultural and social diversity within the territories, which could not have easily been ruled with one existing legal corpus. The Indian Law (*derecho indiano*) was created—valid only for the Spanish possessions in America, Asia and Oceania—to cope with the demands of colonialism and the casuistic nature of Spanish law. It consisted of norms specifically created to govern the colonies (the Indian law itself), continental Spanish

8 Archivo General de la Nación, fonds "Tribunal Superior de Justicia del Distrito Federal", box 490, "Year 1870, Criminal contra Agustin Foro".

law (covering the inhabitants of the Spanish mainland and applied in the colonies when considered necessary), and the indigenous law (collected and thereby constructed from the legal customs of the conquered populations).

Therefore, while the 1871 Penal Code did not recognize distinctions of any kind between the inhabitants of the country, the colonial legal system sought to incorporate local legal customs[9] as long as they were not considered contrary to the interests of the Crown or Church. In the *Recopilación de Leyes de los Reynos de las Indias* we can find a disposition given by Emperor Charles V on August 6, 1555:

> [...] as for the laws and morals that the Indians formerly had for good governance and policing, the customs they observed and retained after they became Christians and which are neither in our Holy Religion nor in the laws of this book, and those they have newly created and ordered to be saved and executed, we hereby approve and confirm insofar as we can add what we consider necessary to serve God Our Lord, and ourselves, and for the maintenance of the Christian police among the natives of those provinces, without harming what they have achieved, nor their good and fair practices and their States (*Recopilación* 1973 [1681], 126).

The legal concepts underlying the Colonial legal system persisted even after the enactment of the Penal Code of 1871. Many jurists of the time were skeptical of the Penal Code's ability, or the ability of any unified code, to cover the full range of possible legal cases. They found this an undesirable aspiration that would be impossible to fulfill. This group insisted on allowing judge's discretion to help fill supposedly unavoidable legal gaps. In this way, they expected judges to judge *by* the law, and not *about* the law.

The 1871 Penal Code still contained the category of crimes against morality. This was a direct inheritance of the colonial law in which the distinction between "sin" and "crime" was blurred. Adultery, homosexuality, and bestiality, for example, were punished both before and after the 1871 Penal Code, but only if these caused a public scandal. As Antonio Martínez de Castro himself explained in the preamble of the Penal Code, the drafting commission considered as a crime only those acts which "si-

9 The Spanish conquest shattered the social foundations of the colonized societies, and colonial rule distorted the social relations within the subject peoples. As the great majority of native elites were exterminated, the local colonial authorities began to appoint indigenous authorities. Yet in so doing, they often ignored ordinances and local custom, choosing "Indians of their confidence" instead (Varallanos, 1959, 315).

multaneously were contrary to moral justice and to the preservation of society", and thus discarded all those acts which, "although involving a very serious offense against morality, do not disturb the public tranquility", like pederasty, statutory rape (*estupro*), or bestiality, "except when committed with scandal, obscenity or violence" (Martínez de Castro 1968 [1876], 161–162).

This example of continuity in the internal legal culture is mirrored in the external one: in newspaper articles, *corridos*[10], and the broad popular narratives about criminality prevalent at the time the offender is usually described as being a victim of evil temptations. In fact, illustrations in flyers and magazines often depicted offenders as literally being driven by the Devil. These popular publications provide further evidence of the endurance of certain values in the external juridical culture, this time related to punishment. Corporal punishment was an essential part of sentences in New Spain, reaching the levels of a theatrical performance. One of the most curious cases perhaps was the 1723 public trial and burning in Mexico City of the skeleton of an ancient leader worshipped by the Nayar. After a year-long trial riddled with irregularities the case ended with two days of public processions, religious services and sermons in Spanish and Nahuatl. It culminated in the burning ceremony and the flogging of seven Nayar captives, which was meant to symbolize reconciliation of the "natives" with the Catholic faith (Ortega 1944 [1754]; Del Valle 2009, 83–132).

Although the Penal Code of 1871 eliminated corporal punishment, *corridos* and illustrations in popular publications depict corporal and supernatural punishments for criminals. For example, in *el corrido del parricida* (the parricide's *corrido*), Antonio Rodríguez, a villager from Real de Ozumatlán and a "disobedient, rude, spoiled and ungrateful son" assassinates Juan, his own father, who has rebuked him for his laziness. During his flight, Antonio, "whom even God cannot forgive" receives his "deserved Lord's punishment" in the form of several "hungry beasts" that devour him (Mendoza 1995, 253–256). The *corrido del rayo de la justicia* (the justice's thunderbolt *corrido*) relates how Manuel, a drunken, "rude and wretched son" kills his own father with a machete. Although warned

10 *Corridos* are popular songs about important social or political events, or people's daily lives.

by Manuel ("don't rebuke me, father, the devil can tempt me to assassinate you"), the father rebukes him and is then killed, but not before cursing his son in the last moment. Hours later, as "God's punishment" Manuel is torn to pieces by a series of thunderbolts (*ibid.*, 256–258).

Corridos reveal the merging of Spanish colonial and post-independence, liberal notions of justice or, more accurately, how liberal notions permeated the external legal culture. Thus, the Belem Galindo *corrido* describes the assassination of a woman at the hands of her husband, Hipólito Mendoza, on October 19, 1883. In response to gossip begun by his own mother, Hipólito shoots his wife Belem in the heart after just ten days of marriage. Policemen come to arrest Hipólito, a judge comes to preside over the removal of the body, and an autopsy is conducted. "Belem is already in the Glory, giving account to the Creator" while Hipólito is in court rendering his testimony. When the verse is repeated, Hipólito is already in prison. But supernatural elements appear: "What could have been the dominant planet when Hipólito was born? Maybe his mother was in sin, or she did not baptize him" (*ibid.*, 76–77).

The persistence of dueling is a final stark example of the endurance of values and customs characteristic of the old regime's juridical culture. It is noteworthy that even jurists, whose professional ethos should have discouraged them from such a practice, fought duels or participated in them as trusted representatives. This highlights a notable divergence between convictions about the legal system and ideas of justice. Although Martínez de Castro condemned the practice in the preamble of the Penal Code in which he considered taking justice into one's own hands a usurpation of state authority, the Code contained a legal loophole to protect duelists (Martínez de Castro 1968 [1876], 161–162). More concretely: While manslaughter (*homicidio simple*[11]) was punished with twelve years in prison[12], or ten if committed in a fight[13] as the aggressor, or six as the as-

11 This is defined as a killing "that is not premeditated (*premeditado*), nor executed with advantage (*ventaja*), perfidy (*alevosía*) or treachery (*traición*). Penal Code of 1871, third book, second title, chapter six, art. 550 (Dublán and Lozano 1879, vol. XI, 657).

12 Penal Code of 1871, third book, second title, chapter six, art. 552, parts I–III (*ibid.*, 657).

13 This is defined as "a confrontation in fact, not of words, between two or more persons" (*la contienda de obra y no de palabra entre dos o más personas*).

saulted[14], killing in a duel was punished with six years for the challenger[15], or four years for the challenged.[16] These considerations for duelists contradict the principle of self-defense, defined as follows in Article 34: acts are not considered criminal when the accused "acts in defense of his own person, his honor or his goods, or of the person, goods or honor of someone else, by repelling an actual, imminent, violent and unjustified aggression (*una agresión actual, inminente, violenta y sin derecho*), unless the plaintiff proves that any of the following circumstances intervened"[17]; these include situations in which the accused himself provoked the assault, in which the accused foresaw the assault and could have prevented it by legal means, or in which there was no rational necessity for the means employed in his defense.[18] Any of these circumstances negate the self-defense argument in a duel. How could Martínez de Castro allow such a contradiction? The reason lies in the classism that permeates his arguments justifying mild measures against duelists. He finds that "no one can believe" that the injuries and homicides resulting from a duel could be put on the same level as those resulting from "a fight to which the fighters are drawn by the almost irresistible force of vulgar concern" (Martínez de Castro 1968 [1876], 161–162).

A revealing case resulting from such class privilege is the following. On November 1, 1879, the daily newspaper *La Patria* published the answer given by the paper *El Mensajero* to the weekly newspaper *El Gendarme*, founded and subsidized by the Government to improve the image of the police. *El Gendarme* had justified the police's passivity against the duelists after the newspapers *La Libertad* and *El Mensajero* had lamented the contrast between this practice and their harsh measures against *gente del pueblo* (lowly people), who were commonly arrested in case of a fight. Part of the answer *La Patria* so approvingly published says, "We see no difference

14 Penal Code of 1871, third book, second title, chapter six, art. 553 (Dublán and Lozano 1879, 657).

15 Penal Code of 1871, third book, second title, chapter six, art. 597, parts I–V (*ibid.*, 661).

16 Penal Code of 1871, third book, second title, chapter six, art. 598, parts I–III (*ibid.*, 661–662).

17 Penal Code of 1871, first book, second title, chapter two, art. 34, section 8 (*ibid.*, 601).

18 Parts I–III (*ibid.*).

between a brawl and a duel, but in the kind of weapons and more or less trivial formulas. Both are equally crimes."[19] The owner, director, and chief editor of *La Patria* was the lawyer, congressman and journalist Ireneo Paz, grandfather of the future Nobel Prize laureate for Literature, Octavio Paz. Around six months later, on April 27, 1880, Ireneo Paz killed journalist Santiago Sierra in a duel. Sierra was the younger brother of Justo Sierra, director of *La Libertad* and future president of the Supreme Court of Justice of the Nation and Minister. Paz was not arrested and never faced any legal consequence.

The Challenge of Legal Positivism

In a curious case of historical irony, the long-gestating Penal Code was "born" just as new ideas about the proper legal organization of Mexican society were taking hold. The new ideological challenger, positivism, considered the Liberal ideas of the 1857 Constitution and the Penal Code to be both historically obsolete and scientifically wrong.

Positivist thought had been present in the writings of several members of the Mexican political and cultural elite since the early 1840s. The great majority of them were former followers of classical liberalism disappointed by the ongoing disputes and social disorder caused by seemingly abstract and "metaphysical" principles, such as natural law and individual rights. This small group began to extol the "organic development" of societies and to condemn the Liberal project as an act of violence against society. They argued that it is possible to discern and analyze the laws and processes governing societal evolution. They claimed that doing so would facilitate the modification of all parts of society, achieving social change in a peaceful, organic and scientific manner (Otero 1842).

In a speech given in 1867 Gabino Barreda, then Chairman of the Committee on Education Reform in the newly restored Liberal government of Benito Juárez, became the first government official to explicitly and fully link the ideas of positivism with governance. In his speech, Barreda formulated for the first time what would later become the official positivist motto

19 *La Patria*, November 1, 1879, p. 3.

during the Porfirio Díaz dictatorship: "Liberty, order and progress". He argued that since freedom of the press prevailed in Mexico, only spiritual and intellectual revolutions could thenceforth be justified. He expressed the hope that material order, safeguarded by the state, would be the reliable path toward civilization and progress (Barreda 1877, 104–105).

Barreda had studied medicine in Paris between 1847 and 1851 before dedicating the next ten years of his life to starting and organizing the Preparatoria National School. In this way, he introduced the ideas of August Comte—under whom he had studied in Paris—to Mexico, where they fermented among the next generation. These lawyers, journalists and jurists twenty years his junior grew up during an almost permanent state of civil war. They therefore often prioritized political stability above all other values including the liberal ideals of individual rights, which they views as archaic and metaphysical. That generation's desire to preserve political stability, which they associated with social peace and progress, led them to promote conservative policies that partly relied on pseudo-biological, racial arguments in their discussion of law and justice issues. Following their rise to power with the Porfirio Díaz dictatorship (1876–1911), the positivist politicians would become popularly known as the "Scientists" (*los Científicos*).

The positivists believed that the legal system should judge criminals, not crimes. Consequently, they emphasized less the penal responsibility of the subject, but more the danger he or she posed to society as a whole. They believed that both the Penal Code and the judges ought to take the offender's life circumstances into consideration. The Scientists were convinced that every person was the result of factors such as nourishment, received education, and the social environment in which he or she had grown up.

It is important to note that mixed in with these ideas were embedded notions about race and social class. Although a Congressional decree passed in 1822 prohibited classifying the "citizens of this Empire" by their origin "when recording their names in every public or private register or document"[20], there were always voices advocating precisely that. "The wise policies of our government have banned forever the odious distinctions between white, black, bronze and mixed;" however, "without knowledge

20 No. 313 in Dublán and Lozano (1879, 628).

of the people, it would be impossible to assess their civilization, morality, qualities, and needs" (Buffington 2001, 52). Finally, Justo Sierra wrote: "The two main factors of crime are essentially the same that form the basis of Darwinism in biological studies: heritage and media influence".[21] In this manner, morality and the presence of criminal impulses become both racial heritage and social issue. These ideas were anathema to the liberal foundations of the 1871 Penal Code from another perspective: they discounted the free will of the citizen. The positivist legal culture excluded these elements and replaced them with social and partially racial determinism. To avoid direct racist discourse, positivists tended to use a patronizing and even sympathetic language, whose degrading overtones can hardly be overlooked:

> An Indian wrapped in a crude *zarape*, a native of those who are by their appearance a sort of problem for the thinker, one of the most degraded specimens of this poor race… In the presence of one of those beings, one may doubt to what point human responsibility exists within them. And if our eyes didn't see how this great race awakes slowly but positively […] we would almost doubt their equal rights, the fundamental truths of democracy.[22]

It is with this description that *El Foro* begins one of its reports from the criminal court in 1873. The ethnic origin of the accused (who was incidentally found not guilty) is presented as primary, though it played no role in the accusation. Founded in 1872, *El Foro* was a newspaper marketed to lawyers, prosecutors, and legal professionals: to the bearers of the internal legal culture. It is therefore no coincidence that the subtitle of the newspaper was *Periódico de jurisprudencia y legislación* (Journal of Law and legislation). This newspaper, founded and directed by Sierra and Pablo Macedo (also an influential lawyer and future member of *los Científicos*) was the first print medium to publish an article by Cesare Lombroso, in 1884.

Comte and Saint-Simon heavily influenced the Mexican positivists, while Sierra's writings reveal the influence of Spencer. Specialized journals such as *El Derecho* and *Revista de Legislación y Jurisprudencia* also made frequent reference to the Italian criminologists Ferri and Garofalo. However, the key reference society at this point was probably France. The positivists

21 *La Libertad*, October 12, 1878.

22 "Jurisprudencia criminal", *El Foro*, June 7, 1873.

accessed European thought primarily through the French language. This, along with Barreda's personal connection to Comte and his age relative to Spencer, explain why French authors were read first. By 1885, however, the influence of the British author had topped that of Comte in Mexico.

As seen, a mixture of social and biological determinism took hold in Mexico, appealing to the classism and racism already present in Mexican society. These ideas found wide resonance across society, including among legal professionals. Advocates of both positivist and liberal ideas engaged in constant debate during this time. It is worth emphasizing that even supporters of positivism had to operate within the bounds established by the Liberal Penal Code. If we remember Tarello's distinction, we detect a clear dissonance between the Code as a source of legal principles, on the one hand, and interpretations and uses of cases by attorneys and lawyers before the court or jury, on the other.

The Jury

An especially illustrative point of contact and friction between the legal system and external legal culture was the jury court, instituted in Mexico City in 1869 and abolished in 1929. There were four main ideas supporting its institution. The first was to let the people, understood as the repository of the sovereignty of the nation, freely exercise and participate in the administration of justice. Liberal reformers considered this to be essential to the life of any democracy. The second was to allow people direct access to the judiciary as one of the branches of the government. In both the executive and the legislative branches, popular participation was indirect, via elected representatives. The third was the belief that juries would ensure the independence of the judiciary from the executive. Finally, the fourth aim was to elevate supposedly apathetic inhabitants to the status of concerned and active citizens (Zarco 1987 [1857]).

For the sake of brevity, I will limit myself to pointing out some important features of the introduction of jury trials in Mexico City. First, it was adopted for common law crimes previously under the direct jurisdiction of the criminal court judges.[23] The Penal Code proscribed the sentence for each offense, in order to limit the discretion of the judge and the influence of the offender's circumstances in sentencing decisions. Following the reform, the judge was limited to overseeing the process and presiding over the jury. Judges also advised jury members on filling out the questionnaire, which not only declared guilt or innocence, but also rated the crime and could recommend increasing or reducing the sentence based on aggravating or mitigating circumstances. The eleven jurors did so after hearing the reading of the first investigations, witness testimonies, face-to-face confrontations of the parties, and closing arguments. The decisions of the jury were irrevocable, indicative of the great powers invested in it.

The members of the jury were chosen by lottery after a series of filters from a list initially including all eligible inhabitants of the city. Jurors had to be literate, older than 25 years, and Mexican-born citizens. They could not be public officials or have an occupation that would cause financial difficulties for the family if too much time were taken off; finally, gamblers, inveterate drunks, or those with previous criminal convictions could not serve as jurors (Art. 61, p. 663).

Some legal professionals complained that the quality of the jury was low and the powers given to it too great. They argued the first point on the basis of the absence of socio-cultural filters, modern terminology, and better jury selection procedures (Rodriguez 1900, 426). Consequently, in 1880 a reform was undertaken to decrease the jury's powers and to raise its socio-cultural profile. Thereafter, the decisions of the jury remained irrevocable only if taken with a two-thirds plus one majority of at least eight votes.[24] An additional income requirement of one peso per day was added to the list of qualifying criteria.[25] As the literacy and income requirements proved to be too exclusive, foreigners with a minimum residence in the country of five years and public employees were also admitted.[26]

Even before this reform it would be an exaggeration to claim that the jury represented the legal culture of the common people (*el pueblo*) since

23 *Ley de jurados en materia criminal para el distrito federal* (Juries Act in criminal cases to federal district) Art. 1 (Dublán and Lozano, 1878, Vol. X, 658).

24 *Código de procedimientos penales* (Criminal Procedure Code), Art. 507 (Dublán and Lozano, 1886, Vol. XV, 53).

25 *Ibid.*, p. 37

26 *Ibid.*, p. 53

the literacy requirement eliminated a substantial portion of the population. In contrast, the members of the wealthy social classes usually sought to avoid serving as jurors, leaving it to the lower strata of the middle class. The 1880 reform, however, reveals the objective of limiting the lower classes' access to the administration of the law.

Conclusions

The sketch provided in this chapter of the juridical cultures in Mexico City around 1871 shows a complex interweaving of ideas, values, and attitudes about justice permeating Mexican society. The coexistence and blending of legal concepts spanning from the colonial regime to the racist and biologically deterministic ideas of the positivists demonstrates the multiplicity of legal cultures existing even within one city.

Crucial for this interplay was the conflict between the centralizing and standardizing attempt to bring all Mexicans under one legal system, and the centripetal effect of the different legal cultures present in the country. For the liberal reformers, only their prototypical Mexican—an urban male *criollo* or Europeanized *mestizo*—was a true citizen of the country and thus the intended beneficiary of the 1871 Penal Code. The customary legal practices of the Amerindian population were ignored while the all-pervading classism and racism continued to affect the poor urban *mestizos*. As we have seen, the new codification was inspired by the penal codes from more than twenty countries, none of which were facing the social challenges Mexico had. The 1871 Penal Code was drafted with a focus on a tiny minority, while the great majority of the population was, in the best of the cases, relegated to the role of passive spectator.

Works Cited

Aguirre, Carlos and Salvatore, Ricardo D. (2001). Introduction: Writing the History of Law, Crime, and Punishment in Latin America. In Ricardo D. Salvatore, Carlos Aguirre and Gilbert M. Joseph (eds.) *Crime and Punishment in Latin America. Law and Society since Late Colonial Times*, 1–32. Durham, NC: Duke University Press.

Barreda, Gabino (1877). *Opúsculos, discusiones y dicsursos*. Mexico City.

Buffington, Robert (2001). *Criminales y ciudadanos en el México moderno*. Mexico City: Siglo XXI editores.

Constitución política de la monarquía española, promulgada en Cádiz a 19 de marzo de 1812. Valladolid: Ed. Maxtor, 2001, facs. ed. of 1820 Madrid edition.

Del Valle, Ivonne (2009). *Escribiendo desde los márgenes. Colonialismo y jesuitas en el siglo XVII*. Mexico City, Siglo XXI editores.

Dougnac Rodríguez, Antonio (1994). *Manual de historia del derecho indiano*. Mexico City: Universidad Nacional Autónoma de México-Instituto de Investigaciones Jurídicas.

Dublán, Manuel and Lozano, José Maria (eds.) (1878). *Legislación mexicana ó colección completa de las disposiciones legislativas desde la independencia de la República*, Vol. X. Mexico City: Imprenta del comercio de Dublán y Chávez and Imprenta y litografía de Eduardo Dublán y Comp.

Dublán, Manuel and Lozano, José Maria (eds.) (1879). *Legislación mexicana ó colección completa de las disposiciones legislativas desde la independencia de la República*, Vol. XI. Mexico City: Imprenta del comercio de Dublán y Chávez and Imprenta y litografía de Eduardo Dublán y Comp.

Dublán, Manuel and Lozano, José Maria (eds.) (1886). *Legislación mexicana ó colección completa de las disposiciones legislativas desde la independencia de la República*, Vol. XV. Mexico City: Imprenta del comercio de Dublán y Chávez and Imprenta y litografía de Eduardo Dublán y Comp.

Lombroso, Cesare (1884). *La antropología y la criminalidad. El Foro*, July 15, 1884.

Martínez de Castro, Antonio (1876). *Exposición de motivos del Código penal vigente en el Distrito Federal y Territorio de la Baja California dirigida al Supremo Gobierno por el ciudadano Lic. Antonio Martínez de Castro, presidente de la Comisión encargada de formar el Código expresado*. Mexico City: Imprenta de Francisco Díaz de León.

Mendoza, Vicente (1944). *Cincuenta corridos mexicanos*. Mexico City: Ediciones de la SEP.

Mendoza, Vicente (1995 [1954]). *El corrido mexicano*, Mexico City: FCE.

Moreno Bonett, Margarita (1997). De la crisis del modelo borbónico al establecimiento de la República Federal. In Gloria Villegas Moreno and Miguel Angel Porrúa Venero (eds.) *Enciclopedia Parlamentaria de México, Serie III Documentos, Volumen I: Leyes y documentos constitutivos de la Nación mexicana*. Mexico City: Instituto de Investigaciones Legislativas de la Cámara de Diputados.

Nelken, David (2004). Comparing Legal Cultures. In Austin Sarat (ed.) *The Blackwell Companion to Law and Society*, 113–127. Malden, Massachusetts: Blackwell Publishing Ltd.

Ortega, José (1944 [1754]). *Maravillosa reducción y conquista de la provincia de San José del Gran Nayar*. Mexico City: Layac.

Otero, Mariano (1842). *Ensayo sobre el verdadero estado de la cuestión social y política que se agita en la República Mexicana*. Mexico City.

Recopilación de Leyes de los Reynos de las Indias (1983 [1681]). Vol. 1, Book 2, Chapter 1, Act 4. Madrid: Ediciones Cultura Hispánica.

Rodriguez, Ricardo (1900). *El procedimiento penal en México*. Mexico City: Secretaría de Fomento.

Tarello, Giovanni (1995). *Cultura jurídica y política del derecho*. Mexico City: FCE.

Universidad Nacional Autónoma de México, Instituto de Investigaciones Jurídicas, Senado de la República (1980). *Actas constitucionales mexicanas (1821–1824)*, Vol. I. Mexico City: UNAM-IIJ.

Varallanos, José (1959). *Historia de Huánuco*. Buenos Aires: Imprenta López.

Zarco, Francisco (1987 [1857]). *Historia del Congreso Constituyent.* Mexico City: Instituto Nacional de Estudios Históricos de la Revolución Mexicana and Gobierno del Estado de Puebla.

Notes on Contributors

Carlos Aguirre, a Peruvian historian, teaches in the Department of History at the University of Oregon, where he is also Director of the Latin American Studies Program. He has published extensively on the history of slavery, crime, punishment, and intellectuals. He is the author or co-editor of nine books, including *Dénle duro que no siente. Poder y transgresión en el Perú republicano* (2008) and *The Criminals of Lima and their Worlds. The Prison Experience, 1850–1935* (2005). He is currently working on a book manuscript on political imprisonment in twentieth-century Peru.

Benjamin Beuerle studied history, philosophy and public law in Berlin, Tübingen and Aix-en-Provence. He received a Franco-German double degree (Magister Artium/Maîtrise) in autumn 2005 from the universities of Tübingen and Aix-en-Provence. The following year, he was a lecturer at the State University of Voronezh (Russia) where he taught German and Western European history. He is now completing his dissertation on the role and content of Western reference models in Russian reform debates (1905–1917). He was funded initially by a scholarship from the German National Academic Foundation. Since 2008 he has been a member of staff at the Collaborative Research Centre "Representations of Changing Social Order" (SFB 640) at Humboldt University in Berlin.

Benjamin Buchholz is a researcher at the Collaborative Research Centre (SFB 640) at Humboldt University in Berlin. He studied Oriental Studies in Frankfurt, Bamberg and Tehran and received his diploma in 2004 with a thesis on the role of intellectuals on the eve of the Iranian Revolution. Benjamin Buchholz submitted his doctoral dissertation to the Central Asian Studies Seminar at Humboldt University in the spring of 2011. This dissertation focuses on the institutional history of Afghanistan's *loya jirga* in the twentieth century. He has published a first set of findings in the article "Afghanistan's *loya jirga*: A Myth?" (in *ASIEN*, 2007). In addition, he teaches courses in modern Afghan history at Humboldt University.

Jane Burbank is Collegiate Professor and Professor of History and Russian and Slavic Studies at New York University. She is the co-author with Frederick Cooper of *Empires in World History: Power and the Politics of Difference* (2010), and author of *Russian Peasants Go to Court: Legal Culture in the Countryside, 1905–1917* (2004) [http://www.nyu.edu/projects/burbank/] and *Intelligentsia and Revolution: Russian Views of Bolshevism, 1917–1922* (1986). She is a co-editor of *Imperial Russia: New Histories for the Empire* (1998) and of *Russian Empire: Space, People, Power 1700-1930* (2007). At present she is working on a study, based on Kazan province, of law and political affiliation in imperial Russia.

Stefan B. Kirmse received his PhD at the School of Oriental and African Studies (SOAS) in London. He works at the intersection of history, social anthropology and cultural studies. He is the author of the book *Youth and Globalization in Central Asia: Everyday Life between Transnational Islam, Global Media and Western Donors* (Campus, 2013, forthcoming) and editor of *Youth in the Former Soviet South* (Routledge, 2011). His latest research project takes his interest in intercultural exchange and Muslims of the Eurasian space into the imperial period, focusing on experiences of law and empire under late Tsarism. Further findings will be published as "New Courts in Late Tsarist Russia: Of Imperial Representation and Muslim Participation" in the *Journal of Modern European History* (2013, no.1, forthcoming). From October 2013, Stefan B. will be a Research Fellow at the Wissenschaftskolleg Berlin as part of the program "Rechtskulturen/Legal Cultures".

Manuel de los Reyes García Márkina, a Mexican scholar, is a Research Fellow at Humboldt University in Berlin. He is a PhD candidate at the Institute for Eastern European Studies at Free University Berlin. Having carried out extensive research in the field of Russian nationalism and national identity, his new research project focuses on "modernisation" and the reform of the legal system in nineteenth-century Mexico.

Lena Gautam received her BA from the European University Viadrina (Frankfurt/Oder) in cultural studies and her Master's degree from Free University (Berlin) in Eastern European Studies in 2008. Lena is currently a PhD Candidate in the department of Eastern European History at Humboldt University in Berlin. Her research focuses on changes in autocratic rule and government on the eve of modernity, and on the Russian Judicial Reform of 1864, in particular. In this context she is particularly interested in the reforms' impact on the relationship between the state and the population.

Ulrike Schaper is a research associate and lecturer at the Free University of Berlin. In her PhD thesis on law and German colonial rule in Cameroon (submitted to Free University Berlin, 2010) she analysed law as a site of political, cultural and social struggle and interaction between the colonisers and the colonised. Her publications include *Koloniale Verhandlungen, Gerichtsbarkeit, Verwaltung und Herrschaft in Kamerun 1884–1916* (Frankfurt/Main 2012) and "Law and Colonial Order. Legal Policy in German Cameroon between Civilising and Public Peace," *Comparativ* 19 (2009), 1, 17–33.

Xiaoqun Xu (Ph.D., Columbia University, 1993) is associate professor of history at Christopher Newport University in Virginia, USA. He has published one book in Chinese and two books in English. The latter are: *Chinese Professionals and the Republican State: The Rise of Professional Associations in Shanghai, 1912–1937* (Cambridge UP, 2001) and *Trial of Modernity: Judicial Reform in Early-Twentieth-Century China, 1901–1937* (Stanford UP, 2008). One of his most recent publications is "Judicial Professionalization in China: In Light of the Republican Experience," in William Alford, William Kirby, and Kenneth Winston, eds., *Prospects of the Professions in China* (Routledge, 2010). He is currently writing a book on an influential newspaper supplement, *Chenbao Fukan*, published in Beijing during 1918–1928.

Index of Names and Places